Faith, Flag, and Family
A Purposeful Guide for Selfless Service
Robert E. Jordan

ISBN 978-1-0980-1676-0 (paperback)
ISBN 978-1-0980-1678-4 (hardcover)
ISBN 978-1-0980-1677-7 (digital)

Christian Faith Publishing, Inc.
832 Park Avenue
Meadville, PA 16335
www.christianfaithpublishing.com

Printed in the United States of America

To my darling Apo and her children's children.

CONTENTS

Commissioning Address Chief Warrant Officer Robert E. Jordan

November 06, 2009

Looking back upon my enlisted career, I can best describe it as unimaginably fulfilling. I have been blessed to serve in ways, and in places, that I thought not at all possible when it was that I first recited the Oath of Enlistment. I often recall those leaders, who believed in me—at times, more than I believed in myself—and encouraged me to better my efforts, to accept the burdens of leadership, and to serve purposefully and selflessly those I was charged to lead. Looking to the future service opportunities, I humbly and with much gratitude forward my naval career now accepting, unreservedly, a commission as a Chief Warrant Officer. I do so with the desire to serve tactically, with select groups of military professionals determined to take the current fight to the enemy, protect U.S. and Coalition forces, and forestall any future attacks against our homeland. As an enlisted leader, I established my determination to lead military personnel and serve in harm's way. I have demonstrated my maturity and self-lessness by answering the call to lead Sailors in the fleet and joint forces in Afghanistan. Now, at this moment and for the foreseeable future, I will do so with a personal vigor and professional passion as a Commissioned Naval Officer. With the opportunity to serve as a Chief Warrant Officer, I state with confidence, that I am ready to assume the leadership opportunities as a naval officer, and lead our nation's best in support of national objectives. I will do so by the best of my abilities knowing full well that wherever this service takes me, I remain a servant to many, and a leader to all, projecting a professional paradigm which I trust others will emulate. Let these words serve much more than a reception of this commission but rather as a service contract with our Navy and our Nation. It is with much pleasure and high regard that I do accept this commission as a Chief Warrant Officer. I am especially thankful for this unique opportunity to serve our country and our community. Thank you and God bless us all.

Preface: A Statement of Service

October 03, 2012

My Beloved Family,

I know that yet another deployment has presented itself to one and all unexpectedly. I know too that you are apprehensive as I again will be involved in an unconventional duty assignment. I also know that my service strains nerves through upset and because of the unknown. Truly, I believe myself blessed and thank you all for your love and support. If I could ease your concerns by telling you more I would do so. Although the true nature of my service is subject to scrutiny, I can offer you that what I do, I do selflessly and for the betterment of a country in turmoil and for the security of my community. The separation, though long and not without peril is worth the sacrifice. I know that all my family contributes to this global effort. For it is the collective effort and support of my family that enables me to go forward far from home for months at a time, into the fray yet never far from those I love. Wherever I find myself, you are with me. I am comforted often as I feel you close. And in prayer, I offer thanks and praise for my family; though far from me, yet ever close at heart you all remain.

Truly I believe compelled to take part in the struggles that exist in this world. Not for fame or glory, but rather for the privilege to aid and assist others; from my labor to benefit the unfortunate and, giving the best of myself, for my part I offer my good fortune to those who are unable to better their own lives. This is an epic struggle with many uncertainties. A precarious situation awaits those who will go forward. There are many who scheme to derail the betterment of these struggling foreign societies. Yet, come what may, we must prevail, persevere, not waver nor abate our efforts to better their lives. My military service is my personal legacy and my signature in life. It is through my military service that I hope to better the man that I am and better still countless other lives.

Know that I pray for your safety and security. More often than occasionally, I ask the Lord for his mercy and grace to surround my family, loved ones and those I hold dearly. Community and friends will provide for you and the Lord will tend to your needs. You are blessed with friends and family who care for you and who are there for support. Their lives will strengthen yours. Though times are difficult, love and laughter will brighten any day.

Know too that I offer myself selflessly in the service of others. What I do I pray will prove significant for and with those I serve. Military service requires much from both service member and family. Yet, as there are those who move forward, those who remain serve too these uncertain times. Your love and support, prayers and consideration bridge the miles that separate. And, warmly received is your compassion and kindheartedness. I ask in your moments of prayer, pray for us all.

To my Beloved wife, thank you for your love and support. Over the past ten years we have endured separation and sadness, love and war. I've traveled to foreign lands and your presence has accompanied me. Wherever my service might lead me, you my beloved wife are forever near. In love and in prayer, our hearts are joined. Though I may be thousands of miles from my beloved wife, you are near; in all that I do your hand is upon me and your smile brightens though storm clouds may they gather. You are my angel and go with me always.

Family, fret not, for as today appeared so too will tomorrow's dawn and in time so too will the day of my return. Think often of the joyous reunion and your heavy hearts will be made lighter. All my love accompanies here and wherever I may be, all my love is extended to family and friends, both near and far, both here and overseas. God bless you all.

Truly,
Bob

Abram Osterhout's Gettysburg Letter

As a young man, my parents provided me a wonderful historical look at our family's ancestry. In particular, I was fascinated by letters written to family members during our nation's Civil War period (1861–1865). One letter, which is transcribed and included within this book, notes the service and sacrifice during the Battle of Gettysburg, July 01–03, 1863. Written by Private Abram Osterhout, who served with the 120th New York Infantry, Company D, assigned to 2nd Brigade, 2nd Division, Third Corps, of the Army of the Potomac, captivated my attention years ago and a transcription of that letter is provided. Transcending generations, this letter inspired me to write my sentiments of Faith, Flag, and Family offered to service members as monthly memos espousing rightful service. As this book is dedicated to my granddaughter, Abram's letter will be known to her as well as her children's children. This book is in fact a gift to future generations of my family.

1863
Monday July 13th

Dear Brother,

It is some time since I have received a letter from you or written you. I have had very little time to write since we began to march and that was the 12th of June. I am well this morning and I hope that all of you are enjoying the same blessing. You have well heard that we have been in battle again before this time. We was in the fight near Gettysburg on July 2, and a very severe it was. The battle at Chancellorsville was nothing to be compared with this one. While shot and shell were falling on like hail stone and men were dropping on every side, I was amongst those that came out unharmed and feel very thankful for it.

Our regiment lost that day, killed, wounded, and missing 202. The loss of our company is killed, wounded, and missing is 22. Only two of them are dead. A few are wounded severely but the most of them are wounded but slightly and will recover. Such dear Brother is the horrors of war and I hope and pray that it will soon come to an end. The loss of our army was heavy in this battle. Yet, we claim a victory. We are now in Maryland not far from the Antietam Battle grounds, and I think too that we have force enough to meet them. Yesterday afternoon we had a very heavy shower and this morning it still looks rainy.

The country is quite hilly through here and good water is plenty, both wells and springs. There is some of the largest fountains here that I have ever seen, which makes it very nice for us soldiers for we need great deal of water. My letter will not be very lengthy this time, but I thought I would write and let you know that I am alive and well and where we are. We are looking for another fight soon and it may be today if you keep track of the Third Corps then you know where we are. Now I will stop my scribbling for this time. Write when you can and remember me to all inquiring friends. From your brother,

Abram Osterhout

WHY I SERVE

July 20, 2007

"Why I serve." Not a question, but rather a statement offered for your reflection and consideration. During World War II, legendary Hollywood director Frank Capra compiled a series of films entitled *Why We Fight*. These films inspired a nation to rally for war, and they inspired both of my parents to choose careers of service. Today, in similar reflection, I offer you the reasons for my service. In doing so, I hope to inspire you to consider your own motives for the path of service that you have chosen.

Because we are at war, your country will demand more from you tomorrow than you offered today. The War on Terror continues to be challenging, and I do not foresee the path becoming any less arduous in the near future. As such, we must be prepared to sacrifice accordingly. I do not doubt that deployments will be longer, and the burdens which we bear will not lighten over time. Still, I am prepared to endure increasing hardship and uncertainty. Even as we struggle, I will serve as selflessly as I can for the sake of others. In a time of war, I serve in order to preserve a way of life meant for all: to deliver hope, unity, and opportunity to the impoverished, downtrodden, and hapless. I serve by recognizing the needs of others before satisfying my own. I serve to enable my juniors to establish themselves: guiding, directing, and mentoring them. I serve to honor those who have worn the uniform and those who serve today. Many have gone before me, and I honor their sacrifices with my own. I serve to learn and understand, to acquaint and refine, and to endure adversity in order to strengthen my resolve. Through my service, I am educated in the ways of the world. Believe me, no institution of higher learning will offer you such a challenging curriculum; none will test you, demand of you, or expect you to offer your expertise as does the military. Such is the common core of military leadership. No other occupation will expect such commitment. No other industry will insist that you depart the home front, bid farewell to loved ones, and face such uncertainty. By the same token, no other organization will honor you in such a way, appreciate your service, and remember you with reverence for all of history. For the freedoms that endure are made possible from the toil and blood of those who thought less of themselves and more of those who serve and fight side by side, shoulder to shoulder.

I trust that from these words, the singular meaning of "I" truly incorporates the equally singular "you." In unison then and in life, we must live to serve others, serve selflessly and allow ourselves to serve altruistically. In so doing, you and I serve our friends, family, community and country, those we love and those unbeknownst to us. I serve to serve you and those you hold dearly. *"Come what may, and it surely will,"* I serve as I am asked and as I am ordered; for I shall meet the demands unreservedly. In perpetuity, I will know that I have served others without reluctance or regret. For this above all else is my reward of *"Why I Serve!"*

THE COST OF FREEDOM

We've heard the statement many times: "Freedom isn't free." But what of the costs?

In today's balance sheet-driven business world, many speculate on the dividends—and wonder if they outweigh expenditures. I am convinced that the billions of dollars spent and invested cannot be tallied with regard to yield or dividends. This war, I believe, cannot be viewed from the short-term perspective. The focus of freedom is from the long view. The costs must be seen as a perpetual roll-over of fused expenses. Freedom is not an end state in and of itself. Furthermore, once freedom is achieved, it must be maintained—so the sacrifice must be ongoing. Along the way, the blood of brave patriots will inevitably be shed, hardships endured by the citizenry, and sacrifices shouldered by all. Indeed, the cost of freedom is high—but what does it cost you personally?

All too often, we feel that by serving in the military we have given our all and done our part. But how much do we really offer? Many service members are in direct harm's way, facing hardships and danger unlike anything that they could have ever imagined. Extended deployments, uncertainties of reassignment, and repeated duties in combat zones, the costs can indeed be a burden. Still, are they overwhelmed? No, because military men and women understand the costs and identify with the hardships. Those in the combat zone realize the fragility of life, and as an all-volunteer force, they welcome their duties and apply their tradecraft admirably. Smartly put, we stand tall in the face of hardship.

So few Americans serve in the military; estimates show that approximately 2 percent of our citizenry serves in the armed forces. Many citizens hope that they too could serve, but for a myriad of reasons, they cannot. Those who have not served honor the men and women of the military for shouldering the burdens of service and thank the military for the dividend from your toil. Service men and women preserve freedom at any cost. You keep our communities safe and our nation secure. You have sworn to uphold and defend the Constitution of the United States of America. You know that the money is not enough; you do it not for compensation.

Knowing this, why do we serve? We serve in order to give of ourselves selflessly and provide for those who depend upon us for their defense and well-being. We serve for the privilege of wearing the uniform. We serve in order to carry on a long tradition of sacrifice with honor, dedicated to something that is difficult at times to understand. We faithfully serve countless countrymen and foreigners alike, without discriminating between them—aiding and assisting the disadvantaged, emissary and adversary along the way. Even in battle, when a combatant no longer possesses the ability to inflict harm, we care for his wounds as well.

Bearing all this in mind, we must ask the original question again: what, really, are the costs of freedom? The truth of the matter is that they are not costs or debts at all. They are credits.

You see, service members give of themselves without expecting a balanced budget. We think in terms of ways and means to secure and preserve the security of our nation, the unity of our countrymen, and the betterment of our communities. We serve to enable a better way in life for all Americans. Perhaps most importantly, we serve not to dominate, but to uplift. We serve with the knowledge that sacrifice is necessary, understanding that there are overarching principles more important than our individual selves. We serve in order to give from our hearts so that freedom may endure.

Ultimately, any attempt to weigh the cost of freedom is counterproductive. I ask that rather than focus on personal offerings, focus instead on your willingness to serve, your ability to shoulder any burden, and your willingness to give more of yourself. Come what may, you'll stand your ground in defense of freedom, never to waver or capitulate. Truly, as a military man or woman, you do not speculate on the costs, but rather you appreciate the commonality of effort—the esprit de corps—and you welcome the selfless desire of others who similarly go into harm's way in order to redress the evil of the world. You do this not for yourself, but for those who will come after you. Believe this: your sacrifice and achievements are truly what compensate the *"costs of freedom."*

FOR WHOM DO I SERVE

Several years ago, a personal experience profoundly affected me in the way I view not only the world, but also how I see my role in it. Walking near the former US Naval Base at Subic Bay, Olongapo, Philippines, I briefly acquainted myself with a little boy whose life is one of the hustle and bustle of the streets. I approximated his age at five years. He was a child of the street, a beggar, a nuisance to some, and a shadow to many. Though the following description will be brief, the impact of his acquaintance will haunt me for the rest of my life.

A cute child of mixed ethnicity, he was soiled from head to foot, with encrusted filth encircling his neck. I believe his parents to have been unfortunates of the time, quite possibly his mother disadvantaged by circumstance and his father unbeknownst to him. His life was one of fetching food, avoidance, and survival. At even such a tender age, he was involved in selling plastic bags at the open-air food market. As I approached him, I took note that he was infested with lice and blind in one eye, with a prominent scar distorting the right side of his face. My heart was made heavy as he smiled at me, exposing the putrefied remnants of infant's teeth. With no shoes on his feet, he made his way around the market in search of those heavily laden. An oversized tattered undershirt was all he wore. In offering him spare change, he gleefully accepted and made his way through the throngs of marketers.

Here now is the meaning of this message: as an exploitable pawn, he and countless children like him are victims in their own right. For many such children, by way of association, indoctrination, acclimation, and solicitation, once acquired by an enemy of the state, their lives are often determined to be expendable, paltry, and meaningless. For a charismatic lie, many will do the enemy's bidding. If necessities are met, then atrocity, brutality, or the commission of both can be made permissible and perversely justifiable. Child soldiers, operatives, or suicide bombers are coerced to commit heinous crimes against humanity with the hope and promise of a better life.

Manipulated through rancor, retribution, coercion, and intimidation, children such as this little boy are often thrust into the violent abyss as mere sacrificial offerings for a cause steeped in malevolence and malignity. It is my hope that national awareness will be raised in order to shed greater light onto this shadowy gray area of armed conflict. For there is more to the loss of life when the innocence is wrenched from those whose existence holds such promise, and quite possibly a new dimension of offering a peaceful solution to an age-old impasse between rivals. Abject poverty oppresses the masses; this is true. However, those impacted most are children who are vulnerable to indignity, sexual defilement, and domestic injustice.

And so, for whom do I serve? I serve for those who have little hope, those who find life so unfair, those whose survival is dependent upon others and whose suffered injustices merit retribution. I serve in order to enrich their lives with hope and civility. With basic needs met, opportunity and education must then follow. I serve in order to preserve a way of life meant for all, to deliver hope, unity, and opportunity to the impoverished, downtrodden, and hapless.

For this reason, the "privilege" of military service is defined as such. Selfless service, sacrificing so others may benefit, this is my service to remedy social injustice and make better the lives of those in need. I trust that you will similarly serve.

WHY THINGS HAPPEN AND WHY THINGS MATTER

Recently, a Sailor came to see me, perplexed and pondering a situation that he had been facing. He looked me in the eyes and asked, "Why has this happened to me?" The Sailor was frustrated and grieving, and his once optimistic outlook was dimmed by a cloud of despair that seemed to overshadow his career and life. Knowing this Sailor well, I took the time to listen and to evaluate his experience. I also identified an opportunity to redirect his self-perception of gloom and emphasize "why things happen and why things matter."

After careful appraisal of the Sailor's trouble—much like that which I have faced personally—I said, "What better way to end one's browbeating and hand-wringing then by accepting the trial and tribulation as an opportunity to rally personally, professionally, emotionally, and spiritually!" Yes, tough times will befall us all, but all love to ask, "Why me?" Why has this thing happened to me? It seems that the world is against me! Common themes to everyday life! All of us have pondered why things happen, but how often do we rally ourselves to come to grips with the bigger picture of why things matter? Just as I told the Sailor, "Now is the time to believe in yourself, rally on, and surmount what appears daunting and insurmountable!"

Whether you believe in the randomness of occurrence or destiny, things "do happen." In life, bad things will occur, and each and every one of us will shoulder the burdens of troubling times. However, when these things happen, the energy exerted to cry defeat would be better employed to rally onward. As leaders, innumerable eyes watch our reactions and activity in dealing with problems. We motivate and inspire people even beyond those in our immediate circle of awareness. If we accept a defeatist attitude, those who look upon us will likewise be "uninspired." Yet, if we accept the inevitable and rally from within, then others will similarly be so moved. There is strength, seldom tapped, within us. Self-belief enables a person to turn inward, inspiring self-awareness and self-confidence while exacting a positive change to their circumstance. And, that's why "things matter"!

When things happen, believe in yourself. Accept your faults and shortcomings, and believe that this is not an insurmountable obstacle but rather a personal rallying point. We must believe that when "things happen, things matter"! Your ability to accept and shoulder additional burdens will strengthen you individually and inspire others personally. Refinement of personal energies, directing our strengths to overcome our weaknesses, and constructing an affirmative emotional stratagem will awaken an inward force that will enable and reward you and those who look to you for guidance and inspiration. Believe this: all "things" matter—and when they happen, accept them as another of life's opportunities to refine your persona and provide a positive example for others to emulate!

IN TIMES OF TROUBLE, FIND PRIDE IN SERVICE

With all the political and uncivil bravado as a constant message, some may begin to wonder about and doubt their true purpose. Backed by political motivations and fueled by personal reward, the voices of our naysayers are everywhere. Media pundits rant boisterously while celebrities spout an endless stream of disparaging remarks. The airways are flooded with anti-American speak that similarly dresses down both the military and our war effort. People openly verbally assault our president and commander in chief, as well as our military leaders, seeking to discredit them all. It can be disheartening, to say the very least. As service members, some may feel overwhelmed and question their commitment to our nation and its national objectives. With the demands of longer deployments, surge tasking, Individual Augmentation assignments, and repeated separation from loved ones, it is natural to ask ourselves if it is worth all the effort and sacrifice. My response and I trust yours as well? Stand strong in the face of it all. Once again, these challenges have presented themselves as opportunities to engage and enliven our purposeful and selfless service.

In my humble opinion, what we need most today are heroes who espouse altruism and unity. Still, military men and women are genuinely modest when the spotlight shines upon them. They know of the personal awards they display on their uniforms or which hang in display over countless mantles at home. Though often personally awarded, these awards are seldom an individual effort. Often, the community identifies heroism with every ribbon attached to one's uniform while many service members are a bit uncomfortable with the moniker of "hero."

Then again, are all heroes so identified by distinguished medals? Many heroes are unsung and continue to serve not for self-identity but rather to serve honorably, identifying with others whose needs have become overwhelming. The truth of the matter is that every service member, through their service alone, can become a hero to others. Far from the battlefield, heroes emerge when a bright smile, an extended hand, or a sincere gesture of benevolence are freely offered to those in need, who want, or seek a role model.

As service members, we must collectively commit to redress the popular culture of negativism and the slander and enmity levied against us as a military. We must not allow ourselves to be complacent and let pass an opportunity to express our political views through voting. We must unite and involve ourselves in community-based advocacy as sponsors for community projects, adapt-a-school programs, neighborhood beautification, and veteran's programs. We must take every opportunity to portray and espouse purposeful selfless service here at home and abroad, offering charitable organizations all that we can in order to benefit those in need.

Importantly, we must honor the service of others by flying the American flag at every opportunity. Remember the days after the tragedy of September 11, 2001 and the proud displays of patriotic unity. Many of my neighbors may not know my name, but they can identify my house as being the one where the American flag flies every day of the year. My hope is that my house and my identity will once again become opaque by the increasing number of flags flown on my street by both service members and like-minded citizens.

How, as a military, can we redress the disparagement against us? First, we must amplify our behaviors, our speech, our appearance while broadening our service to community and country. Whether on the battlefield or on Broadway, we must conduct ourselves well beyond reproach. We must commit ourselves to redressing criticism through community advocacy at home and abroad. We must support and defend our country and those we are charged to serve in accordance with doctrine and protocol. We must stand firm and tall, yet offer compassion at each opportunity. Your patriotism, professionalism, and compassionate community sponsorship will send a clear message to our critics and political rivals, all of which we serve purposely and selflessly.

WHY WE ALLOW DIVERGENT
AND DIVISIVE VIEWPOINTS

Years ago, Iranian President Mahmoud Ahmadinejad spoke at New York's Columbia University. It was a shameful and disrespectful display of the rantings of a megalomaniac (or cunning political tactician) with his venomous and hateful rhetoric—one who conspires against us was permitted to lash out against America, here on our own soil! And, New York City police officers, many of whom are military reservists, were tasked to provide essential security for Columbia's honored guest! How and why would American officials permit an "enemy of the state" to speak frankly and openly against the United States within its borders and within a prestigious hall of academia? Who would be in attendance, welcoming Ahmadinejad to the stage, agreeing with his statements as a rallying cause against US foreign policy? Why would political leaders allow such divisive viewpoints to he voiced? How is this possible to offer reception to an outspoken enemy while elevating his status to one of celebrity?

For some time, I pondered an answer. I searched my conscience and my heart. I embraced this question academically, spiritually, and with temperance. I balanced reason and displeasure. And, then it came to me, an answer of forethought and fortitude and an answer that in reflection I knew was both right and just. So here, now, is that answer: Americans would invite, welcome, and provide a venue for Ahmadinejad not because of who he is, but rather because of who we are! America, a *"shining city on a hill"* for all to gaze upon, an enviable example of freedom and liberty, of humanity and humility, of compassion and of obligation, and of opportunity and promise—this is who we are, for all to admire, for others to envy, and for some to vilify. We tolerate those with whom we disagree. We allow divergent interests and viewpoints allowing free speech by right and affording ample opportunity for conflicting speech to be heard. We provide opportunity of worship to all religions. Although we might not agree with our neighbor, we coexist because we subscribe to the inalienable truths of freedom. Americans understand that our diversity is in fact a union that binds us together. It is the American spirit that unifies, accepts, justifies, and appreciates the human condition of individualism, choice, desire, and multiplicity.

America allows both adversaries and enemies to speak out against us not because we are intimidated, but because we are strong. We permit conflicting and discordant viewpoints to be voiced in both private and public venues because of tolerance. We again define what makes America great when we permit such viewpoints. Though we are constantly vilified by our opponents, it is in no small measure that envy is the basis of their displeasure. America offers unprecedented opportunity, shares its great wealth, and is quick to offer compassion and aid to those in need. Nations from around the globe know of our consideration, for it was Americans who created the CARE package filled with nutritional essentials and sundries. America is the world's first responder to disaster and famine. Often cited for our supposed disingenuousness, meddling, and intolerance, we coexist in relative harmony. Importantly, we choose our political leaders, affording the opportunity of public service to all of our citizens. Regardless of the theatrics and mudslinging that so often come with politics, we choose our leaders without revolt or revolution and without coercion or insurrection. We welcome all people from all religions and accept transformation as a human condition. As we seek to redress the evil of terrorism, former Secretary of State Condoleezza Rice launched the State Department's annual report on religious freedoms and stated, "Religious freedom is integral to our efforts to combat the ideology of hatred and religious intolerance that fuels global terrorism." Interestingly, the State Department's annual report on religious freedoms noted "continued deterioration of the extremely poor status of respect for religious freedom" in Iran.

We afforded Ahmadinejad the opportunity to speak and for those who admire his words to listen; yet again, another opportunity presents itself to define American greatness. We define ourselves by tolerating a man who—though his words vilify—sought an international trek that only served to delineate that which makes America grand. Ahmadinejad's words, although cheered by some, will soon fall upon the ears of Americans whose right it is to choose not to listen. He returned to Iran having enjoyed diplomatic immunity although knowing that his political and military ideals would be accounted for. So then, after careful thought, I offered this to the Sailor who asked why the likes of Ahmadinejad should be allowed to speak in America. We allow divergent and divisive viewpoints because of who we are: significantly and truly yours, America!

DEFINING A SHIPMATE

Shipmate: a term of fidelity and commitment and a historical statement voiced by those who have gone to sea. Sailors have referred to one another as shipmates for centuries. The mutual bond between shipmates has united and defined them. The term *shipmate* cannot be appropriately defined by simple terms. Shipmate is an amalgamation of personal and professional traits of the human condition. In recognition of this seafaring alliance, I think it appropriate to define this term of union between those who have before, today, and will presently be drawn to the service on the sea.

A shipmate assimilates his or her personal identity into an organization of inclusion and acceptance. From the moment you don the fabric of our nation, you have risen above all past inequities, injustice, personal shortcomings, and faults. You are welcomed aboard an organization whose purpose it is to enhance personally and strengthen your affinity to our nation. You are not an employee of an organization. You are not a stockholder of a corporation. You are a stakeholder in a military force whose mission it is to support and defend your family, community, and country. Yes, you will learn of its prowess and might while you extend the benevolence and compassion of a concerned nation. Your sacrifice will enable those who have been subjugated by tyrants to embolden their desires for freedom. Your actions and contributions will make possible self-evident truths that become opaque in light of hunger, desperation, and deficiency. You are not just a workforce: you are ambassadors of our nation. Wherever your travels take you, no matter how far your destination, you are compass points of the light of freedom. You represent that which others desire: freedom of choice, opportunity, abundance, and obtainment. And, through tutelage and mentorship, you offer them the ability to rally the wherewithal that enables a single individual, family, community, or country to free them from the burden of oppression and define for themselves their personal cultural identity.

Shipmate is an inclusive term. Its meaning is plural. As individuals enter recruit training, they become shipmates. Individuals from all parts and points from the world are so united. A shipmate is a welcomed family member who lives, learns, toils, sacrifices, laughs, cries, sweats, and bleeds through trial and tribulation, who triumphs over adversity as a collective spirit as sacrifice is endured by all. When one shipmate wavers, all shoulder his burden because they are all united in purpose. When one errs, responsibility is shared by those appointed to guide others in the right direction. When one falls, we all cry. We are a family bonded together by the fabric of our flag. You are patriots, celebrities, and yes, some are heroes. Perhaps you are even veterans, whose sacrifices have enabled for others a better way and guaranteed freedoms to endure.

Shipmates are committed in purpose and desire. They are devoted to mission and its execution. United by principles that reward hard work and focused desire, a shipmate is guaranteed unprecedented opportunities to excel and advance. Your yearning to succeed will afford you the opportunity to lead and serve as our Navy extends the honor and privilege of advanced leadership and service opportunities. When one leads, those who follow are guided by one and the same, a shipmate who will endure more of the collective burden willingly and selflessly.

These words define who we are as shipmates. I believe that these words define the attributes of Sailors from ship to shore, from those in flight to those who serve beneath the waves. We are shipmates in an ongoing global struggle, and I am confident in the abilities of my compatriots. I know for certain that in a time of need—whether in a firefight or fighting a fire, when professional pursuits momentarily overwhelm and life's challenges become burdensome—there will be a shipmate who will be standing ready to lend a helping hand to yet another shipmate. For this is the true reward of serving together, accepting the sacrifices, enduring the hardships while experiencing the benefits of being shipmates in the service of our Navy and for America.

DEFINING PURPOSEFUL SERVICE TO AMERICA

The ideal of selfless service may at times be clouded by selfish desires and personal pursuits. Military service sets a person apart from all other occupations. No other occupation demand from its members as does the military. In a time of insecurity, long deployments with uncertain return dates, separation from loved ones, and the risks associated with combat often rouse sentiments of self above the collective. Yet, do we not volunteer for the privilege of military service? Have we not accepted what may come? Why, then, are some at times among us so indifferent and are apathetic to mission and purposeful rightful service? After September 11, 2001, one would have to be oblivious to the events of the world for a civilian to join the military without recognizing the demands and tasks associated with the armed forces. Still, service members must appreciate the balance between military tasks and personal desires. As a naval leader, you must live honorably, courageously, and be committed to the mission. Subordinates perceive your every move: your actions, behaviors, and your self-defined limitations that establish a benchmark for others to emulate. Each day, there are opportunities to selflessly serve others. Each day, your actions and behaviors are being evaluated and often replicated. If you advance personal pursuits above and beyond service to others, then your behaviors detract from the premise of "Mission First, Sailors Always." Either way, your decision to act, whether aligned or contrary to rightful service, will be emulated.

As you serve, strike a balance between professional commitments and personal pursuits. Live to serve others, recognizing their plight; offer the blessing of your service. Lest we forget, societal rewards include you too as a citizen. You must extend a hand, connecting your hopeful heart to that of the hapless. Service promotes the betterment of your social setting and expands the breadth of society, empowering others to serve their fellow citizens. Communal service elevates the society that you serve. Realize that selfishness overshadows the ability to appreciate contributions that benefit the society of which you are a member. Altruism permits society to advance while egotism rarely benefits anyone. The humanity of selflessness advances society far beyond the limitations of arrogance and social insensitivity. In all that you do, you must represent the professional paradigm for others to follow and emulate.

Selflessness is an enviable trait that will be emulated. Military members must transcend purely selfish pursuits. Many desire while others demand your expertise, as well as your assistance. Believe that we define ourselves by the contributions we freely offer society, not by that which society extends. A dear friend once told me, "One's good name is worth more than all precious jewels." Your benevolence, compassion, and commitment to others will define you while enriching society. In so doing, you will most certainly and with purpose serve America.

OVERCOMING INDECISION

Indecision drives nothing; motivation, although the fuel of determination, yields little without the first perpetual step forward. Yet, capricious advance often leads one in the wrong direction. Plans less rigid are those of mastery. Flexibility, adeptness, and foresight are elements of decision that afford answers to a questioning soul. I've often heard, "No one in the Navy does anything for me!" What a puzzling statement!

When examined, an underlying meaning to the utterance is shrouded in frustration. I once again direct you to review my opening paragraph: "Indecision drives nothing; motivation, although the fuel of determination, yields little without the first perpetual step forward." Rather an odd statement, don't you agree? I think that the meaning behind the phrase characterizes frustration, browbeating and hand-wringing. We know that this statement is, of course, entirely false. The Navy offers incredible opportunity for all to take advantage of. Personal and professional programs abound. Nevertheless, if you analyze the statement, "No one in the Navy does anything for me," you'll learn that the words "no one" have a self-centered focal point. Frequently, the "no one" is an utterance of oneself. And here, then, is the crux of this message. Indecision not only stalls our progress, but in a competitive world, it drives others onward well ahead of those who experience indecisiveness. When a person believes in self, formulates realistic goals, and is willing to work hard and persevere, accepting that the measure of an instant passes one day at a time, then indecision is overcome by the mastery of personal determination and vocation. Being decisive is the basis of goal orientation and the ability to readily accept the burden of leadership. In life, you define yourself by your ability to make decisions and your willingness to accept the outcome. Knowledge, prudence, and practicality spur along ideas, ideals, and outcomes.

THE FABRIC THAT BINDS US

Once again, a Sailor came to me expressing concern over the apparent apathy and indifference of others. The Sailor's comments focused on those who display a lack of commitment to our core values, the needs of the service, and the needs of others. I was moved by this Sailor's genuine concern for those who truly could and certainly should but choose not to commit themselves to purposeful selfless service. I pondered an answer centering on the decline in societal standards, the pervasive media influences, or distinct personal shortcomings. After much deliberation, however, I thought it better to concentrate on a cure rather than the cause. Yet, rather than identify the behavioral changes and requisite attitude adjustments, I thought it best to focus upon how we as leaders should infuse ourselves as an essential force, one whose own actions and behaviors exemplify our core values, whose leadership does not waver due to the occasion, and whose moral convictions establish a standard for others to emulate.

Look at our national ensign, displayed and revered. Truly one of the world's most recognizable symbols, the American flag is a banner of freedom, opportunity, and justice. Our flag is an icon of both might and compassion. Yet, for all its strength and unity, the flag is a fabric, meticulously woven, weave by weave, stitch by stitch. The intricacies of the weave bind the entire fabric. Strength united, our flag has weathered many a storm. "Old Glory" proudly waves atop buildings along Broadway and on the field of battle as a symbol of hope, endurance, unity, and victory. Nevertheless, with careful inspection of our flag, you'll notice there are minute irregularities, strained stitches, and minuscule inconsistencies. Looking at the imperfection, one might believe that a tear at the heart of the fabric is forthcoming. What, then, binds the fabric and prevents the shredding of the material? It is the strength of the collective weaves, the adjoining thread that holds the imperfection wholly together as one piece. The vigor of the amalgam binds the material together. From this analogy,

I trust you to identify that it is the strength of one—the character of the individual, the charisma of a single person—that has, time and again, proven to be a rallying force for both those who display traits unbecoming and for those who also feel the strain of others who fail to grasp hold and shoulder their share of the collective burdens faced by command and by our communities.

Although often associated with rank, leadership is not solely reserved for those wearing numerous chevrons, anchors, or devices. As military men and women, we all are leaders and must seize every opportunity to lead when called upon. When a Sailor is in need or in trouble, when personal burdens overwhelm, when separated from family, when bad news arrives, when pressure builds and outside influences derail, purposely united, we must strengthen our grip, sharpen our focus, and offer ourselves to aid and assist, to enable others to see the proper path, to step off in the right direction, and stave off the troubles that may inevitably draw us apart. As an exemplar for others, leaders must accept the scrutiny of others and must accept that their faults will be focal points and their errors magnified. These are challenging times that require leaders to rally for the benefit of others, own their errors, and pledge to refine who they are professionally. As leaders, our actions, strength, unity, and purpose; our identity and empathy; our tenacity; our professional signature, if you will, truly is the fabric that binds us.

DEALING WITH LOSS

A Sailor recently asked me, "How can leadership help their juniors cope with personal loss? In what ways should leadership reach out to them and aid them when they need help?" These are troubling times indeed. Events chronicled in the news, violence etching disturbing images in our minds, leaders must look to communicate with Sailors in an open forum to discuss these pervasive societal challenges. Leaders must be personally in tune with their Sailors and discuss such matters candidly. Regardless of divergent views, all are united in identifying grief and loss and offering support and understanding through compassion and empathy.

We must all view misfortune as a part of our existence. Events, whether here or abroad, unprovoked and premeditated: can any sense be made of the madness perpetrated by those who are misaligned or fanatical? I think not. Yet, we must in turn grieve united. Such violence on the world stage is now equal to the graphic depiction on mass-marketed video screens. Yet, our resilience will enable us communally. We must believe that the scars from such tragedies will heal in time. Although not erased, nevertheless with understanding and collective compassion, we will rally to strengthen the bonds that unite families, classmates, communities, and our nation.

Death of a loved one is a tremendous burden. I know its weight. During past deployments, I've lost family members. The first was my brother. After returning from Afghanistan, I learned that my brother was soon to pass. An urgent message arrived via official notification from the American Red Cross, and I was put on an international flight home. I learned after telephoning home and before making my way to a connecting flight that my brother quietly passed away. In 2006, my father also departed this life. In all sincerity, my father was my hero. Although he had been sick for years, he stoically shouldered all burdens, offering his knowledge and confidence during my daily telephone calls. My father was a World War II veteran, and we shared a strong affinity because of our military service. His passing was a tremendous loss for me. At his funeral, I was honored to eulogize my father. Shortly thereafter, my father-in-law suddenly passed away. This came as quite a shock as well. When death calls unexpectedly, the family distress is overwhelming. Again, I was sent home to attend to family matters. And, once more, several months after my father's death, sadly my mother passed. Yet, again as family united, we dealt with matters collectively; and as in the past, I was especially thankful to the Navy for their part in easing my pain.

The constant in the paragraphs above is the welcomed support that the Navy offers to those who experience loss of a loved one. For this we must be particularly grateful. From immediate grief counseling to travel arrangements, for the cards and flowers that arrive, for the phone calls and the consideration, my respective chains of command have offered my family wonderful support. My family and I are especially thankful.

As leaders, being attuned to our Sailors' personal lives is essential to taking care of them. Effective communication, empathy, and consideration are indispensable. There is a certain trust that must be earned and shared between those that experience loss and those who offer assistance. This trust, however, comes long before the Red Cross message arrives. Leaders must gain this trust through professional development and the knowledge of programs, policy, and support services. Importantly, supervisors must willingly and compassionately discuss personal loss with dignity and reverence. One's burden is not to be shouldered individually; it is a collective loss that must be shared with our Navy family members.

Life's clock ticks away without our intervention. We truly do not know when time will inevitably stand still. My heartfelt advice is this: communicate with your loved ones and with them that which needs to be said. If a family fracture exists, mend it. Life is too short. Better to mend fences than later build bridges. Trust in your leadership and chain of command. Policy exists that will enable you to rejoin your family and attend to their needs. The chaplain offers grief counseling, and guidance is available for family members. There are professionals who stand ready to assist you and those you hold dearly.

Estate planning and preparation of personal and family wills are also available. Most importantly, Sailors must believe that they are not alone in their grief; they must feel that their leaders are willing and able to assist them and their family members professionally, caringly, and completely. When tragedy visits, Sailors must know that their leaders are united to ease their burdens and extend a caring hand in times of trouble.

GIVING THANKS

Often times, when we give thanks, we do so in the past tense. This is especially true during the holiday season, when we give thanks for the many blessings that have been bestowed upon us. We express gratitude to spiritual entities or thank our lucky stars for our good fortune. Time and again, however, we offer praise for our good health, wealth, and wisdom: our spouse, a job, a lucky lottery ticket, or an adventure experienced as we realize that from it all, we have been made stronger, better, and wiser. We often exclaim, "I'm so thankful for…," and with a renewed sense of appreciation, we thank for all that we have, all who we are, and for what we've endured.

Nevertheless, we learn valuable lessons though at times continue to make mistakes. After reflection and careful consideration, from what has been, we base resolutions in the hope that we can prosper. We think ahead fantastically as all things are made better in our mind's eye. We often see ourselves bigger, stronger, thinner, and taller, with thicker hair, without bodily imperfections, younger, bolder, emboldened, and blessed with celebrity. As we long for instant change yet forgo machinations, repetitions, and redundancy, the journey along life's path would better serve us if we could travel by warp speed to our own private paradise. We give thanks for what is, but really we mean that we are thankful for what was rather than what can be. We spend considerable time looking toward the future, yet we think of others who foretell it as tricksters and showmen; paying attention and money to those who portend to tell our future, we seldom believe in ourselves as the master of our destinies. Whether you're a believer in divine intervention or the fickleness of fate, life does not permit us to sit idly by waiting on either bounty or recompense. We've been blessed with unprecedented opportunity. As we reach forward for the reward of that enviable golden nugget, we must first pull ourselves up by the bootstrap. And, that's life; be thankful for it!

So then, be thankful for the ability to change, as life is not static, nor should you be. Be thankful for your abilities, your intellect, and the wherewithal to accomplish what to others may seem unobtainable. Be thankful for your strengths and, yes, your weaknesses, for both bring about an appreciable self-awareness. Be thankful for your courage to meet the unknown, to seek out the uncertainties in life, and to preserve when facing adversity. Give thanks for your compassion, your empathy, and your ability to extend your hand further than three feet. Give thanks for the ability to change yourself and others. Give thanks for your decision to serve humanity by serving your community, your country, and the nations of the world. *Be thankful for knowing that no matter how bad it gets, it's always worse for the enemy.* Be thankful for your decision to serve purposefully and selflessly, offering yourself as an example for others to follow. Give thanks for what life is and the awareness of self and how your behaviors impact others, appreciably and favorably. Give thanks for life and how you live it. Be thankful for everything you are and all that you have because life is fleeting and passes in a moment's notice. Give thanks for your ability to consider others first and offer yourself genuinely and unconditionally to those in need. Be thankful that you are a citizen of the greatest, most powerful, and most benevolent nation on earth, where openhandedness is the precept for public relations, care and concern are fostered, and opportunity is boundless. And, give thanks for the ability to judge first yourself, view the future with optimism, and both encourage and enable change within you in the service of others. Give thanks not only for the past and the present, but also for the future and your ability as one person who can influence change personally, professionally, familiarly, and globally. Sincerely, then, I give thanks for all you do. Thank you for serving our nation with commitment and sincerity.

THE BLESSINGS WITHIN

Often we reflect upon the holiday season and fondly recall the exchange of gifts, the festive atmosphere, and the family reunions. We think back to a time of innocence, of our youth, and happy times, times when the world seemed much smaller and unblemished. True, there are those who may have experienced less than others, feasted less on that which was hoped for, and received fewer gifts than others. In our youth, we expect that others will provide for us and, during the holidays, family and friends would surely extend themselves to suit us. The efforts to wrap our share of gifts were no match for our determination to unveil what was ours, the things that we wanted, that to which we were entitled. Of course, not all of us received equal measure; some were gifted with much more, and others received much less. Yet, for the vast majority, the holiday season is fondly reflected upon because the memories of those long-gone days are cherished more so than any discarded toy or outgrown item of clothing.

My point here is that in our youth, the holidays were defined by what we received and less by what we gave. I, too, once thought that blessings were tangible things. My health, a good job, prized possessions, money, love, and the benefits derived from them—these were indeed blessings to be thankful for. I thought myself fortunate, as though the blessings bestowed upon me had made me bigger and better: complete. Human nature being what it is, however, we take our blessings for granted. True, we receive a great deal in life. Yet, it is from within that we are enabled; if we first realize this and then act upon it, the reward bestowed upon others will indeed benefit us all.

A true blessing in life is the ability to benefit others from the benefits bestowed upon each of us. And, this is the true blessing of military service. An interesting view I submit, one that I recently discussed with a friend of mine. Military service and the profession of "warship vice worship" was the opposing talking point that was argu-

41

ably presented to me. My friend's position was this: "We've defined ourselves socially, politically, and nationally from the past years of armed conflict…where is the blessing in that?" Admittedly, I was taken aback. Not in capitulation, but to rally my response: "In all things, good and bad, those things difficult and those things which we would rather not be it at all, there are blessings in all things." I put forth that in war, true, there is devastation, destruction, and death. Neither side of the conflict is exempt. But truer still, in war, there is much opportunity for humanity! And, this is a true blessing indeed. First, your sacrifice, dedication to duty, and commitment to purposeful selfless service are true blessings. As military men and women, we stand ready to support and defend even those who disagree with our cause, a cause that ensures that the discord of our fellow countrymen is heard and whose rights are protected. Our ability to care and nurture the disadvantaged, poor, sick, and those who have known only turmoil are thankful for the blessings that we extend. Our commitment to leave our native shores and travel to those distant in order to deliver a better means of living, a better life, laying the foundations of good governance and economic opportunity, all are blessings that once received can be extended to the masses. We are blessed when we extend the benevolence of our nation to those in need and then watch a child's smile beam with a renewed sense of happiness from a once-hapless heart. In every opportunity and with every endeavor, the blessing of opportunity is evident.

As a man, I've replaced my childish selfishness with the desire to extend myself further in all that I do. Through my military service, I have learned that to count my blessings is to measure my ability to meet opportunity with optimism and with purpose. From within, I refine my ability to serve others. Believe me: as I count my blessings, with each day you are so accounted for. Your service, your compassion, and your willingness are among the blessings that I tally and that I praise in thanksgiving. From your daily service, I am so blessed and moved to do more each day. I am especially thankful for your commitment to purposeful selfless service.

CHARACTER: LOOK BEYOND YOURSELF!

I recently addressed a group of Sailors and the topic focused upon selfless service. As a sidebar, the mention of character was voiced by a young seaman. The gist of the conversation was that character is a defining personal trait. True, character defines who we are, what we do, and why we do what we do. As there is more to a person than their outwardly appearance, one's character is truly not necessarily a personal attribute so individually defined. Who we are, what we do, and why we do it extends well beyond ourselves. Indeed, "character extends far beyond our own line of sight." Each and every day, our personal actions, behaviors, and contributions are observed, noted, and frequently even emulated by others. As human beings, we naturally look to others for guidance and direction. And, herein lies the lesson that I imparted upon the young Seamen and which I now share with you. Through selfless, purposeful service, we can set the example for others, inspiring them to follow and initiate their own service. Character is a measure of one's being, a definition of both who and what we are and what we are made of. Character is an individual trait, but it can foster an organizational, societal, or even universal epiphany.

Yes, it begins with one person, but its potential influence is limitless. Making every effort to do what is right, even in the face of insurmountable adversity, to realize that the internal battle within may rage on long after the external battle has quieted, never wavering, but serving magnanimously—now that's character! Character is standing tall when faced with hardship. Bending, yes, but not breaking, challenging mediocrity and all the while realizing that the right thing to do is often a supreme ideal, yet still easily obtainable when strength of mind and purpose are driving one onward.

Character is defining oneself without saying a word. It is motivating others as they observe you doing your best. It is not just leading from the front, but rather extending a hand to those at the back of the pack. It's not just verbally motivating one who is weakening; it is also shouldering another's burden, affording them self-belief as they put their trust in you. Character is realizing that the most important person in one's life is someone else. Character is one's signature in life that enriches others before self. Character is an enviable trait that will be emulated, thereby heartening others to do more through their own struggles and sacrifices. Thomas Paine once wrote, "Reputation is what men and women think of us; character is what God and angels know of us." Through our actions and deeds we shape our reputation. Truly, goodness or vice will be emulated by others through their perceptions of us. May it be the former rather than the latter that you exemplify to others as they pursue their own direction along life's path.

Character is also giving more of self than what is expected in return. Rather than the personal, it is an offering to the greater good that clearly defines character. May you define yourself similarly, positively, and with distinction! Give more of yourself, and in so doing, your endeavors will reward others as they benefit those beyond their own line of sight. Character is an enviable trait that clearly defines more than ourselves but rather, when emulated, defines a greater sense of being for others.

THE PIVOTAL CROSSROADS IN LIFE!

As a command representative, I recently accompanied a Sailor to court. The Sailor had been issued a summons to appear before the magistrate. Over the years, I have accompanied more than a few Sailors before the bench. Whether a mistake, a task forgotten, or wanton disregard for the law, these Sailors have presented themselves before the magistrate accepting the mandates of the court and followed through with the prescribed corrective action. As a command representative, I stood by them, ensuring that the command would make certain that the mandates were fulfilled. There is, however, so much more to the experience than that which I have described above. For the Sailor, the experience enables them to stand accountable before authority to be both judged and served. In uniform, you represent so much more than yourself; and due to this circumstance, your every transgression is magnified. More is expected of those in uniform, as they individually represent the entire organization and the totality of our nation. To the civilian observer, the uniform represents many things, some based on personal experiences, to others an acquired fiction, and still others their perceptions based on personal bias. What they may not know nor understand is that the uniform is not ordinary cloth but rather the fabric that binds us together. And, of course, to earn the right to wear the uniform, there comes a higher degree of personal commitment and adherence and acceptance of what is right. And, yet there is more to the story here.

As I sat waiting for the Sailor to be called forward, dozens of citizens presented themselves before the court. Many of them were young men and women, without means of employment and with no money. Some bore a history of past transgressions that made them seem destined for a future of incarceration. Some had violated the conditions of their probation while others were repeat offenders who had already been punished months before. One after another presented themselves before the court with a disheveled appearance and cavalier attitude, and when sentenced to jail, they appeared not par-ticularly bothered by it all. In fact, one young man appeared before the court, inappropriately dressed, with a sense of frivolity and more than a scant scent of alcohol on his breath. He was reprimanded by the court on all counts. And, yet there is more to this story.

When the Sailor was called before the court, both of us stood in deference, representing more than each of us and addressing the magistrate respectfully. As a command representative, I addressed the court on behalf of the Sailor, providing a personal representation of the Sailor's integrity and ability. The Sailor professed sincere regret, apologizing to the court and to the police officers.

While this young Sailor was appearing before the magistrate, I observed another young man; he too was inappropriately dressed, though with less the sense of frivolity, as he appeared in awe of what he observed. Certainly, he took note of what is most probably the thing he most longs for: rightful direction, enabling purpose, the incentive of personal responsibility, and the reward of seeing past himself and focusing on serving others. And yet, with a defined application, life's proper path presents itself before each decision and with each step forward.

And, here is the meaning of the story. The Navy offers a better way in life for all who serve and for those who desire to positively and meaningfully change their lives. Each day, we all approach those pivotal crossroads where our choices or indecision not only influence but also impact our lives as well as the lives of others. The Navy offers training, tradecraft, and personal growth through diverse and challenging experiences. There is an innate trait in all of us—some though fail to realize—that there is no finer public service than that of serving others. Personal accountability is a standard measured with a high water mark. Much more is expected of those who serve, for we serve something larger then ourselves: we serve all others. Remember, when you face a crossroad, focus your attention on the right direc-tion, and the proper path will be before you.

ARE YOU A VIP!

As we are inundated from all means of media of the red carpet, the royal treatment, and special considerations, we at times revel in fantasy as we too wish we could walk in the footsteps of celebrity. Fame and admiration of adoring fans, the recognition of worth, and the glamorous life are the subject of daydreams and aspirations. What must it be like to be instantly recognized everywhere you go? As admiring crowds hoping for a momentary indulgence, we think of the good life that rewards icons of stardom. It is easy, in light of this, to lose sight of yourself and the value that you bring to the world. We think of these people as VIPs, and we don't see that we too are very important people. For you, as well, are a VIP. Your service to America is very important, purposeful, and significant. You are held in high regard, and a grateful nation sincerely thanks you for your service.

As a VIP, you are important for certain, yet there is more to being a VIP than importance alone. Consider the following:

Virtue. As a servant of our nation, being a person of virtue, you are incorruptible, and you believe in the virtue of being in the service of others. Altruism is the foundation from which you stand. Considering others before self, you serve with unselfish resolve. You believe in yourself and your appreciation for the lives and contributions of others. Your actions and generosity are traits that serve as enviable examples that others will emulate. Yet, rather than being first in line or taking life's red carpet in stride, you'll allow others to pass before you, offering those in need a helping hand. Surely you understand that others may take the spotlight, but you are fulfilled knowing that it was you who made prosperity possible for others.

Integrity. You faithfully endeavor to serve knowing that your conduct defines your personal signature in life. Your moral compass tests straight, and you strive to stay the course. You realize that others expect you to do what is right, to guide them, lead them, and provide them the way when their personal aspirations may cast them off course. In the service of others, their needs come before your own. You aspire to advance not your own cause but that of others. You are resolute in your beliefs. And, you see the land upon which you stand as being more precious than your own shadow cast upon it. You stand upright though the burden of leadership may be weighty, and yet you are willing to take on the burden of others because it is the right thing to do.

Professional. When you are under no gaze but your own conscious, you conduct yourself as if in the public spotlight. Why? Because you are a professional, and in so doing, you know it is expected of you. You subscribe to putting forth the extraordinary, even when the task might be mundane. You believe that to waver is to fail those who demand much from you. You are resolute in your ambition. You are confident, yet you are not conceited. You are demanding of others without becoming overbearing. You care for those you are charged to lead, for within them all, you know that their best can be inspired as they emulate who you are.

Although the inclusive definition of a VIP may be perceived as a lofty ideal, if you believe in yourself, seek to broaden your service while empathizing with others, and sacrifice on their behalf, you will inspire others to define themselves as you seek to be and as they hope also to become.

MAGNIFICENT AND MAGNANIMOUS!

Without question, the United States Armed Forces are truly magnificent. No other military can match our organization, operational capability, logistic support, and the combat effectiveness of our adaptive military force. At any given time, our military proudly displays the flag and projects its majesty, safeguarding individual liberties, enabling good governance while maintaining free trade. The United States military's combat effectiveness is unprecedented, and our military capability is undisputed. The mere presence of the US military causes immediate notice and pause. A rich heritage demands standards not to be paralleled but rather elevated. Our military strength is emboldened by the valor of those who have toiled, sacrificed, and shed their blood in the service of country, believing that what they have done make possible the prosperity of others. Our enemy knows our strength, certainly knows our might, and recognizes the folly of their intent when above the horizon our national ensign appears majestic atop a mast or embroidered on the shoulder of a battle-worn uniform. Our military is rightly awe inspiring. What, then, causes our enemies to rally against such preeminence? Though envy is a powerful emotion, I believe it less a rally against the magnificence of the United States military but rather in response to our magnanimity.

What our enemies fear most is what they cannot themselves provide. Our military is chivalrous rather than chauvinistic. Our benevolence is worldwide. We offer compassion to those who have for so long shouldered the yoke of tyranny. We humanely offer essential services and extend the compassion of the American people to those who know little of a people well beyond their own comprehension. We seek not to enchain, but rather to uplift. We offer not despair, but encourage smiles—and by design, we offer hope to those who are hapless.

Yet, more than our presence, it is our flag that evokes such hostility from our enemies. We often witness our flag torn, set ablaze, and tramped upon by those who are spurred along by fanaticism. A distorted view, our enemies publicize a notion of imperialism as they seek to defame us—not because of our presence, but rather due to their own inabilities and, yes, their own distorted views. Extreme are their ideas, radical their beliefs, intolerant of equality are they. They publicize the injustices and the vices of America, though we champion unparalleled opportunity, religious tolerance, liberty, charity, and goodwill to all. We seek not to isolate those thought by some to be undesirable, but as a touchstone, we espouse social inclusion. Above all else, I believe what antagonizes our enemies most is that our flag proudly waves: not with spiteful intent, but rather in spite of their best efforts to pull asunder.

We offer those in need deliverance. We extend ourselves to those who have been besieged, and we are a light for those who live in darkness. We are willing servants to those at home and abroad, and we care equally for both emissary and adversary. For when an enemy combatant can no longer sustain the fight, we offer him compassion, humanity, and kindness. We acknowledge that words alone cannot justly express the gratitude of those whose lives our military benefits. It is the union of a glance, a palm's embrace, or a penetrating smile that signifies the appreciation of those whose own kind seeks only to distort our cultural character. Accountability and transparency serve as our operational paradigm, none of which our enemies subscribe to. Unlike our enemies, we conduct ourselves holding dear to the guiding principles of law. And, to those who are enemy, we extend legal provisions provided by our nation's founding document, the Constitution of the United States: a document our enemies seek to manipulate in their own defense. Despite this, we remain magnificent and magnanimous, defining military service through endeavors on behest and behalf of all.

CELEBRATING OUR CULTURAL VOCATION

Several years ago, I visited one of the top cybertechnologies companies located in California's Silicon Valley and was fascinated by the sense of a business culture that the company embraced. The high-tech ultramodern layout of the facility was impressive. Company representatives were articulate and savvy with regard to human resources, their customers, broadening the bottom line, and seeking new world markets. Spreadsheets and product demonstrations were striking, yet it was the human capital of the company—a testament to its ingenuity—that was most notable. When asked about the recruitment and the entry-level compensation package offered potential employees, what was revealed was a number nearing six figures. The pay and benefits package appeared not to be the sole draw for potential employees. It was apparent that it was the "cultural amenities," which, when packaged along with salaries, piqued the interest of candidates and fused longevity and company loyalties. The intrinsic value of incorporated work, unity of effort, productivity, and importantly a sense of inclusion, worth, and demand fostered an atmosphere of efficacy that transcended the corporate structure throughout work sites both here and abroad.

For just a moment, I thought, "How is it possible that the Armed Forces, in the dynamic world of recruitment, can attract young adults who too are inspired to ameliorate their personal standing, earn a living, while being included within an organization that believes both in its corporate vision but also empowers its workforce to fulfill its vision by charting its future?" And, then of course, in retrospection, I answered the previous rhetorical question that I had asked myself. For the answer is based less on what the military offers, but rather what individuals present: a united effort, a melding of divergent skills into a common purpose, fused with honor, purpose, sacrifice, and compassion. Let me be first to admit that the compen-

51

sation that our Armed Force receives, although adequate, is far from enough. The same twenty-two-year-old college graduate who enlists in our military receives a base pay that equates to a wage slightly above the federal minimum wage. Believe me, I was thirty-four years old and a university graduate who willingly enlisted knowing that the pay and benefits paled in comparison to that which I had earned previously. Like so many others, the sacrifices are realized when we review our very first Leave and Earning Statement! It is, however, our culture of purposeful selfless service, the desire to defend that is held dear, and the occasion to benefit the lives of others that motivates above all. In return, we delight in the rightful recompense of a smile from another who looks to you as a hero, a lifesaver, a champion. It is the inclusion within a constituency of patriots that rallies an inward desire to belong to a collective that has shed the selfish sense of pure individualism and who unreservedly don the fabric of our nation. It is the realization that a personal effort truly has merit while enabling the lives of those here and abroad who depend upon us; whose cries of distress, without us, would go unanswered; and whose liberties would be denied. Without our efforts, the weighty burdens of despair and disparity would flourish. Because of our service, to those subjugated, we freely offer the chance for a better life; now empowered, they are moved to make a better way in life: free to choose and free to decide their own course.

So then, it is who we are, what we represent, and what we provide that is cause to celebrate. You are guardians, lifesavers, and champions; you are heroes who, united in purpose, know that remuneration is less the focus than that which is provided to community, country, and those for whom we serve.

WHAT'S YOUR NEXT MOUNTAIN TO CLIMB?

From the Summit of Every Mountain, There Is Far More Beyond

Several years ago, I enjoyed the pleasure of being in the company of David Breashears and listening to him speak about his experiences on Mount Everest. A director and filmmaker, he led the Everest IMAX film expedition in 1996. Drawing from his life experience in bouldering, climbing, and mountaineering, he authored *High Exposure: An Enduring Passion for Everest and Unforgiving Places.*[1] From the pages of *High Exposure,* it is apparent that his ability to overcome trial and tribulation, while surmounting life's impediments, were not necessarily overshadowed by his multiple trips to the summit of Mount Everest. The book is a testament to David Breashears's courage and determination.

During the conversation, David spoke of the triumph of being atop the world's highest peak perched at 29,028 feet. He also addressed the art of leadership, respect for others, and decisions that affect the team. Interestingly, he also focused upon the ability to motivate self and others to muster the herculean effort to get to the summit and return from a place he described as the "death zone." "There is so little oxygen above 25,000 feet that the human body is unable to adapt; Every moment spent at that altitude is time the body spends starved of oxygen," he writes.[2] The discussion centered less upon David's personal achievements and rather on his application of leadership upon those he was charged to lead on an expedition to the top of the world. His ability to organize, encourage, and reassure others while weathering the inevitable storm was measured by rousing others to move forward. Whether it be ascending the steep slopes or descending from a place of fleeting life, achievement is measured in but a few precious steps and minutes. It is the ability to look beyond the next stride, to recognize consequences of a misplaced step, and to deduce the proper path to follow that are crucial elements of leadership.

Although the numbers of mountaineers who attempt to climb Mount Everest have grown exponentially over recent years, most of us will never take the first step on the rise to the top of the world. Yet, we all face imposing impediments along our life's journey. I've climbed Mount Fuji three times, and although the summit is less than half the height of Mount Everest, it was for me a defining point in my life. This was, to date, the highest mountain that I've climbed—but all the same, other personal and professional obstacles have appeared as challenging. Some of these impediments were tangible while others have been some of my own making: self-imposed, daunting as well as haunting, overcome by no less the measure of grit than that which required surmounting Mount Fuji. As a leader, the challenges and burdens associated with guiding others, offering care and development while compelling them to achieve that which they may think unattainable or, by defining limitations that forestall their hopes due to practicalities and physical constraints, lend ink to our defining professional signature. The passage of life is a long journey far beyond any single goal attained along the way. As leaders, we must recognize that accomplishments may be singly defining, but represent a momentary respite from which we embolden ourselves and others to forge ahead. There is much more to be accomplished after the goal has been obtained. Much can be taken away from Breashers's words: "Getting to the summit is only half of any climb. Getting back down is everything—the finish line is at the bottom, not on the top."[3]

As leaders, we have to inspire others as we drive ourselves onward. We cannot succumb to becoming tyrants. We must guide others toward achievement, recognizing that not every endeavor will yield the desired goal. We must not allow ourselves to be individually transfixed on a goal at the expense of others. Acknowledging that the long haul is wrought with setbacks, we must recognize life's broad experience and define our ability to lead by casting off blinders that channel our vision directly ahead. Breashers reminds us, "If you stop long enough to listen, the mountains always have something to teach you."[4] Mountains that stand before us, both real and metaphorical, are not improbabilities, but rather challenges to be overcome. As leaders, we must view a goal from a collective ideal fostering personal and professional growth for one and all.

K+C (E) = SM2

A Formula for Success

On a recent transatlantic flight, I was reviewing random thoughts and somehow I returned to my junior high school days and the challenges of math class. Funny how the mind drifts—sort of like it would regularly while sitting in Mr. Tokarchik's math class! All of a sudden, my thoughts merged, and I found myself thinking about the present and the challenges faced on a daily basis. Often, Sailors will ask me career advice, and considering the divergent paths and different focal points, I considered a formula for success. Now, I must admit that Mr. Tokarchik often cited that I would apply my own unique formulas to solve those daunting math problems that he assigned me. I would somehow factor and figure the answer to the computations—honestly, more often than not, my best guess would be applied. It was more so the application of a formula that was the problem to be solved. I would spend considerable time working the problem rather than concentrating on the solution. Somehow, I managed to solve those endless math computations—though forty-two years after graduating from Kingston High School, I still struggle to balance my checkbook! But all in all, I've faced many challenges and solved more than my fair share of those I call my own, as well as those presented to me by others. The formula presented here is a theory void of complex algorithms or quantum hypothesis; it is, however, accomplished and universally beneficial. It is a true leadership principle offering a blueprint for success. The practical application of this formula for success emboldens the individual and benefits those who receive its appliance and functionality. Here now is an analysis of the computation for the formula for success.

$$K+C (E) = SM2$$

The *K* represents the requisite knowledge of a leader and naval professional. Knowledge is earned from many an endeavor. Personal and professional attributes based on formal education or, as my father always equated his success to, the school of hard-knocks; it is knowledge that enables a leader to be a factor for individual success. We educate ourselves not for ourselves alone. We educate ourselves in order to educate others. We are schooled and so we should school others. Of course, not all knowledge comes from the pages of formal text. Practical application is always the end state of any computation or theory.

The *C* represents credibility based upon one's know-how and proven accomplishments. Credibility is the mainstay of one's professional signature. Practicality, resourcefulness, and personal integrity are standards that define one's authority in a given matter. As leaders, our credibility, which fuses personal and professional traits, incorporating our ethical and moral attributes, is a benchmark that so defines our behavior and, importantly as a leader, so outlines the behaviors of those we are charged to lead. Our credibility must be an enviable example for others to follow. Credibility is an amalgam of faithfulness, personal responsibility, and determination that enables us to stand against that which would divide during the challenges of any examination of self and of our ability to lead others.

The *E* represents experience, which is the standard from which we are measured. Our time-tested knowledge of mechanics, applications, and theory bolster our knowledge and credibility. Juniors and peers will measure your abilities based upon your experience and demonstrated application of that which they seek to learn. As leaders, we are obligated to impart our experience upon those who are seeking direction. We provide the valuable lessons learned along our life's journey, understanding that the best advice is that which we should not do while enabling others to do what is right along their own journey in life.

The *SM2* equates to being a subject matter mentor who trains personnel to obtain core competencies, who instructs a workforce to acquire operational knowledge of complex systems, one who trains personnel to develop and formulate standard operating procedures and unify proficiencies into a cohesive fusion center of excellence. The formula for success is a multifaceted union of the human experience and represents a triumph of assembly and purpose. Yet, with any theory, refinement, examination, and utility will define a purposeful solution to the plan of any day and the problems that will inevitably be encountered. As with any theory, however, the formula is only validated through practical application and examination. It is now your time to test its utility through performance.

AMAZING GRACE

"A Standard for Leadership"

Coincidentally—or, perhaps, by design—I once, on the same day, overheard three versions of the iconic hymn, "Amazing Grace." I first heard a haunting rendition played on an echoing bagpipe, another sung by Chris Tomlin, and then I listened to a previously downloaded version performed by guitar virtuosos Carlos Santana and Jeff Beck on my MP3 player. As my interest piqued, I thought about how grace can be incorporated into my practiced leadership principle of espousing selfless purposeful service. Contemplating the word *grace*, I realized that much like the song with many performed versions, the word too has many meanings. From the mechanics of movement to moral fortitude and theology, grace defines elegance, action, mercy, and favor. As a principle of leadership, one's grace should endure as the song itself. It is here that I hope to further the principle of grace as a facet of leadership that I trust you will incorporate in your efforts to manage your day-to-day challenges.

As naval leaders, we face myriad situations and stand before personnel with divergent backgrounds. We must consistently rise above the standard and strive for an adaptive ability to formulate a course of action to meet the needs of a unique workforce. Not a reactionary, but rather as an activist for resolution, a leader must demonstrate the ability to both mitigate while navigating through the dilemmas that face those they are charged to lead and manage their own challenges that they too face. Navigation must not be meandering. A leader must be enabled to enable others, uniting the efforts of those who follow in order to define resolution. Now that's grace.

A decision made, I trust others will follow suit. The most difficult aspect of human nature to manage is, of course, free will. As a leader and an exemplar for others, we must enable those we are charged to lead to change their minds, forgo free will, and submit to our directives. Moral fortitude permits us to bear self-imposed burdens as well as saddle the encumbrances of others. Standing firm, confronting adversity all the while admitting when at fault, a leader's rally must be a fusion of self-discipline and principles. As the follower confidently embraces the reason to step forward in the face of hardship, rather than considering a decision to be rash or impulsive, those who follow do so not blindly, but faithfully. A leader is so defined when mired by the concerns of others and knowing the way ahead to be arduous, yet navigating the perils and precipices with motion and poise. Such is a measure of a leader's ability, resilience, and yes, such is a leader's grace.

As leaders, we must, of course, resort to our own abilities, realizing our inner strength, a determined spirit if you will, while recognizing the guiding force of our individually held spirituality. From my own experience, I write with confidence that many of my most difficult decisions have been determined by both inner fortitude and consultation with divinity. During challenging times such as these, it is my consults with God that I am provided with the vision to faithfully step off in a direction that I trust others will follow. Admittedly, at times, I may be lost, hesitant, and unsure of the course to take. At times such as these, I do, however, trust that my faith will enable me to know that where there is darkness I will see the proper path and lead others in the right direction. Now, my friend, that's amazing grace: "To be once lost but now found, was blind, but now I see." May you too see the right way that is before you and lead others properly and with rightful conviction.

HEROES NEED APPLY,... THEMSELVES

I have spent much time contemplating the events of our time and the media's fascination with celebrity and negativism; I find it distressing that in our celebration of media icons, a relative few know the name of James Dunham, a true American hero. One need only look at the media to be bombarded with the negativism that is often linked to pop icons, societal elites, corrupt business executives, and questionable political leaders. I find it saddening that a great number of people are drawn to, identify with, and emulate the behavior of such idols while there are many in harm's way, selflessly serving and carrying out their duties while providing for the impoverished, the needy, and those longing for a better way. It upsets me that many know those antisocial and irreverent media types, but few know Corporal James Dunham who was awarded the Medal of Honor posthumously for his extraordinary valor while fighting in Iraq.

Many who have been recognized as heroes served selflessly well outside of their chosen discipline. Whether by design or circumstance, heroes rise above the din, break away from the pack, and extend further a hand to another in need. Motivated by adrenaline and altruism, heroes let conscience, not caution, determine their actions.

Heroes are simple folk who have served significantly. The following is an excerpt from the letter to the regimental commander recommending Corporal Dunham for the Medal of Honor: "Realizing the enemy possessed a hand grenade Corporal Dunham may have been able to avoid his fatal wounds by simply moving away... His personal action was far beyond the call of duty and saved the lives of his fellow Marines. He is worthy of the highest recognition and honor of our nation."[5] Corporal Dunham: an ordinary young man who displayed extraordinary valor.

I offer you here another exemplar of a hero. In 2004, after delivering much-needed supplies and clothing to an Afghan orphanage, a place where hardship and scarcity were commonplace, a remarkable act of consequence was etched in my mind. Although a stark place, when a hand is extended, the brightest smiles signify that America's benevolence is welcomed and appreciated. Our team spent a couple of hours distributing items to the children, interacting and shaking hands, photographing soldiers and orphans, and enjoying quiet moments of cultural discovery. With our visit ended and our convoy on the move, I noticed a boy running toward us. The boy was running with his hand in his tattered jacket pocket. I must say that more than a few members of our team were concerned. However, as the boy ran toward my vehicle, and under guarded eye of the others, he reached into his pocket and offered me an apple. This boy, whose extraordinary act of kindness and thanksgiving, knowing the perils of his actions, sought to selflessly sacrifice a significant portion of his meager daily ration to me. In my mind, this boy's selfless action of extending a hand, unselfishly denying his own needs in order to benefit another, signifies courage truly noble in purpose and heroic in result.

Often, the collective notion of a hero is one who displays superhuman strength, endurance, and ability. Truly Corporal Dunham's actions signified this as he threw himself upon a grenade in order to shield his counterparts from the explosion. We often question ourselves, wondering if we are such a person. I offer two points: First, you are stronger than you imagine, and your willingness to serve others sets you apart from those selfish and those who seek the limelight. Second, a gentle hand extended to those in need; the ability to provide for others; the willingness to serve where your duty calls while enduring harsh conditions, isolation, and danger, in the hearts and minds of many, you are known and believed to be a hero. You protect all that is dear to us; you forward peace and prosperity and provide hope and promise to those who suffer under tyrannical rule. Today, heroes are very much needed. Commit yourselves to your duties and serve broadly; extend yourselves in the service of others, apply yourselves, and your heroic deeds will be imparted upon those whose lives will be made better because of your actions and your abilities.

There are many ways to act heroically. Whether in a firefight or fighting a fire, as a community advocate or a volunteer at a veteran's hospital, a hospice aide or a teacher's assistant, a companion to the elderly or a civil servant, your service is vital to the defense of our nation. The impact of your commitment to excellence and dedication to duty extends far beyond that which is immediately apparent to you. Your service to our nation during a time of war is praiseworthy. You follow in the footsteps of service members who have met the enemy and the challenges of their time. They sacrificed so much in order that we should persevere. Be confident in believing that in their eyes, you are their heroes who now serve where our military demands. Thank you for your service, your actions, and your willingness to give more of yourself to those whose needs are great and whose time is now. A true hero serves with purpose and with immediacy, selflessly, and without reservation.

THANKSGIVING

"In Reflection, We Give Thanks, in Anticipation, Offer Praise for What Will Be"

Reflecting upon the Thanksgivings from my past, I readily recall the anticipation of the feast: the wonderful aromas that would waft about the house, the banter of voices, and of course, the Macy's Day Parade broadcast on the television in the corner of the dining room. With the windows translucent with steam, the curtains would be pushed aside by my mother in wonder of what her boys were doing out there in the cold air of upstate New York. My brothers and I would be unaware of the chill as we played football in the yard, the frosted ground hard beneath us in our gang tackles and the frequent pile-on. First, mother would call us to come inside, and then father would summon us. Cleaned and ready, the blessing said, the festive meal would begin. No surprise on the menu, our meal, however, was steeped in tradition as a family united; we enjoyed our dinner and time together. Focused on the plenty piled upon my plate and with good will permeating the dining room, I could not help from time to time but to give my brother a swift kick under the table. Not malevolent, but rather mischievous as I recall, but neither my brother nor my parents considered my act as anything less than out of place for such an occasion. Yet, it was my brother who would readily scheme to retaliate at the right moment; perhaps when it was that that bulbous mound of mashed potatoes gingerly aloft on my fork and nearing the height of my chin would he kick off his revenge. And, so it was around the holiday table at the Jordan household.

Many things change with time. Over the course of my military career, I've spent few Thanksgivings at home as my military service has taken me far afield. Over the years too, the place settings at the family table have diminished. Grandmother, my great-aunt, my mother and father, and my brother have passed on. Several years ago, the Jordan home stood empty of all but a few boxes, remnants, and forgotten keepsakes. Surely the new owners will sit at their dining room table at Thanksgiving and count their blessings offering praise for all that they are blessed with as well.

What I've learned over my life is that Thanksgiving is not solely reserved to the last Thursday in the month of November. "In reflection, we give thanks; in anticipation, we offer praise for what will be." So then, what am I so thankful for? I am thankful for my health and abilities and the opportunities to serve my family, my community, and the global population. I am thankful for the love and support of those near to my heart and to the encouragement of those thankful of my military service. I am thankful for the opportunity to serve with those who consider their uniform as an individual statement of pride and collective testimonial to unity of purpose. I am thankful for being enabled to serve others in response to their needs, forgoing my individual wants without regret. And, we should be thankful as Americans to recognize our divergent views while still displaying a unity of purpose that binds us as a nation. Envied by the world, we should still be thankful that although vilified by some, as Americans, we extend a hand to all in need, not to hem in, but rather to enable, not with chauvinistic intent, but rather forwarding the ideals of freedom, individualism, and opportunity that as Americans we are thankful for.

So with days of Thanksgiving, I offer thanks and praise for the blessings of the past and the opportunities that exist. In reflection, we give thanks in anticipation, offering praise for what will be. It is here that I extend my sincere gratitude and appreciation to family members who support you and our force. May you all enjoy the blessings of the day, and may your days to come be richly blessed. As we gather around the table, let us offer thanks and praise for all things borne from the goodness of our endeavors, and for that which we are prepared to do in the service of others.

A MERRY CHRISTMAS, CAROL

December 20, 2008

The holidays are a time of wonder, hope, and reflection. True, this is the season that represents many things for many people. For those of faith, the season is a time of congregation, prayer, and rejoicing. For families, it is a time of togetherness, anticipation, gifts, and reminiscing of holidays past. For the little ones, it is a time of wonder, fantasy, and looking forward in anticipation of things to come. It is a time of magic for most, yet it can be a time of despair for some.

As a boy, for me, Christmas was shared with family, listening to holiday songs on the radio, with the Christmas tree all aglow, snuggled in my bed as I would hear distant sleigh bells that my mother would ring in the early morning hours—and know that the holiday would begin early with presents to be opened and others to be exchanged. And, later in the day, giving thanks for all we shared, grace would be said before the bountiful meal would be short-lived. As a boy, I was blessed to receive that which I needed rather than all that I wanted. Those were magical times that I will always cherish.

As I ventured about the globe, the world presented itself in terms of stark contrast to my childhood experience. As an adult, I viewed the world in terms of reality rather than a world of childish fantasy. I've seen the disadvantaged and viewed abject poverty. I have seen children as young as only a few years old working in the streets. I've seen children clothed only in tattered remnants of discarded clothing; I've seen children standing ankle deep in mud thickened with frost without the benefit of shoes. I've seen women begging in the streets with outstretched arms, offering others a severely deformed child. And, I've seen girls forced to offer themselves to men in order to enrich those who enslave them. Some say it's a cruel world. Yet, each situation presents opportunities to serve others, to offer ourselves as a solution rather than a cause, and to extend the benevolence of our service to those less fortunate.

There are many who are homeless, who endure the frigid nights and face the cold hearts of those who pass by. Seeing them as nuisances, we turn away from their pleas. Hopeless and hapless they are. No debate on the reasons why, we just look beyond their sad eyes. What I offer here are two divergent perspectives of the holiday season: both individual and, with the times, all too traditional. There will always be those who are advantaged, and there will be those who are hindered by much more than inconvenience. There, too, will always be a way to offer remedy. Of course, there will always be a choice. I offer the reader a poem that I penned for a memo released in December of 2008, entitled "A Merry Christmas, Carol."

City streets aglow with holiday good cheer,
Bells ring, kettles fill, an empty stomach and hope lie still.
Just off the lane, another side of times so merry;
There, out of place, dark and dank, many are wary.
Store windows attract those who yet long for more;
Around do they step, certain not to tarry.
A world of wonder viewed wide eyed,
There within a cardboard box doth Carol lie, her frosty tears fall among hushed cries.
Shoppers dash to and fro, overlooking her outstretched hand;
Defiled, alone, no loving embrace, where warmth emits from a rust encrusted steam grate.
Who knows what tomorrow may bring; anticipation of gifts, of home,
Family warmth around the fire, but there within a box, numb to a life so dire,

Another empty day long to transpire, hunger but a fleeting desire;

As the city wakes to yet another dawn; for-
lorn she lays, her breath to retire.

No longer the need to hide, on gilded wing
doth Carol ride;

Cold and hunger forever no more, from the
street to Heaven's door.

May the joy of the holiday season transcend throughout the
year, and may the joy that you experience be passed on to those unbeknownst to you. May you find the time, the means, and the purpose
to extend a simple gift, an offering from the heart, a compassionate
donation to those in need. Do more than offer to pass spare change,
but rather embrace those who receive your charity. This is a gift that
surely will be warm-heartedly passed on. I thank you for your purposeful selfless service to those in need, and I am thankful for your
societal contributions. Blessed are those whose lives you touch, and
blessed am I to serve with you. May providence prosper you and
those you hold dearly.

WITH THE NEW YEAR

January 01, 2009

With optimism and hope, we look forward to the coming year. With the holiday season gone for yet another year, we settle in for a long winter, and we yearn for the approaching spring. With the lengthening days, we set into motion the way ahead. What the coming days have in store, we may not know; but as we chart our course, we believe that we'll navigate past all obstacles, overcoming all impediments and bypassing all disappointment. We desire all things positive: the best of health and welfare, financial success, and our just reward. We project that we'll look back a year from now and realize that our eventual achievement was unfettered. Yet, before we get to the finish line marked by the New Year's end, in reality we will face many challenges, hurdles, and yes, trying and perhaps troubling times. It is less the reward that measures success, but rather the struggles that were rightfully handled that defines one's accomplishment.

Life is a series of events that are both timely and random. These events are defining moments that identify the person. Truth told, not all events will realize immediate results of our liking. We'll detour off our charted course. We'll choose the wrong path; we'll make mistakes, some more costly than others; and we'll face the consequences that are the result of our actions. Some will experience repeated successes while others will struggle being impeded by the burdens of the journey. We'll often question the reasons, the why, and the means to the success of others. We look inward and question our abilities, our intellect, and our place in the world. But take to heart that questioning is the first step toward refinement. Interestingly, according to Bill Gates, "Success is a lousy teacher. It seduces smart people into thinking they can't lose." I prefer to measure success not by rewards earned, but rather by the methods employed to obtain it. A measure of success should include an apportionment of endured hardship, for success is an amalgam of life's experience rather than those things that result from it.

It has been said, "To err is human." Consider, then, the error of our ways. Often, these experiences define who we are. I too have exercised poor judgment and made many personal and professional mistakes. Yet, I have learned from these experiences. These events in my life provided me with the means to lead others by first addressing my shortcomings and vowing to enhance my abilities to serve and mentor others by focusing on my faults while providing others an example to follow through my personal and professional success. My grandmother once told me, "The best lessons in life are those things that we must not do again." Believe me, I have learned much from my lessons that often exacted quite a toll upon my travel through life. I've learned greatly from trials and tribulations. I believe that I've learned from these experiences and in time provide others in the naval service with an example of what not to do while demonstrating that yes, "to err is human" yet too successfully overcome is the sign of a leader that defines success.

With the year ahead, I wish you all rightful abilities, the where-withal, the courage to overcome, and the realization that it is fitting to extend a hand to those who follow in your life's journey. To those who follow, teach them well. Your tutelage, your insight, your fore-sight, and your wisdom will enable in them the drive, determination, vision, and focus to find their way in life. Teach them those things that must not be done and enlighten those you're charged to lead of the trials you've endured, and you'll enable them the ways and means to succeed.

ON THE PROPER PATH, CHOOSE
THE RIGHT DIRECTION

With the journey of life before us, we often hold to the notion that we know the right direction in which to proceed. Admittedly, at times we walk blindly, oblivious to opportunity yet focused upon that which forestalls our advancement. Anecdotally, as a young boy, I recall that my father and I once stood beside an upstate New York canal watching ships slowly proceed along the inland waterway. I remember a deckhand who was walking aft as the ship advanced, and due to the forward motion of the ship, he appeared to remain parallel to where I was standing along the waterway. Looking at me, he said, "Boy, this is the story of my life. I walk and walk, but never seem to go anywhere!" Similarly, how often do we all experience such inertia as the world passes us by? More often than occasionally, I've thought that I had spun my wheels and making no progress as due dates and deadlines, opportunities further outpaced my efforts. Dismayed, I thought I'd never "get there from here"; only after falling further behind did I realize that I'd stepped off in the wrong direction although the proper path was at my feet! With this realization, I'd refocus, admit to a temporary setback, "buck up," and drive on.

I am constantly reminded of what my father used to say: "It is far better to change direction than to be haunted by those things that could have been." My father also taught me that adventurous foresight is far better than dogged resistance to change. Believe me, I've at times resisted change and stubbornly thought I knew the right way. It was only after experiencing a daunting challenge and with deep introspection that I'd evoke the lessons etched in my mind that my father had taught me years ago. Rather than admit to defeat, I'd permit myself to change course and step off rightly. Over the years, I've learned that plans are but vague dreams that materialize before our eyes, only becoming realities due to our ability to define the precepts of accomplishment.

Another lesson that I've learned is that we are defined not so particularly by the past, but by how we accept the future. It is what you will do rather than what you did that defines you. It is one's ability to pause, evaluate, and reflect before taking that anxious and optimistic first step that will stand as a defining point in life. Undeniably, the way ahead will be trying. For some, the journey will be perilous while for others the progress will be rich with repeated success. Yet, for most, the passage will be wrought with challenges, with periods of mediocrity, and the occasional high point. Importantly then, it is not where you find yourself but rather how you got there that defines the journey.

Over time, I have learned that more than coincidence, things happen. It is a matter of faith that enables me to accept that although my path may be predetermined, as I progress, I must look beyond myself for direction. Self-confidence may be superficial, but it is faith that is supernatural, empowering me to press on, permitting me to meet the challenges that wait upon me. As things do happen, things do matter. We truly define our direction by the way in which we meet our life's trials. On the proper path, we must then step off in the right direction; guided by our ability to do what is right, that which is just, and that which will benefit more than ourselves, it is the way that we progress that will define our journey.

May the New Year be one of good health and good fortune for you and your families. I wish you much success in your personal and professional endeavors. Understand that both of your struggles as well as your achievements benefit those you are charged to lead. Clearly, it is your determination, your perseverance, and your ability to shoulder the burdens of others along your journey that will enable others to follow your advance. Remember this: as you step off, others will surely follow.

A PARABLE: THE COFFEE CUP

More than a few years ago, as an instructor at the Navy and Marine Corps Intelligence Training Center, I was talking with a student who was a bit older than most and who was having trouble adjusting to military life. His academic performance was mediocre at best, and he was continually being counseled for his lack of military bearing. He told me that he considered his military service as menial and his efforts insignificant. Additionally, he stated that he thought he was being taken for granted. He then told me that his civilian employer appreciated his service so much that when he left to join the Navy, he was presented a gold leaf coffee cup as a memento for his years of service. I then asked him where the coffee cup was now. He thought long and hard and finally replied that he did not know exactly. "If my memory serves me correctly," he replied, "quite possibly it was stored in a cardboard box back home?" Here was a perfect opportunity to impart a bit of chiefly wisdom.

In response, I offered the Sailor that the difference between the civilian sector and the military is that in the Navy, your hard work is recognized and rewarded daily. Mission readiness is paramount, and each and every Sailor plays a necessary part of the collective whole. While your service at the civilian job provided for you, the Navy enables you. And, where the coffee cup now resides is unknown, your naval efforts will be recognized by an entire nation. As the coffee cup gathers dust, your efforts are rewarded with ribbons and medals that you display daily. And, displayed they are over one's heart; for it is that a grateful nation thanks you for your service and your sacrifice. A grateful nation honors all military personnel past and present with national holidays: Flag Day, Memorial Day, the Fourth of July, and Veterans Day. You are not just an employee, you're not just a part of the Navy, you ARE the Navy! Throughout our nation's great history, you have been there. When we remember the USS *Maine*, you were there. When we remember Pearl Harbor, you were there.

When we remember the Battle of Midway and Coral Sea, the great battles of the North Atlantic and the USS *Samuel B. Roberts*, yes, you were there. When we remember the USS *Pueblo*, you too were there. When we remember the Riverine Operations of the Mekong Delta and the USS *Forestall*, you were there. From Iwo Jima to Inchon, from Bougainville to Beirut, we were there. When we remember the USS *Reuben James*, the USS *Stark*, and the USS *Iowa*, you were there. From the streets of Mogadishu to the hills of Panama, you were there. Recalling Desert Storm and the awesome display of naval operations, you were there; and lest we forget the USS *Cole*, you too were there. And, in remembrance of September 11, 2001, weren't we all there? Whether on the high seas, the mountainous regions of Afghanistan, in the streets of Iraq, and in the skies above Syria and where Special Forces are located, we too are there and will remain until the mission is complete, the fledgling democracies affirmed, and the people standing united and resilient.

A grateful nation honors all who have served and will never forget you. An employer soon forgets those who depart, yet America stands ready to defend your contributions. Military service is the grandest of all public service. Selfless and noble are our efforts that benefit those far from our side, yet always near to our hearts. And, never forget, where you serve, others have served, toiled, bled, and died to secure your right to self-determination, your rights to live and love, raise a family, work, and rest easy, knowing always that there are those who willingly at all corners of this globe stand the watch to preserve our freedoms.

We must accept that life is a struggle, a constant and sometimes precarious endeavor. Yet, as the colonial revolutionary Thomas Paine wrote in January 1777, "That which we obtain too easily, we esteem too lightly." Timeless philosophy and words of wisdom, which truly denote a fact of life once realized, enables accomplishment and appreciation while serving others. My fellow compatriots realize the distinction, the honor, and the privilege it is to serve this country by serving in the United States Navy: the world's greatest navy, unparalleled from sea to shining sea, and in so doing, offering others the nation that you represent with vigor and with virtue.

WHAT WILL BE YOUR LEGACY?

As we make our way in life, we will from time to time look over a shoulder and reflect upon our life's journey. During these moments of retrospection, we focus upon times of struggle and at times, from the outcome, failure. True, we remember the good times and we revel. Yet, it is those times which we hope to forget that we commonly revisit. In hindsight, we dwell on the things that could have been or the way it should be, realizing that though the past cannot be changed, we often do not appreciate that the way ahead can be amended. It is far better to plan your future success than dwell upon those times that resulted in disappointment. Though success can at times be elusive, success is readily at hand. As we look ahead, we must consider our legacy: that which defines who we are personally and that which defined by the journey is characterized by both our failures and our success.

Over the years, I have offered counsel to Sailors who regrettably suffered a debilitating injury and felt that their dreams of service, achievement, and success were now dashed. These Sailors faced a daunting obstacle, standing before an apparent monolithic challenge, the way ahead appears truly overshadowed and for some their dreams shattered. Sailors from the fleet, those attending "A" school, and those enduring the challenges of Basic Underwater Demolition/SEAL (BUD/S) training have called upon me for advice when faced with broken dreams or broken bones. I offered them the following: such times truly define who we are. At times such as these, your confidence, resilience, and perseverance will reward you. Though your aspirations may not materialize, from the experience you will better yourself, sharpen your focus, and define the person you are. Although a detour taken, success is at hand for those who reach for it. In so doing, you will begin to define your legacy built from personal tenacity, discovery, determination, grit, and gumption.

Following the theme of legacy, I recall a conversation with an older gentleman some years ago. The advice given me resonates still today. This man's life was defined by repeated success in business. He shared these accomplishments by providing for his children's educations, futures, and fortunes. His five sons graduated from veterinarian collages and were working for private firms or for the US Department of Agriculture. This humble man, who worked his entire life, investing well and providing for his family, could have easily afforded much more for himself, but he chose instead to provide for others. He also readily offered others a helping hand and advice rich with experience and foresight. This was his legacy. Despite the fact that he was a man of money, he chose to selflessly serve his family, forgoing prestige and notoriety due him from his success. He chose instead to sweep the floors where others beneath his statue walked. He once told me, "As you journey through life, you must from time to time look over your shoulder to see where you've been as you make your way to where you're going." As you do, you etch your name upon all that is your life, enabling you to redefine yourself as you go. For when your life nears its end, your signature, your very name, will be worth more than precious stones and gems.

In life, it is far better to consider your legacy long before the end of your journey. Now is the time to give more and forgive more, exemplifying that which is right and just. Be passionate about a cause, be compassionate toward others, lead others rightly, guide others directly, and truly extend self in the service of others. Your legacy is self-defined; begin now to scribe your legacy rather than one day wishing you could erase those things that cannot be changed.

EASING FAMILY CONCERNS

Amid the war in Iraq and Afghanistan, the turmoil in the Middle East, with deployments to the Horn of Africa, missions that include antipiracy and maritime security operations and operations against the violent extremist organizations, as well as the ever-present financial crises and social discord within our country, we would do well to ease the concerns of our families. With the uncertainties associated with service deployments coupled with the current economic insecurities and other troubling events, many children said goodbye to parents and other loved ones who now serve overseas. Parents and family friends must be prepared to help these children through these difficult times.

The thought of armed conflict can be especially disconcerting for our families. I remember watching war footage on the nightly news during the Vietnam War era. Being an adolescent, my perceptions of violence and war were changed from those images. What I watched on the nightly news was nothing like that which I saw on the big screen at the Saturday afternoon matinee. I remember how divisive the war was and the volatile discussions we often had at our dinner table. I harken back to a vivid memory of choir practice at the local church just up the road from my parents' home and recall the organist who stopped in the middle of her accompaniment of the choir and, with tears streaming, uttered harsh words against Lyndon Johnson, the president of the United States. You see, her son was at the time fighting in Vietnam. For me, it was a telling moment of passionate dissent and congregational compassion. I recall too my father's reaction to the political and social atmosphere of the country during the Vietnam era. As life's cycle would have it, I'm blessed to be more like my father every day. Reflecting upon what he taught me— to question policy and actions beyond my years of understanding—I offer you advice from a perspective of age and experience just as my father offered me.

Just before my second of five tours of duty in Afghanistan, a teenaged family member asked me why did I have to go there again. She also told me that she was scared. I thought about my response and how I would frame it in order to comfort her. I replied, "I'm going there so you won't have to be scared." She was puzzled by my terse words. Here, now, is the meaning of my heartfelt statement. Our service to our country is far broader than we image. Yes, we serve our families and we serve our communities. We serve our nation and people in far-off lands who live under the harshest of conditions, people whose only hope is to eke out a living and improve the lives of their children. They, like our families, hope for safety and security and a better way in life. What we do for our families and families unbeknownst to us is accomplished through selfless service. We join collectively the hopes and dreams of countless people, just like my teenage family member, who I trust believes that my service is universal and benefits many immeasurably. I encourage you to talk with your family and reassure them that wherever you are and for however long you're away, you serve them as you serve others: altruistically, and with purpose and principle.

Today, family members are inundated with media images from war-torn regions: despotic leaders calling for the destruction of our way of life, of American flags set aflame, political effigies trampled upon in streets; it is unfortunately happening both here and abroad. Images of those maimed or those whose life has been lost can be traumatic. When questioned, family elders should guide discussions, but not dominate. Stick to facts when discussing current events. Refrain from offering opinions children could interpret as unsupportive of a parent or family member serving overseas and in harm's way. Take note of your children who may display extreme levels of anxiety or fear. Importantly, be calm. Children take emotional cues from parents and other significant adults. Don't speculate on subjects that could cause heightened fear and anxiety, such as potential outcomes of military operations. In discussions or debate over foreign policy, emphasize that under our Constitution, citizens have the right to express unpopular opinions. Remind children that it is not fair to blame all members of a religious or an ethnic group for the actions of a few or their government.

With the turbulent times in which we live, we should reaffirm the family structure and spend time with one another, putting aside our individual interests and coalescing more often than occasionally the family spirit, one that more frequently looks outward in different directions and with divergent viewpoints. Come together and talk to one another; amid the speculation, there is a certainty to focus upon: there are better days ahead. In the immortal words of my father, "Every day offers an education: school yourself, and teach the other guy a lesson!"

DEFINING YOUR PERSONAL CREED

Many organizations author a mission statement, denoting a guiding code for its members to follow. These standards establish conduct that is proper and exemplifies honorable service. The US Navy established its own exemplars of service, conveying the core values of honor, courage, and commitment, which are etched into our minds and serve as a guiding force behind every action. Every Sailor understands and appreciates the Sailor's Creed, which embodies the fighting spirit of the Navy. Furthermore, the Navy ethos cites service, integrity, and decisive leadership as principled standards of performance. And, the six articles of the Code of Conduct are stressed upon entering Basic Training and reinforced throughout one's career. The themes of these principles serve as linchpins, binding us as a Navy and as a military service. Much is asked of us each day, and more will be demanded from us in the future. Adherences to these conventions empower members to be successful in their personal endeavors. Yet, from time to time, a Sailor will choose to exercise free will rather than good judgment and knowingly contradict both military uniform codes as well as civil law. Unfortunate and regrettable, such action cannot be readily dismissed. All Sailors are advised of the articles of the Uniform Code of Military Justice (UCMJ). The articles contained within the UCMJ serve as directives that socialize the organization. As a microcosm of society, adherence to defined conduct unifies and forwards the Navy on a proven course positively directed in the service of our country and the international community.

As the values expressed above serve as overarching themes for our service, I believe that a personal creed should be defined by each of us. This personal creed self-defined and personally subscribed to will serve as an individual foundation from which to stand upon. Your personal creed, after much contemplation, should be written down and reviewed often. As every Sailor should assemble a binder containing copies of their personal awards, certificates of training, and periodic evaluations, so too should they insert their personal creed accompanied by copies of the overarching themes of service including the Navy Core Values, the Sailor's Creed, the Navy ethos and the Code of Conduct. Your personal creed will serve as a pledge—a commitment, if you will—to dutiful, purposeful, and selfless service. Your personal creed should be reviewed and revised as you professionally mature. Your service will take you afar, and as you serve abroad, so too will your personal creed broaden. As you establish yourself and accept your leadership potential, your ability to influence others through your behavior and actions will require you to amend your personal creed. As we serve others, we constantly redefine who we are. Varied experiences encourage us to broaden the breadth of that which we offer society.

You may ask, isn't a personal creed quite a lofty ideal? I think not. I put to paper my personal creed years ago. It was truly individual, mine and mine alone. Yet, as I spoke with Sailors, I realized that others too could benefit by doing the same, and as my service opportunities increased, so too did the defining principles of my personal creed. I then realized that as I redefined my personal creed, I should share it with others. As I forwarded my personal ideals to others, I would be committed to adherence of these principles. Thus, the first letter on mentorship entitled "Why I Serve" was published. My beliefs and my commitment to service put to paper and forwarded to first five Sailors twelve years later reached over five hundred individuals around the globe. My intent in offering my personal creed was done so in order that others may too define their service personally. I strongly encourage you to define your service by refining your personal creed. Putting to paper your very own ideals of committed service will enable you while enlightening others as well. In return, they too will exemplify the overarching themes that serve to guide us all, and in so doing, others too will follow collectively. And, in unison, then, commitment to rightful service begins with self-defined concepts of exemplary personal behavior.

THE POWER OF INFLUENCE

We are but an infinitesimal part of a complex whole. As mere human beings, the universal powers unknown to most affect each and every one of us, molding and shaping everything in our world. Powers so incomprehensible can only be theorized by grand supposition. So awesome are these forces of nature, so grand in scale that when we search for answers, our questions only mount. Still, in times of trouble, when overwhelmed, look to the night sky and behold the countless stars above. Realize how relatively insignificant you and your troubles are.

Insignificant we are, but far from irrelevant. We have been gifted the power to think, to reason, and to change. Our ability to imagine a better way, to analyze, and to improve our standing has established our place on this planet: a place of preeminence over all earth's creatures. We have been gifted with this ability to imagine and to influence our life better, as well as to improve the lives of others. Who we are is shaped in part by the influence of others. This influential pressure, though powerful, does not have ultimate authority over us, for we are free to choose and to chart our own course. Much can be said of the authority of others over our lives. Negative, capricious, and at times destructive, such factors are ever present. Yet, our ability to reason, to see through the dimness, to press on when others would have us go the wrong way, this ability to rationalize is what will keep us on our chosen path.

We are shaped by trial and error, by tribulation, experimentation, sage advice, and luck. Very few of us truly have an original thought. We socialize, develop, and mature due to the influences put upon us. Influences in our youth shape us and define us. Still, have we not made mistakes based upon how we formulated our ideals and beliefs based upon the sway of others? We choose to exercise free will, at times knowing that the outcome may be detrimental. Yet, it is this free will that presents a duality of conscience, as we also can decide to act contrary to the status quo and make our own way in life. The power of influence is truly universal; the decision of what is right or that which is wrong is also a duality of both morality and effect.

As servants of our community and country, and as military professionals, the right way is defined for us. There are countless policies, doctrines, and instructions written to guide us in every endeavor. Such writings shape the professionals that we are. Right and wrong are clearly defined. The Laws of Land Warfare are tantamount to the doctrine of ethical treatment of unarmed combatants. Clearly, there are lines of demarcation not made faint due to the fog of war. Ethics, principles, and morality are common threads that bind us together. Yet, there are other influences that are designed to depreciate the foundation from which we stand. Social, political, and public effects seek to hamper the travel upon the moral high ground that we must take. For it is easy to make the wrong decision and easier still to go the wrong way. And, here now is the overarching influence that molds us as servants of our nation. As representatives of what defines America, our values, our morals, and our abilities lead us on an arduous journey. The difficulties mount, the requirements made stringent, and the separation from those we love certainly put us on a course charted by a representative few. Who we are and where we go will define not us alone, but America as a whole. The power of influence has molded us, strengthened who we are, and has made us better citizens, providing each and every one of us with opportunities to shape the ideals of others. Whether in combat or involved in civil affairs, delivering humanitarian assistance or providing disaster relief, the power of influence truly is held in hand. An offering from the heart, a brief smile, a grasp of another's palm, forwarding the benevolence of our nation defines who we are, what we represent, and that which we offer others: the influential spirit of America.

REMEMBERING THOSE WHOSE LIFE MADE YOURS A BETTER ONE

We all share a common capacity to love and to give. As children, we are nurtured and cared for, and we grow stronger because of the encouragement, direction, admonishment, and admiration that we receive. Those in our lives who impart upon us that which is right and wrong, by way of tenderness and tenacity, have allowed us to traverse a path wrought with trial and tribulation. Truly, they are deserving of our respect. Though there are special days for special people, Mother's Day signifies a day of remembrance, reflection, tribute, and praise to women who have set in motion each of us on our intended path in life. True, not all have had the benefit of a mother's charm. With extended, blended, and disjointed families, some may not share such a bond. However, there are special women in each of our lives who have molded us, taught us, and enabled us to grow and succeed. A caring hand has been extended, a smile has brightened a saddened heart, and a careful measure of discipline and adoration has shown us that life is a balance of emotion and logic. Whether a loved one or one who is admired—a sister, a teacher, a neighbor, a wife—those in our lives who have cared for us, who have taught us, who have molded us, and who today admire who we are, are deserving of such tribute. It is only fitting that we extend to those in our lives a heartfelt offering that truly will touch theirs.

Given the uncertainties of military service, separations from our loved ones are inevitable. Over the years, I have endured separation and sadness, love and war. I have waved goodbye to my wife and family as I traveled to foreign shores. Wherever my assignments led me, my family remained forever near. In love and in prayer, our hearts are joined. Though I may have been thousands of miles from my beloved wife and family, they were nearby. Our families are united in all that we do as we serve our nation and our Navy. It is appropriate, then, to acknowledge those in our lives who have shaped our very being; who have guided us, who have encouraged us, and who have stood by us regardless of the miles that exist between us.

I recall my mother, who endured the turmoil caused by three growing boys and her many sleepless nights, some caused by me alone. Yet, over the years, I learned from watching this how love overcomes all. Reflecting upon my turbulent teenage years, my mother weathered many a family storm. It was her faith, steadfast and true, that enabled my mother and blessed our lives. I know no greater degree of patience than that which she herself offered. Always a tender hand was extended, and no matter what life presented, her loving kindness and gentle way truly enriched my life as within her arms I found a respite from the troubles in my life. As I grew older, in triumph and disappointment, her love healed many hurts and inspired me to be a good boy and a better man. As I remember, she would forgive and comfort even in times that delivered suffering. My mother always found a way to understand and to reassure. One day before my mother's passing, I told her, "Take care, God bless, and all my love to you." In her voice, I knew that as she said goodbye she prepared me for the day to come. Within her weakened response that I struggled to hear, intently I listened for her last words. I realized the following day that her words were by design that I should hear her say, "Goodbye, and I love you too." On this Mother's Day, I could not but pause and realize that love transcends time. I hope you too remember to reflect upon those women in your lives who have likewise touched your heart.

TWO QUESTIONS TO ASK YOURSELF

I often speak with Sailors who have begun their naval careers. Over the years of my service, I have been asked a myriad of questions. Often, the questions are very similar, as young Sailors hope to learn of the Navy, associated travel and experiences, and service opportunities. From time to time, a Sailor will ask a question that requires considerable personal reflection and introspection in order to formulate a concise answer to the question posed. I recall a time when a Sailor asked me not one such question, but two. In such a forum, I realized that these two questions demanded definitive answers. Here presents special moments, defining instances in times whereby a response will identify the person who you are underneath the outward appearance of uniform and of rank. Here now are two questions routinely asked of me.

Given your career, do you hold any regrets? My answer: Yes, yes I do. I regret at times not working hard enough, not working longer into the night, and remaining at rest when others woke, at times being selfish and on occasion not thinking of others while focused on myself rather than concentrating on the needs of those I was charged to lead. My goodness, have I not exposed personal inconsistencies and shortcomings? Yes, of course I have. Yet, know that because of those times that I have fallen short of what I expected of myself, it is what I do today that inspires me to do more. In fact, the purpose of my writing is to forward a personal contract to many denoting my sentiments of service—how to serve others and for whom do I serve. I hold to the notion that if I lose my focus, someone will surely remind me of what I have written and espoused and then declare me a fraud. In time, I surely would rather be remembered for the effort expended to achieve than that which I could have achieved but thought better not to apply myself.

"Given your religious beliefs, how do you justify what you do in support of the global war?" My answer: Those who are enemies do not have to be! Those who conspire to again do us harm, to once more slaughter the innocent, to cripple America, and then revel in the agony that their conspiracy wreaks, have acknowledged that they are the enemy of our nation. Because of their actions, they will be dealt with accordingly. We are a peace-loving people who champion the rights of all. America has extended the benevolence of her people to those who were once our enemies. We seek not to incorporate those who differ intrinsically from us but rather seek to enable the poor, the disadvantaged, the needy, and those fledgling governments enabling their appointed leaders to define for themselves a better way of coexistence. The enemy of America, once no longer able to carry the fight, as a noncombatant, is assured that they will receive the care and kindness that America provides for its own. We hold true to the doctrine of war, yet we also subscribe to the laws of armed conflict. Radicals, extremists, and zealots seek to punish, to cripple and inflict unmerciful injury upon all Americans. The enemy of America employs a corrupt sense of belief while conspiring to impart fear in order to target those they wish only to further subjugate. America employs a measured response, seeking to end hostilities while incorporating the amelioration and emancipation of the indigenous who have suffered for all too long under the sway of enemies of humanity. My religious beliefs empower me. Still though, my beliefs also enable me to extend myself to those who welcome the deliverance that my efforts provide.

From time to time, questions put forward provide the means to define oneself. Of course, these are times that the spotlight clearly illuminates you. The audience waits to hear a response, clearly defined, logically presented, and lasting in its impression. Always speak from the heart and let your words be guided by your conscience while your actions define who you are: an American military service member, determined, empowered, yet compassionate, empathetic, and at all times, determinedly just.

TOUGH DECISIONS, RIGHT DIRECTION

I often converse with Sailors who have chosen the wrong path in life. Such decisions ultimately result in complex consequences. For one Sailor in particular, an abrupt course correction resulted in a different professional path. On the occasion of such an unforeseen event, I told the Sailor this: Understand that the way ahead is very demanding. Understand too that this service is truly selective. Although you have made costly mistakes, I am however confident that you will learn and grow and, of course, be a better leader because of the experience and the newly prescribed path.

You may be aware of the way in which the Navy and its leaders care for their Sailors. Mentorship and guidance is best directed from those who have shouldered the burden of leadership as well as learned valuable lessons along their personal and professional journey. Understand that the best lessons in life are those we should not repeat. I can tell you that I have learned much from my own experience. Recognize that as a leader, you will always make time to deal with and assist another in need. However, the focus must be on the mission and on those who are serving in harm's way. When distracted by internal or external forces, one's focus is blurred and operational commitments unclear. Yet, as the mission is paramount, so too is the guidance, counsel, mentorship, and motivation provided in order that Sailors right themselves. Your behavior is not uncommon. Your mistakes are not unique, and the opportunity to right yourself will be determined from a rightful course of action that is designed to provide you many opportunities to excel, mature, advance, and grow into a Navy leader.

Over the course of my career, I have served in varied operational environments offering a wide array of service opportunities. My first Chief Petty Officer once told me, "Worry less about your own career, consider the careers of others, and your career will manage itself." Each command that I have served provided me multiple occasions to serve others, learn, and advance. I served aboard the amphibious assault ships USS *Wasp LHD 1* and USS *Saipan LHA 2* and two tours aboard the aircraft carrier, USS *Dwight D. Eisenhower CVN 69*. Believe me, the opportunity to serve as a Sailor at sea is especially demanding. At sea, a Sailor will have many chances to learn and mature professionally. During your tour at sea, you will avail yourself to numerous possibilities, which include becoming a warfare special-ist, a Damage Control Petty Officer, and a work center supervisor. You will face many challenges and face experiences truly unique to those who serve at sea. If you commit to excellence, you will advance in rank, and you will be enabled and expected to lead others as they too chart their own courses.

Think about that! You will advance in rank and become an enlisted leader, with an impressive résumé ready to then meet the challenges of advanced professional training. Believe me, I reached the enlisted rank of Master Chief Petty Officer because of who I became while serving at sea. Understand that while serving in the fleet, the opportunity may present itself to serve uniquely within oper-ational environments and perhaps well outside that to which you are accustomed. This too I have done. While aboard USS *Saipan*, I was assigned an Individual Augmentation (IA) tour to Afghanistan! So the future is bright, and you are truly the master of your own destiny. Few other young adults outside the military hold such a promising future. My advice to you is this: go to sea, earn your qualifications, advance, and willingly accept the burden of leadership. Ready your-self for the challenges of a fantastic career that awaits your next step.

There will be mentors at sea who will be readily available to assist you in your pursuit of excellence. Whatever your career aspi-rations might be, believe this: everything is possible, and each goal is obtainable. Time is eternal; measure time by opportunities rather than watching the clock. Measure time by your accomplishments and achievements rather than by missed opportunity. Focus on your goals, and the route taken will lead to your eventual goal.

MY FATHER WHO ART IN HEAVEN

June 21, 2009

As a child, like boys often do, I searched to identify with a hero: a man larger than life, full of verve and adventure, strong and direct, a gifted man whom others idolized, and a man who I wanted to become. For me, early recollections focus on the television icon Vic Morrow, who played Sergeant Saunders on Saturday morning episodes of *Combat!* Long before I knew of the real-life heroics of Audie Murphy, who was awarded the Medal of Honor for valor in World War II, I idolized him as Second Lieutenant Murphy in the blockbuster movie *To Hell and Back*. There were others whom I considered heroes: Neil Armstrong, who first stepped foot upon the moon; Captain Kirk of the *Starship Enterprise*; and John Wayne's Rooster Cogburn. There was Broadway Joe Namath of the New York Jets, Jerry Grote who caught for pitcher Tom Seaver of the New York Mets, and Joe Kapp of the Minnesota Vikings who once threw seven touchdown passes in a single game against the Baltimore Colts. And, then there was my neighbor who lived across the road. Wayne, who taught me never again would I hold the end of a spark plug wire while another yanked the pull cord of a lawnmower, would go off to Vietnam and come home a changed man with a heart colored purple.

Yet, as I grew, I knew that my hero, the one man who stood above all others, was very close to home and closer to heart. That man is my father. He was an iron worker, had worked in an explosives plant, a truck driver, and veteran of World War II, a hunter, a fisherman, and a trapper; he did the kind of work that real men do. A stoic man who, hours before his passing, told me while we spoke over the telephone that he was just a bit uncomfortable. It was after his passing that I learned that he could not hold the receiver to his ear. Although he couldn't muster the strength to lift his arm, his only complaint was that he was uncomfortable! I often consider the strength in that statement.

As life's cycle would come full circle, from a boy reading my father's *Blue Jacket's Manual* to the day when I left for Basic Training, my life would be on a course set forth many years before. With all my naval experiences, travels, and war service, my father has been with me. His sacrifices to our nation during World War II would in no small measure ensure that I would serve nearly fifty years later. On the high seas or with "boots on the ground," my service continues to unfold. I am the man I am because as a little boy, I glanced through his manual and looked upon his service photographs. I remember the day I left the recruiting office and I turned to salute him. The world has changed so very much since that day. In everything I do, I know that my father is with me. When faced with challenges, I ask myself how my father would want me to act. Though time and distance separate us, he is with me every day and in every way. As a boy, he was my hero. As a man, my father remains that hero. I hope that one day I might stand as tall as him, equal to his strength, and always guide my family and those I am charged to lead and serve the way he guides me still today. When challenges mount, I know that his hand is upon me. And, I know that he has blessed my life.

Few men know the fortune that has blessed my life of knowing my hero as my friend and my father. I am thankful for having such a powerful force in my life, and I remain thankful for the wonderful experiences that we shared. As always, I salute him for being the best father, as the quiet man who from a distance kept his eye on me years ago and who will do so thereafter, forever and a day. It is my hope that you too may know such a hero in your life. As life is fleeting, may you take time to honor those men who have guided you, directed you, and who have shown you the proper course to follow; for we are better men from those men who were at their best for us. Remember this: when we look into our father's eyes, we see ourselves from within the soul to which we are bound.

MARCH ON FOR LIBERTY

The Fourth of July commemorates the signing of the Declaration of Independence. Signed by the colonial founders, this grand document noted that independence was an unalienable right and a self-evident truth and a destiny worth the struggle that would soon follow. The American Revolution would further embolden the spirit of a nation. Independence earned, the struggle would not end there. Independence must be protected as it expands. Time and again, America would face challenges to its hard-fought liberty. Throughout the years, Americans would rally 'round the flag to defend principles, doctrine, and law. Much blood would be shed in order that we today may benefit from the struggles of yesteryear. Yet, the American spirit is not egocentric by nature, for we are a people who foster democratic values and support those who too seek their own independence, which is from our creator given that all should be free. Truly then that once earned, independence must be kept secure. Perhaps our greatest president, Abraham Lincoln, penned the defense of liberty best when he wrote, "Our defense is in the preservation of the spirit which prizes liberty as a heritage of all men, in all lands, everywhere. Destroy this spirit and you have planted the seeds of despotism around your own doors."

Americans honor liberty, prize its rights of citizenry, and debate the direction to further our united way of life. Such debate has at times been acrimonious and egregious. At no time in our nation's history has such a debate fractured such a great divide then during the Civil War. One hundred fifty-six years ago, the turning point of our own Civil War would occur, leaving a scar on our history that only time and reverence could mend. A distant relative, Abram, who served with 120th New York, during a brief respite while the army marched to meet the Confederates once again, took pencil to paper to scribe a letter to his brother on 13 July 1863. In his letter, he described the events of the historic battle fought at Gettysburg.

Abram detailed being on the battlefield and noted that the fight had been a very severe one at that. He had also experienced the battle at Chancellorsville, where both Union generals Barry and Whipple were killed. Describing the battle near Gettysburg, 03 July 1863, he wrote, "While shot and shell were falling on us like hail stones, and men were dropping on every side, I was amongst those that came out unharmed and I feel very thankful. Our regiment lost that day, killed, wounded and missing, 202. The loss of our company, killed, wounded and missing is 22... Such Dear Brother is the horrors of war and I hope and pray that it will soon come to an end. The loss of our army was heavy in this battle, yet we claim a victory."

This July Fourth, as we again celebrate our independence, there are many from among us who are engaged in an epic struggle. We fight for our continued security, prosperity, and way of life. We fight for those who also seek what we hold as self-evident. It is our American ethos that instills in us that all those who are not among us as Americans are with us as a collective race. Selflessness and sacrifice are touchstones from which the foundation of America is built upon. We volunteer, we promote liberty without prejudice, and we give more of ourselves so that liberty can endure. So then, in order to guarantee all that we hold dear, we must march on for liberty. In order to assure independence, the march for freedom continues, here on the home front as well as on foreign shores for those who desire to live free lives of their own. As we celebrate our nation's independence, may our spirit be encouraged, may our focus become sharpened, and may our abilities be made grander as we fulfill our national objectives supporting freedom for others around the world.

WHERE'S ROWAN? THE TIME IS NOW!

On February 15, 1898, the battleship USS *Maine*, at anchor in the Cuban harbor of Havana, was sunk by an immense explosion. Two hundred and seventy-four Sailors lost their lives due to the detonation in the forward ammunition magazine. An official US Navy inquiry determined that the explosion and sinking were due to an explosive device, likely a naval mine, detonating beneath the forward section of the battleship. Such an act of aggression against the United States could not go unanswered. Although much debate has occurred as the exact cause of the explosion or who may have been directly responsible for the blast and sinking of the USS *Maine*, this event spurred President McKinley to declare war against Spain. And, so the Spanish-American War commenced, and the rest is history!

Prior to the declaration of war, President McKinley needed a note delivered to the Cuban rebel leader, General Calixto Garcia, whose forces, seeking an independent Cuba, were engaged against the Spanish military. The note, of critical importance to the rebels, was seen by President McKinley as vital to the cooperative engagement between the United States and Garcia. Lieutenant Andrew S. Rowan was chosen as the man who would deliver the message to Garcia. Without asking for directions, without a dossier detailing Garcia's description, without knowing the whereabouts of the general, Lieutenant Andrew Summers Rowan nevertheless did in fact deliver the message to the rebel leader and "secure[d] secret information relative to existing military conditions in that region of such great value that it had an important bearing on the quick ending of the struggle and the complete success of the U.S. Army."[6]

Where's Rowan? The time is now! If tasked with a daunting challenge, would you answer the call? Would you think of the assignment as a challenge or a chore? Would you take the next step forward, or would you throw up your hands in surrender? Do you consider your service as vital to satisfying national objectives, or do you think of what you do as insignificant? When called upon, would you step forward? Or would you stand down?

A good friend told me several times to read *A Message to Garcia*. As I did, I realized what an incredible story it was: a story of sacrifice, bravery, trust, and faith. I ponder on the countless obstacles, daunting challenges, and perils encountered along the journey that Rowan encountered. I wondered about the mission, the jungle, the mountains, and the unknowns that had to be faced. I mull over Rowan's motivators. Was it money? Was it recognition or prestige?

I don't think so. I believe Rowan delivered the message to Garcia because to do so was vital to the war effort, redressing the loss of American lives aboard the USS *Maine*.

A solution to a problem is a culmination of the ways, the means, and the wherewithal to accomplish that which is at hand. To do so, you must exercise ability, agility, intelligence, and your charter. You must put your back into it. Yet, you've got to have heart! You must see it as an affirmative rather than a possibility. You've got to look at it and believe: this can be done because you are driven, you are able, and you have faith that you will succeed. Why? Because America needs you too! As the souls of those lost to the conflict cry out for remedy, you hear their pleas and answer their call. Your service is not self-serving. You are under contract of a grateful nation whose citizens need such an advocate. For with every assignment, there is one person who is thus enabled, empowered, and emboldened to accomplish that which is tasked.

Where's Rowan? The time is now! Now more than ever, the call has been forwarded for such a patriot, for such a mission, for such a cause. It is now up to you. When called up, may you too answer the call without reservation or hesitation. For his actions, Lieutenant Rowan was awarded the Distinguished Service Cross.

MAINTAINING CLEAR FOCUS
ON YOUR PERSONAL VISION

A good friend and I recently exchanged several emails. After pleasantries were passed, as with most personal conversations, the focal point shifted to matters of "what should be and what ifs." Often, in times of uncertainty, we look outside of ourselves for guidance and direction. Yet, the advice we receive all too often is that which we knew all along. Life is a matter of balance. Time and again, the remedy for uncertainty centers upon not necessarily where you "need" to be, but rather where you need to place your footing in order to get there. We all have dreams and aspirations, some of grandeur and some of fame; mostly, though, these hopes are desires just to get "there," somewhere to a place better, a place with less hassle and fewer requirements, a place perhaps where cares go out with the tide. Yet, even a place of tranquility is visited by a midday storm. With looking forward, it is how we place ourselves in preparation for the unexpected or the inevitable, how we ready ourselves for the future while we enjoy the moment, and how we envision ourselves tomorrow while we seize the day.

It has been said, "Every plan has a purpose." Accordingly, as life is a matter of balance, clearly then what we set our sights upon needs to lead us in the right direction. But life is filled with uncertainties. And, yes, no matter our preparations, there will be disappointment in life. No matter our predictions, it will one day rain on our parade. Are the odds against us inevitable?

Indeed, if we lose our focus, it would appear that way. But every storm has a silver lining. Take to heart the immortal words of Dr. Martin Luther King Jr., who said, "We must accept finite disappointment, but never lose infinite hope." With life, there will be trouble, and there will come calamity. We may ask ourselves why. Now, I do not forward the idea that I have all the answers to life. Still, though, consider this: with each question, does not an answer come? You know, as I reflect back upon my college calculus class, if you factor long enough, you'll figure it out. I will tell you that it is far better to be prepared for problems than to be overrun by them. Here is one bit of advice I'll share that was passed to me by my grandmother who once told me, "It's not where you stood, but how you stand that prevents a fall." Believe this: it is hope that balance is built upon, and with hope, we won't lose sight of our personal vision.

Talking with my friend, I offered that at many times in my life, I have teetered as life's balance was a bit off kilter. Struggles and failure have visited me more often than occasionally. Yet, it was how I stood rather than where I stood that enabled me to right the wrong, turn the corner, and get back on the proper path. Believe me, I'm neither an angel nor a saint, but I do know that faith is my life's balance and serves as the fulcrum from which equilibrium is achieved. If life is a pathway whose direction is predetermined, we remain able to choose a divergent path. At times, the way chosen will lead us astray. We may receive that which we longed for, but not what we originally hoped for. Wealth, riches, fame, and all things we long for, but what we hope for is tranquility, stability, and longevity. As the familiar old adage goes, "Be careful what you wish for; you might just get it." But hope is something that we need not wish for; it is innate and ever-present. "Hope springs eternal," as they say. And, as for me, I have wished that I could be many things. Many of my boyhood heroes I have wished to become. True, I have desired wealth and fame, but truer still is that I am neither wealthy nor famous. As a boy, I did hope and continue to hope for this day to be more like my father who served his country during World War II: a good man, strong, dedicated to home and family, stubborn, determined, and able to be both critical of self and laugh about himself too. So you see, as my father served, so too do I. So it goes with all things in life: I hope to be, and I eventually, with hope, I am.

A REAL-LIFE GHOST ADVENTURE

September 08, 2009

There seems to be a good deal of interest in the paranormal these days. Several television shows, though entertaining and investigative, attempt to document actual hauntings and capture on film true ghostly figures, explaining the mysteries of what makes most of us grab the covers and pull them over our heads. Whether actual or figments of our imagination, as much as we might not admit, we do get a kick out of being spooked.

Once, years ago, I returned to my childhood home for a brief visit and after my parents passed away and before the sale of the property was final. I can write that strange things occurred in this house. Though I was always comfortable staying the night, I did look forward to an adventure from time to time. Visited by images from the past, I see myself as a child, a teenager, a young man, and as I look upon myself in the mirror, I see the man I've become. Long since vacant of furniture and other amenities within this house, there remained a wonderful sense of family, of holidays, of happiness, of trials and tribulations, and much joy. Each time I arrived in the driveway, I look for the familiar curtain to be brushed aside as my mother patiently waited my arrival. As I entered, the musty smell of a house closed tight quickly identified that I was home. And, there, by the window, the rocking chair remained where my mother would wait to greet those who entered from the porch. From the corner of my eye, there was this boy who scampered about being chased by an older brother. From the kitchen, I could hear my father demanding that we quiet down and not run on the stairs. Turning the corner, three of the family dogs followed fast on the boy's heels. In the dining room and the adjoining living room, I looked upon the spaces where family gatherings, discussions, and lectures had taken place, all as the dinner table was set. Turning to the left, the living room and there my mother played church hymns on the baby grand piano.

How was it all possible? My mother and father had long since passed, my brother had departed years ago, and the family dogs were all memories a bit more than faded. As I meandered throughout the house, in room after room, there were people who faded in and out of sight. From the upstairs bedroom window, I could see myself ride my new bicycle in the driveway, which I earned by selling Christmas cards door to door. Neighborhood children played in the yard, long since any of them actually set foot on the property. The house welcomed me as I greeted the others appearing before my eyes. On the walls, there were no more photos of family, graduation certificates, or paintings of historic landmarks. And, of course, the paint faded by many years had taken on a warmer hue because of the love that remained within this cozy Victorian-style home of my childhood.

So then, you may ask, what is the relevance of this memo? It is who we once were that, in part, makes us the people we are today. As the years pass and you do find more time to reflect upon years gone by, you'll realize that from those earlier times, the person you once were continues to inform your identity. For me, as I've surpassed my sixtieth year, I do spend much time in reflection of who I once was. To have gotten here, I had to pass through those days of yesteryear. All the good and those times I'd rather forget have contributed to the man I am. Here then is the relevance of the memo: you too are the person you are (and for many, the person you'll become) from those experiences from years before. Believe me, I was mischievous as a boy and adventurous as a teen; and although not troubled, trouble I found. From it all, the guidance I received instilled in me that all actions yield consequences and it would serve best to be prepared for outcomes intended as well as those unforeseen. Importantly and really of revelation is the discovery that we all have the innate ability to change course and learn from our mistakes. Hopefully, this will happen long before the consequences are set in stone.

Each of us defines ourselves from the experiences from our youth. It is far better to establish who you'll become by your actions of today. Often, the ghosts from our past are at times less than pleasant memories. To forgo future hauntings, it would be best to live life justly, live life rightly, believing that you'll regret the consequences of your actions, while contrary behavior can be made right by living life today honorably. But what of "A Real-Life Ghost Adventure" and those things that go bump in the night? What about those shadowy figures lurking and those things unexplained? Well then, as I settled in for a long night and made ready for what awaited me, with all good ghost stories, to cut a long story short, after much thought and consideration, some things are best left a mystery.

THE MOST AMAZING DESIGN: LIFE!

At every moment of every minute of each day of our lives, we are granted a wonderful gift: the gift of thought. We are who we are because we think. We imagine, we create, and we dream. And, from our thoughts, we build, design a better way, and create our very lives.

Our ability to identify a problem, appreciate the challenge, and overcome an impediment is part of what differentiates us from other species. As we realize the hazards of swimming upstream, for example, we'll eventually build a causeway and go up and over rather than attempt to face the rapids that propel us backward. We can identify right from wrong, and better yet, we can better people along the way.

Still, we may also choose not to change, remaining less than responsible, and still wonder why the world is passing us by. Given time, we appreciate that our future is in our hands and that we are each architects of a grand scheme that is our life. What enables us is a sense of accomplishment, of doing the right thing the right way, which is, of course, at times the hard way. Given our efforts, then, lives are made better. As we prosper, so do others. No other species can understand their situation, adapt, and with determined resolve, change the way they think and live.

When I was a boy, I recall being told that our lives were predetermined with every step plotted on a grand course. One day, as I was riding my bicycle, not paying attention to where I was going, I swerved into the gravel, lost my balance, and fell to the ground. I experienced the revelation that "that which is in motion stays in motion." I also learned that "road rash" is a bit more painful than a minor skin irritation! From that experience, it was revealed to me that to avert an outcome, I needed to pay attention, and fate could be altered. Now, some might say that it is destiny revealed as we avert such an unpleasant outcome. Yet, there have been times when although I knew that unpleasant outcomes awaited, I chose not to step away as the inevitable bore down on me. Through perception, realization, and common sense, we can avert an outcome and press on to far greater experiences.

I enlisted in the Navy when I was thirty-four years old after graduating from the State University of New York. I joined the Navy to gain a bit of worldly maturity before pursuing a law degree. Prior to enlisting, my future seemed to be predetermined in a good way as I was employed, educated, and healthy. I remember informing my academic adviser that I decided to enlist in the Navy and forgo law school. His reaction was a combination of bewilderment and hilarity. Many of whom I had known thought too that my enlistment was certainly a personal crises identified. Many close to me thought that my future was predetermined, set in stone, and awaiting my next step. Yet, I decided to trek off on a pilgrimage and enter the military where most were half my age. There were naysayers, and there were those who thought I was destined to fail. On the contrary, I was determined to succeed! My naval experience has been incredibly rewarding. Although there have been many challenges and more than a few occasions where I have had to take a step back, I rebounded and pressed onward to achieve much more than I could have envisioned at the time—enjoying rewards that have not been mine alone.

Over the years, I've learned that we must consider the future broadmindedly rather than myopically. While the path ahead may at times appear to be a one-way street, I encourage you to seize an opportunity when an alternate route presents itself. I offer these words in order to inspire you to pursue your dreams, push yourself in a new direction, and prepare yourself in order to overcome the unexpected. Believe that failure is not finite, but learn to see it as an opportunity to reassess and seek out alternate paths. The darkness of failure is not blinding. When you fail, you are given two choices. You can allow yourself to be overcome by gloom and miss a fleeting ray of hope, or you can focus on the foreseeable and search for the brilliance of a good idea. You can be weighed down by despair or cast off your burdens to take charge of your future. I trust that your ideas will inspire you to look beyond today and pursue your dreams. You must believe that tomorrow holds the promise of that which is obtainable only when keeping pace with time.

BEYOND THE FOCAL POINT

How we look upon the world truly defines who we are. Our beliefs, our hopes, and our aspirations, our dreams coupled with our intent, denotes our signature on life. As we stand and gaze upon the horizon, our vision intensifies on a finite point. We often focus our attention on the far-off point while the peripheral becomes faint. This focal point, more often than not, is a vision of self: a private reward, an achievement, celebrity, wealth, fame, or accomplishment. As we proceed along in life, our energies are honed, and our distant desires become more precise. With each step, however, we pass life and opportunity by. Our pursuits often become selfish and our vision distorted as our purpose becomes narrowed by individual interests. As we pass by opportunity and occasion, we limit ourselves by forgoing others. Since each dawn provides for a new beginning, may it be today that you broaden your vision on life.

As you concentrate on your life's focal point, there is no better time than now to see things more clearly and expand the breadth of your vision to serve in a broader way. Understand that as you navigate through life, there are countless opportunities to serve others. As we focus less upon ourselves and more intently upon others, we enable those whose vision may be ill-defined, distorted, by hunger, conflict, disease, or social injustice. With the fast pace of life, we are often overtaken by events while we pass by others in need. The world turns at a set speed, and the day remains twenty-four hours long. No matter how we try to increase the pace, we cannot influence time. Annoyingly, how long is it that horns blow after the light turns green? And, how quickly do the same horn blowers react crudely to another's overreaction to their own momentary lapse at the next light? We regularly focus upon time, "our time" rather than how best we could improve the last moments of others in need. John F. Kennedy once said, "For time and the world do not stand still. Change is the law of life. And, those who look only to the past or the present are certain to miss the future." Certainly, we define time by the linear measure or the measurement in one dimension only. So then, now is the time to look beyond your own singular focal point and redefine your vision with multipolarity or that which is characterized by more than two centers of interest: yourself and your own future.

Expand your focal point, and view the world around you in an impassioned way. Slow your pace in order to aid and assist those in need. Give more of yourself to those who require your talents, your understanding, and your kindness. Serve broadly and volunteer. As there remain twenty-four hours in a day, serve others for just a mere few minutes more daily. Put the needs of others before your own desires. We all are enabled to extend ourselves further than we think possible. We are stronger than we believe ourselves to be. We all harbor emotions of goodness, empathy, and altruism. Yet, it seems that it is not an instinctive response to extend oneself for the betterment of others. We must adapt and develop the means to nurture a grieving stranger, to provide for another when we have at times little for ourselves, and accept the burdens of another when our own journey is heavy laden. In serving others, the effort is taxing to one's system and a burden that may impede our own way. But from such encounters, we are made stronger, wiser, and better. And, when our journey is done and we near our life's end, the adventures and the experience will most certainly enrich the detour along our own pilgrimage in life through the selfless service provided others.

ANOTHER STEP ALONG LIFE'S JOURNEY

November 02, 2009

As we move on in years, opportunities were presented for our avail. Whether by chance or by design, we are enabled to take hold of a prospect and step off knowing that whatever may come, our decision is emboldened by our resolve to advance further along life's path. With any journey, there will be trials, tribulations, and pitfalls. The way ahead may be arduous, at times, perilous and a digression into the unknown. We must weigh the possibilities, the chance of reward, and the prospect of failure. As a boy, my beloved father told me time and again of his regret at having not taken a chance on a venture that later with hindsight proved to be especially rewarding for those who allowed themselves to take hold of such an opportunity. I've learned much from my father, and rallying the courage and spirited onward by faith and anticipation, I have taken more than a few chances in life. The way has not been easy. Hard work and sacrifice seldom are. The rewards have not always been tangible in the short term, but more often than not, in the long term, the rewards have certainly been appreciable.

Throughout my years, I've listened to my mentors who guided me, inspired me, and who moved me to a pace beyond my next planned footstep. Whether it was operating a beef cattle farm, to returning to college, as a Sunday school teacher, or enlisting in the US Navy, I've sought the advice and counsel of my mentors; and with reliance on faith, with all intent to succeed, I took a chance in order to embolden my life in the service of others. And, so it was in 2008, when my mentor suggested that I seek a commission as a naval officer in order to broaden my military service did I accept a possibility of a new direction to follow.

My naval career has been unimaginably rewarding. I could not have anticipated the experiences that awaited me, and I would not have thought that I would be one day a Chief Warrant Officer. My enlisted career was wonderfully fulfilling. I served at sea as a Petty Officer, as a Chief Petty Officer, a Senior Chief Petty Officer, and as a Master Chief Petty Officer, traveling to many countries that in my previous life I had only dreamed of. I have been introduced to cultures that were unbeknownst to me. Interestingly, to me and my compatriots, the indigenous taught me and those I served with as foreigners and as redeemers. Hearts have been touched and lives brightened. I've learned that the Navy offers unprecedented opportunities for all who are willing to apply themselves, prepare themselves, and accept the burdens of leadership. And, I know that from these experiences, the Navy has enabled me to be a better man and a public servant. As I was commissioned as a Chief Warrant Officer, I was especially eager to again step off in a new direction. Though charged to lead the way, I extended a hand to all who might follow my lead. The honor and privilege bestowed upon me, I pledged to serve as a professional paradigm and I most certainly hoped that others sought to emulate. I am especially thankful to those who have motivated me to best my last effort in order that I should serve purposefully and selflessly, confidently focused on the careers of others. May you too serve with principle and intention, offering the best in you to those who are so deserving while seizing every opportunity to expand your service in the service of others.

HAVE YOU FOUND WHAT YOU'RE LOOKING FOR?

As a young man, I looked to a few as heroes. I have written of those who have inspired me, enabled me, and those who definitively changed my life. Many of my heroes I have not met. Men such as Audie Murphy and a few fictional characters as portrayed by actor John Wayne come to mind. Harkening back, I once received a postcard from Richard Nixon in response to a letter that I forwarded to the former president when I was ten years old. I don't know about Mr. Nixon as my hero, but to have a postcard from the president of the United States, well, to my classmates, I was a hero of sorts. Another hero from my childhood was a decorated Vietnam veteran who lived across the road. Considering Vietnam and another hero, a few years ago, I enjoyed the privilege when I met Senator John McCain in Afghanistan. Even closer to home, my mother and father will always be my heroes. Yet, as I traveled to distant locales, I have met more than a few heroes, selfless servants of our country, of a foreign community, and many unbeknownst to me; yet for only an instant, their actions became indelibly etched on my mind for a lifetime.

My military service has been especially rewarding. I have served with boots on ground and upon cold steel at sea. I have met many people that I admire. I have served five tours of duty in Afghanistan. And, yes, I have been blessed to meet heroes there. With each consecutive tour in Afghanistan begun, I sought heroes. Men and women who inspired me, who sacrificed so much for our country, those separated by time and distance, on formidable soil did they live and fight; still as they think of home, they believe in one another. There is a unique bond between the armed forces: a bond like no other.

Not all heroes wear a military uniform. I seek those who have faced tyranny and twisted logic and endured. For we are among men and women who seek a better life, one where they can pray and prosper as it is intended for them. In Afghanistan, I sought those who could enlighten me, who could inspire me, and those who encouraged me through my tireless efforts, in their service, to recognize their culture, ideals, and identities. I sought patriots whose sacrifices emboldened a national spirit, who sought to educate men and women in technologies that the generation before did not know and who searched for social tranquility free of societal disorder. Heroes are among us, men and women who seek less for themselves but more for their society. Free of prejudice and distortions of justice, there are those who will further sacrifice for future generations. Heroes will do this without greed, fraud, or vice. It will be men and women who believe in a national identity while recognizing differences, seeking an inclusive social system based on acceptance, tolerance, and unity while appreciating their unique cultural differences.

So then, who are these heroes? An elderly man in tattered clothes sweeping the streets of Kabul before sunrise; teachers who offer children an education free from domination and distortion; students and shopkeepers, artisans and professionals, all who are venturing in new directions; entrepreneurs and family role models; and the men and women volunteers of the Afghan National Police and Armed Forces—yes, these are heroes. Heroes, too, who have traveled far or sought refuge aboard and who return proud to be Afghan, seeking to better the homeland that they once watched collapse before them.

Yes, I have met such heroes, and they have made me a better man through their unique perspectives and our cultural differences. How about you, have you found what you're looking for? I have learned much while serving in Afghanistan, and the following well-known Afghan proverb truly defines a vision that we should all embrace: "What you see in yourself is what you see in the world."

FLAG DAY

Flag Day—for some, this is a day of antiquated tradition while for others, it is a day of irreverence and defiance. For most, however, it is a day to celebrate: not just a cloth mended together by needle and thread, but rather the fabric of a nation, melded by blood and sacrifice. There will always be the naysayer, the opposition, and a counterculture within our society, those who find it in themselves to speak out against the very culture, their own inclusive government, and a way of life that provides and protects their very right to voice their displeasure. They fail to see the paroxysm that is the foundation from which they stand. A subculture, true, but there is one symbol above all else that inflames their sense of separatism. It is Old Glory: our American flag, a symbol of justice, moral authority, and a universal emblem of hope against which they rail.

Of all things American, it is the flag that waves above all else. Our flag is an enduring symbol of freedom and opportunity, the symbol of the most powerful, compassionate, and giving nation on earth. The American flag is an icon of liberty and self-determination, and thus, even when burned in defiance, she yet defends the freedom of expression that enables such an act. Interestingly, and of contrasting symbolism, when the American flag is to be retired, it should be reduced to ashes, with reverence. It is the intention behind the act that determines its outcome.

My neighbors may not know my name, but they know where I reside. Each day, the American flag is displayed in my front yard. I am proud of my family members who served in the military over past generations. I can trace my family's military service to the Revolutionary War. I hold letters from members of my family who fought in the Civil War, and both my mother and father are veterans of World War II. My wife's grandfather was killed by Japanese forces in the Philippines during World War II. Although defending his homeland, he fought with American forces. In our home, we reverently display the Purple Heart Medal and a citation on behalf of the United States signifying that Paciano Balabis was killed in battle. My wife's other grandfather and an uncle were killed during a Japanese air raid. Though a Filipina, my wife is an American who too honors the stars and stripes that at our home fly every day for all to see.

It is not a display of hubris when we fly our flag. It is not a mark of insolence as some might take it, but rather a sign of veneration for the cloth that has empowered a nation to be fruitful, beneficial, and when necessary, powerful. For those who decry injustice, in times of need, they welcome the sight of that same flag of ours, which at other times infuriates them. Empower your families to fly the American flag, for once proudly unfurled does she wave. As with every day, our flag is a symbol that demonstrates patriotism and your standpoint as a grateful American, who is prepared to assist all in their service and for their benefit.

YOUR LIFE'S CONTRIBUTION

May it be your contribution that is the measure—the standard, if you will—that we value rather than what we receive in return for our efforts. As a young man, and throughout my time with my father, he would often tell me, "Butch, it's not what you've done, but how you did it that makes 'cents' to a man's worth." Though my father passed away over twelve years ago, his sage advice resounds today. I've said many times, "Life is not about what you've done, but rather what you're willing to do." So then, in conversations with Sailors, I am often confronted with the hopes and desires of special recognition for work yet to be done. Of course, we all do enjoy recognition from time to time, but should the recognition be special, or should what we have done to deserve the attention be exceptional?

The awards we receive are awards earned. How can it be then that we often consider an award prior to earning it? Often confused is an award and a reward. Selfless service should be the reward provided others. Selfless service is our vocational design. What we do for others is the true testament to our service. During one particularly restless night, the following phrase came to me: "There is much to be said about the meaning behind two phrases, 'because of' and 'just because.'" So it should be when we consider our contributions and consequential recognition.

But what of fairness, and what about so-and-so and the all-too-familiar "I know this person who…and the inevitable, that's just not fair"? At my age, I can say with certainty that life is not based on fairness. Consider that benchmarks have been made less strenuous, and envy, a powerful emotion, has all too often caused selflessness to shift from a state of altruism to one of ego. Still, you must look inward to justify your actions and behaviors. That is the real measure of self-worth. There are many among us who want to be someone they are not, and there are others who consider falsities nothing more than an expression of free speech. Yet, although they need not answer to others, they must ultimately answer to themselves. I guess they can do in the same way as an older person looks into the mirror without wearing their glasses in order to see someone they are not. I speak from experience on that note.

The point here is simply what is right. Consider less what you receive, and reconsider what you are willing to give. Work harder, work longer, take on more of the burden, volunteer, and do much more than your share. Why, you may ask? Do so not for the desire of special recognition, but rather and simply put, because you are truly able.

THE TELLING FACTS ABOUT DIVERSITY AND ACCEPTANCE

Though we are all created equal, by our very nature, differences do exist. While statistics illustrate that disparities are present, if we consider social, economic, class, and creed, dissimilarity is common throughout our society. Within our Navy's cultural climate, we as leaders recognize that our organization is strengthened by a diverse workforce. Education, life experience, and individual socialization are factors that are balanced within the military service. We enter the service of our country from unique social constructs. Crossing this threshold, we then become equals as servants of our nation and a force of good for our world community. Our Navy is made up of varied ethnicities, differing social classes, and spiritual beliefs. Just as importantly, our service is a blend of shades: blue, white, khaki, and camouflage patterns.

It is expected of us to be accepting of those who may be different, yet who are likewise committed to serve. Religious affiliation, gender, and sexual preference must not lead to discrimination or separatism, as all are afforded the opportunity to serve in the military without harassment. This inclusion will mandate assimilation into a culture of tolerance and acceptance whereby professionalism is the paradigm that all will follow. Importantly, irrespective of sexual preference, a Sailor's willingness to serve will be the unit of measure. Service and sacrifice, professionalism and commitment to duty will be the hallmarks by which all Sailors will be judged: not skin tones, spirituality, or sexual preference.

Our military provides all entrants unique opportunities to expand, enhance, and excel. Self-actualization is accomplished by one's pursuit of excellence. The Navy's selection process for advancement and promotion is based on established precepts that set excellence as the equilibrium to selection criteria. Rather than focusing on a remedy based solely upon gender or race, it is prudent to seek those candidates who have risen above their peers, excelled academically, and who have consistently demonstrated a leadership paradigm that others emulate. True, a broader base provides for cultural richness. But again, it is intuition, aptitude, ability, and the inclination to serve broadly and selflessly that is most desired in our leadership. These high standards are not measured from a precipitous rise. True, the parallel is established at the high mark, but the criterion is balanced though it does require one to initiate the first step up. Such is not a limiting factor for consideration, but rather a consideration for those seeking to advance themselves and, in so doing, serve others rightly and as representative models of behavior.

Significantly, teamwork is a critical component of our armed forces. Whether in a firefight or fighting a fire, what is most important is the bond between those on the line. Maintaining a professional ethos is paramount to the success of any evolution. As professionals and members of an elite military organization, this trust must not be weakened by bigotry, racism, or personally held beliefs or biases. As a team, we must accept the hand of a teammate, regardless of differences, as we stand shoulder to shoulder with those whose differences are made somewhat opaque by the fabric that binds us.

WHAT'S IN YOUR HEART?

We all know the meaning of Valentine's Day. It is a day of romance and of giving: of cards and chocolates, roses and pleasantries. The symbol of the holiday is the heart. Much has been made of this symbol. The heart has been commercialized and marketed in a way of gift giving and receipt of tender bequests. Yet, there is much more that can be given from the heart. Trinkets fade and, after a few days, end up put aside, gathering dust, to be forgotten in the weeks ahead. True love comes from the heart, but what too resides within? Some say it is the soul, a mystical eminence that proves to be one's unique identity. The heart can fall physically ill and be repaired, removed, or even replaced; but the soul transcends time and space, and manipulation. The soul is one's personal identity: character, kindness, and consideration. I believe it is within the heart that one's soul resides and promotes who we are, who we can be, and who we should be. Many will say it is the mind—one's personality—that dictates a person's identity. Much has been said of the power of the mind, and much study has been devoted to its definition. With all certainty, I will not counter those who know much more than me about the mind. However, my point here is to forward my thoughts about one's personal offerings originating from the heart.

So then, what's in your heart? Benevolence, charity, humanity—do these personal traits define who you are? When you extend a hand to another, is it to offer rather than receive? Is it empathy rather than apathy that defines your personal interactions? Do you worry less about your career and consider the careers of others foremost? True, many individuals are strong willed, and many others are weak minded. I think it is the heart that enables a person to do the extraordinary. Consider those who run into a burning building to save a stranger; now, that takes heart! It is the soul that enables one to address adversity rather than take a path less arduous. Consider the heart of a person who will sacrifice himself for those unable to fend for themselves.

A few years ago, I had the privilege to meet two Medal of Honor recipients. These were humble gentlemen. When they spoke, they did so with confidence and not bravado. When they addressed others, they forwarded their sincere appreciation to the men and women who serve this country. They were focused less on themselves and their gallantry. Listening to their heroic tales, we can only speculate if we too would serve in such a capacity: when the odds are overwhelmingly against us, sacrificing ourselves in order to save others. Certainly, these men thought less of themselves and considered the lives of others to be paramount.

As an example, upon receiving the Medal of Honor, Staff Sergeant Giunta, the first living recipient of the Medal of Honor since the Vietnam War, humbly stated, "Because of this day, I lost two great friends of mine, and although this [award] is so positive, I would give this back in a second to have my friends with me right now." Are you such a person? Would you sacrifice yourself for another? Would you lead others to a place that another would circumvent? Are you a person who considers the lives of others before your own? Could you forgo fame, prestige, or special recognition to do the extraordinary? Could you move forward when your mind tells you to run the other way? Would you hesitate knowing that whatever comes from your actions would likely be realized posthumously? When the time comes, will your heart be strong enough, be bold enough? Of course, it is not possible to answer these questions until you're confronted with such a decision. However, now is the time to bolster the heart that is within your chest through the service of others. As with any endeavor involving the heart, it is a selfless act that will embolden your heart and enable you to face the inevitable with honor, courage, and commitment. So, then, what's in your heart?

THE LAST DOUGHBOY

According to Wikipedia, the term *Doughboy* is an informal term for an American soldier, especially members of the American Expeditionary Forces (AEF) in World War I. The term dates back to the Mexican-American War of 1846–'48. The last Doughboy, Frank Buckles, served in WWI and died at the age of 110 on February 27, 2011. The extraordinary sacrifices of our servicemen and women from that long-gone war are today seldom considered, rarely taught, or for some, believed to be irrelevant. True, there is a national WWI monument in Washington DC. But I am sure that many young Americans pass by the monument offering homage with no more than a glance. Memorials symbolize the significance of life, stand in recognition for societal contributions, and serve as a testament of sacrifice and honor. As time goes by, monuments fade and lack their original luster due to the elements, current events, and a generational conscious.

The passing of Frank Buckles etches in the nation's consciousness the monumental contributions of so many to a far-off war referred to as "over there." Being sixteen years old, he was turned away by the US Marines and the Navy, but later enlisted in the Army in order to go "over there." During the war, he served as an ambulance driver in both England and France and assisted with the repatriation of German prisoners to their homeland after the war. During World War II, although as a US citizen, Frank Buckles was taken prisoner by Japanese forces in the Philippines and was held for over three years at the Los Baños internment camp. With his retirement long after the end of the war, he raised cattle on his farm in West Virginia. Frank Buckles was active in veterans' affairs and served as the honorary chairman of the National World War I Memorial Foundation. He was buried at the Arlington National Cemetery. Frank Buckles's life and service stand as a testament to selfless sacrifice and humble honor rather than celebrity. He endeavored that we should not forget the service of those who fought in the "Great War," not for himself, but rather for those who willingly gave their youth and their lives to a cause much larger than themselves.

Many do not know of Frank Buckles. Today, we are fascinated with societal oddities, focused on disturbing trends and those whose vices are center stage. These celebrities capture the attention of the masses though their irreverent and at times bizarre behavior and mindless rants receive more attention as they act out. Paid millions of dollars an episode for television shows that offer no societal value, yet still inexplicably captivate the attention of millions, these self-serving eccentrics are known around the world and adored by fans. Many others are constantly in the news for nothing more than hedonistic and self-destructive behavior and best categorized as burnouts rather than momentary flashes in the pan.

I thought it only fitting that as we recognize the personalities of others, we should reflect upon a man of true character, of grit, of fortitude and of resolve. It is, then, appropriate that we acknowledge and honor a man whose quiet determination, wit, and reverence are lasting testimonies to a life of selfless service dedicated to others. Frank Buckles was such a man: a quiet man, one who sat with presidents honored by his presence. In his memory, it has been written: "Frank Woodruff Buckles' life spanned the awesome, horrible, fantastic, dreadful Twentieth Century. He saw and experienced much. As America's last surviving veteran witness to the First World War, his life experiences and perspectives are an artifact in our day which often lacks perspective."[7]

WHAT MY PARENTS TAUGHT ME

April 14, 2011

I have always been fascinated by my parents. Their modest storybook lives intertwined since childhood; their shared sense of sacrifice, conservatism, modesty, and sacrifice captivated my interest as a child and still today as a man. Tales of living through the Great Depression, World War II, and the Cold War are etched in my mind. As a child, I realized that my parents were dedicated to serving their church and their community while focusing their attention toward their children rather than pursuing their own desires. We lived modestly, not going without, but making sure that we stretched most things at times beyond what others might have thought practical. They taught me to think about the future and prepare for what may come.

I recall our cellar and the back room designed as a bomb shelter where canned goods were stocked in the event the Russians launched a preemptive nuclear strike. I must admit that though my parents practiced civil defense, even as a child, I didn't really take to the notion that that room would offer our family refuge from a nuclear blast and the subsequent fallout. However, the back room also served to secure precious commodities, which included dozens of fresh-baked chocolate chip holiday cookies that my mom would store there in order to keep them safe from the grips of her three boys. My parents taught me to be prepared and set aside items of necessity in the event of hard days, bad weather, and the uncertainties of an unpredictable future.

I was always very close to my father. To me, he was much larger than life. I looked up to him as a child, and as an adult though taller than he, I still looked up to him. He was then and is today my hero. Faced with adversity, he pressed ahead. A man who loved his family and his home, he and my mother rarely ventured far. My father

119

taught me much. Most of all, he taught me to make time. When faced with challenges, I would look for his guidance; he would always tell me, "There are twenty-four hours a day, and you've got to make time." Even when I was working two jobs and attending college, with seemingly impossible time constraints, my father would tell me, "Butch, if you think there's not enough time, you better make it for yourself." I didn't think it possible, but of course, he was right. My father taught me to establish priorities, refine my trade, and develop prudent time management, all the while preventing myself from forfeiting my eventual reward of accomplishment that my toil and sacrifice would permit. Of course, he was right all along. In all that I do, I know that my father's advice resounds. I often think of him and believe that he would be pleased with the man I've become. Still, if alive today, he no doubt would still subtly tell me that there is yet time to do just a bit more.

My parents taught me what is important in life. I am who I am because of them. I learned from them that even as the years go by and one grows old, as a worldly perspective fades and one's view diminishes, and with many days spent together, there is no need to grow tired of the one to whom you are bound in marriage. Though my parents were stoic and resolved, from time to time, I would notice that as the years passed, their love for one another did not. They grew up together, went to school together, were apart during World War II, reunited after the end of my father's obligatory service, and married April 16, 1946. Their union withstood many a storm. Over the years, they taught me that a sense of humor is very necessary, as life is at times less than fair. Hard times and tragedy befall every marriage, and life's struggles often yield temporary despair. Yet, hope remains, and with laughter, a dark day is brightened.

Other than the war years, the longest period of separation they endured was the months between my father's death and the day that my mother died. The last time I saw my mother, she lay in a hospital bed. Nearing death, she was joyous as she recalled long past loved ones by name. Her fond recollections prefaced her eventual reunion with those gone before her but with whom she would soon be reunited. My parents taught me to cherish the days that you're given and always strive to make more time for those you love. Though the days are fleeting, love is everlasting. *Their inspiration enabled me to better myself and, in turn, better the lives of others.*

A SENSE OF HONOR IN MEMORY OF
THOSE WHO SERVED BEFORE US

Recall the meaning of Memorial Day. Memorial Day was officially proclaimed on May 5, 1868, by General John Logan, national commander of the Grand Army of the Republic, in his General Order No. 11 and was first observed on May 30, 1868, when flowers were placed on the graves of Union and Confederate soldiers at Arlington National Cemetery.[8] There are many who today confuse Memorial Day with Veterans Day while there are others who misrepresent Memorial with a 30 percent storewide savings event!

In my years of naval service, I have traveled far and learned from people whose culture and customs were unbeknownst to me. I also acquired a deep sense of purpose and selflessness. I know no higher honor than that of representing the United States of America while wearing the very fabric of our nation. I have served with the finest among us, and I have known those who have been wounded and others killed battling enemies of our nation. It is for those brave warriors that I recall the true meaning of Memorial Day, and it is them for whom I serve.

Yet, I have also known veterans who consider themselves before those whom we should truly honor. Yes, these veterans are patriots who have served our nation in a greater capacity than others, for these veterans volunteered to serve our country knowing full well the arduous nature of military life. At times, I have heard more than a few veterans who, near retirement or having already retired, exclaim what they feel was due them, what was owed them, and what more they deserve due to the very nature of the service that they volunteered for.

I cannot relate to this. I will soon begin my twenty-sixth year of military service. I entered the military at an age when others were beginning to sight their own retirement. At age thirty-four I enlisted, and today at age sixty, I can write that my military career has not been easy—mostly by my own doing. I volunteered for service in combat environments, serving five tours of duty in Afghanistan. As for me, the arduous nature of the military has benefited me personally and professionally. My health and well-being are what they are because of the benefits derived from my military service. As a result, I prefer to honor those who have given more than me by thinking more of what I owe them than dwelling on that which others believe is due me.

As I too begin to picture retirement—likely sooner than later—I am thankful for the man I am, the health I enjoy, and the shape that I am in. I am honored to have been with true warriors, and in retrospect, I relish the fact that I have inspired those who thought less of their own military service. As these words bear what I hold dear, I will think of those more deserving than me. The highest honor comes from the privilege and protecting the constitutional principle that I volunteered to support and defend at the behest of others. I am but a humble servant whose service is an honorable vocation, and I am indebted to our nation for the very privilege of serving, owing more to those who have done more than me.

HONORING OLD GLORY AND OUR NATIONAL ENSIGN

Are you aware of the origins of Old Glory? Originally made sometime in the 1920s and presented to one Captain Driver by his mother and the ladies of Salem, Massachusetts, the captain is reputed to have chosen to fly the flag—which he named "Old Glory"—from the mast of his sailing vessel. Surely, Old Glory withstood many a storm on his journeys at sea, and it reportedly also survived attempts by Confederate forces to capture and likely destroy it during the Civil War. It is the flag's resiliency that defines it as an iconic symbol of who we are as Americans and as a nation. Our flag is much more than a stitched fabric; it is an icon of who we are.

Over the years, our flag has been identified with struggle, sacrifice, and the triumph of the spirit. Many photographs exist of our flag, but the iconic photo taken atop Mount Suribachi, located on the small volcanic island of Iwo Jima, captured the attention of our nation like no other photograph before. The photo permitted Americans who knew of the mounting casualties from the Pacific theater to unite and rally around those men, our military, and our national objectives. The photo was a moment in time where struggle, bloodshed, and loss were not linked to the flag; rather, the raising of Old Glory atop that volcano symbolized that above all odds, beyond all momentary limitations and mounting casualties, the flag's fabric, as is our national spirit, is hard-wearing, powerful, and personifies victory.

Our flag has ventured deep beneath the world's oceans and has been placed on the surface of the moon. I recall watching a grainy black-and-white television picture where Neil Armstrong took those historic steps. I witnessed the bicentennial celebrations while I was in high school and recall the incredible outpouring of nationalistic pride: the parades, picnics, and celebrations. I further recall the Vietnam War era and the political and social unrest. I recollect that during those days, an American flag proudly waved at our local church in remembrance of those from our rural community who had served and in recognition of those serving in Southeast Asia. I remember the awe-inspiring support for the US Armed Forces during the first Gulf War, the displays of patriotism and reconciliation with our Vietnam veterans. In fact, the patriotism from those days was a motivating factor that led me to enlist shortly after finishing my undergraduate studies. I now recall the terrorist attacks of September 11, 2001, and the iconic photo of firefighters from the New York Fire Department hoisting our flag amidst the rubble of the World Trade Center. This photograph defined all that we are, our American spirit, and our way of life once again tested, yet defined as unbreakable.

Consider the tornadic event that befell Joplin, Missouri, years ago. After the weather cleared and from the rubble, yet again another iconic symbol appeared. There among the debris and carnage, multiple American flags, tattered but proudly swaying, a symbol of strength and renewal, proudly waved to again inspire the spirit and define the strength of the American people. What is this symbol that inspires so many, defines us as a nation, spiritually, cohesively, and universally? This is much more than a piece of cloth sewn together by machine. This flag is our identity, embraced and emboldened; it is our national persona on display for the all the world to see. It is an emblem of strength and of benevolence, of justice, and of goodwill. Old Glory represents both what and who we are collectively, a proud people, diverse yet unified by the fabric of our nation, an enduring symbol of our eternal American character for all to behold.

ARE YOU PREPARED TO DO THE EXTRAORDINARY?

Only a fraction of Americans swear to support and defend the Constitution of the United States as a member of the military service. In so doing, we realize that we are expected, much more than the citizenry, to do that which is necessary in defense of our nation. Though we are expected to go above and beyond, I believe that fewer still realize that within them resides the ability to do the extraordinary.

Each military member is transformed with the acceptance of an ethos that places our nation and those we serve before ourselves. We can no longer turn our heads in the face of adversity, turn the corner to avoid confronting insurmountable obstacles, or fail to extend a hand to those in need—even if all appears lost. As the oath is spoken, so it is that we are transformed, supplanting selfishness with a determination to serve others whose struggles would beforehand likely foster a response to turn away. We are different; we have matured and view not the world as a sphere that begets opportunity for personal reward, but rather consider challenges as the means to fulfill our vocational aspirations of serving others. We are not elected to such a position; we are volunteers who serve, knowing that the needs of others become foremost the consideration of the collective. Those among us have done the extraordinary; displaying uncommon valor, heroism, and astonishing courage, yet the esteemed World War II general and later General of the Army Omar Bradley best defined such heroism as bravery "the capacity to perform properly even when scared half to death." Among us are those who chose to move forward because of duty vice a sense of self-preservation in order to preserve the life of another. Such an act defines what some have done, what we are, and what the rest of us should do despite the costs—first acting without calculation or without reservation. This philosophy is a constant definition of who we have been, who we are, and who we will always be as members of the United States military.

I recently spoke before a group of Sailors many of whom have yet to report to their first operational command. They asked questions and expressed their concerns. They wondered what the next few years of their lives would yield. They forwarded questions but in actuality question themselves. Many of their questions I have before fielded by others in their position. A young Sailor once asked me, "Sir, what do you fear the most?" I suppose I could have taken a less-than-honest path and replied "nothing" or conjured up some false bravado. But that would be a far cry from the truth and not the man or the officer I swore to be. My response offered to the Sailor was that I fear not serving to my fullest potential; rather, I fear falling short of the expectations of those I am charged to lead.

I contemplate this every day. I've served in Afghanistan, and as a detachment officer in charge, I was responsible for the lives and careers of those under my charge. I am responsible to my superiors, to the command that I directly support, and the command to which I am assigned. I am also responsible to the families of the Sailors that I lead. Believe me, my thoughts are weighty. Yet, my thoughts inspire me to do more for others: to serve them at my fullest and to do whatever is asked and whatever it takes to do my best. I serve not for individual benefits or recognition. I serve for the privilege of being asked to or, if necessary, demanded to do the extraordinary for those I serve with and for those I serve: for the poor, the sick, the oppressed, and those who seek a better life.

Because of my actions, my behavior, and my sense of service, I trust I motivate others as I have been motivated myself. I ask others if they are so stirred, and if not, I advise them that it is their duty to locate a trusted mentor to guide and direct them. There are many whose actions can motivate. Being so guided, prepare yourself to serve with distinction each day and prepare to do what is asked and then ready yourself to do a bit more.

The same Sailor who asked what I fear most followed by asking if I am scared of death. I told him how I quell my anxiety by reflecting on the words of Lt. Gen. Thomas "Stonewall" Jackson: "My religious belief teaches me to feel as safe in battle as in bed. God has fixed the time for my death. I do not concern myself about that, but to be always ready, no matter when it may overtake me…that is the way all men should live, and then all would be equally brave." Come what may, I define my life the way I live it, and in so doing, I pray that when called upon, my life in some small way should be an inspiration to all.

CELEBRATING OUR INDEPENDENCE AS WE SHOULD, IN THE PLURAL SENSE

We are a nation because of our independence. I admit that the previous sentence may at first seem self-evident, but there is a broader meaning that at times is shunned. Independence is often considered an individual right. Now, I am not to dismiss one's rights to self-determination. On the contrary, I will, however, put forth my sentiments concerning independence and the plurality of the term as I believe it was intended. Our founding fathers were deeply spiritual intellectuals, scholars, and free thinkers. In crafting the Declaration of Independence, the founders sent forth a document that would inspire a union of people seeking their destiny. The year was 1776; though the day of the declaration is at times contested, our nation celebrates this monumental occasion on the fourth day of July. Our history, our national identity, our achievements, and our collective sacrifices are to be celebrated. Our founders intended that through our independence, "we" would be free from tyranny; that as a country, our collective spirit would be emboldened; and that in union, "we" would set off to make a better way in life for all who would for each year to follow celebrate our independence.

From the Articles of Confederation to the ratification of the United States Constitution, the founders thought carefully about the text and, knowing the significance of documents, recognized all too well that independence and liberty would be tested from within as well as from external forces. Yet, without well-planned thought—these documents and a democratic republic—our independence may well have cascaded into anarchy. The Constitution was adopted on September 17, 1787, by the Constitutional Convention in Philadelphia, Pennsylvania, and ratified by conventions in each US state in the name of "the People." The Constitution has been amended twenty-seven times; the first ten amendments are known as the Bill of Rights. Over the years, our nation has been tested by external forces and divided as a result of internal social upheavals. But from it all, our nation became stronger with a national determination that improved the lives of "We the People."

I grew up in the turbulent 1960s, the Vietnam war era, a time of political assassinations, and witnessed a man walking on the moon, observed over the years the ebb and flow of a sense of national unity, of common purpose and pride in our nation. I was a teenager when I witnessed our nation's bicentennial celebration. In my twenties, I recall the turbulence of the political environment, wars and strife, and the assassination attempt of our fortieth president. I also remember the collective mourning of our nation after the Challenger spaceship disaster. In the early nineties, I witnessed the Gulf War and, in particular, recall the day after Pres. George H. W. Bush's announcement of war, as I was driving to the university and listening to talk radio and heard Kate Smith's rendition of Irving Berlin's "God Bless America." After graduating from the University of New York at Albany, I longed to serve my country and chose to serve in the military rather than pursue a law degree.

Over the years, I've witnessed much social upheaval and turmoil. As I grow older, I believe that becoming more conservative and possibly a bit wiser than my youthful days, I have taken note that the popular ideals of independence have shifted from the "we" to the "me." Much individual revision has been made of rights and laws and the original intent of our founding fathers. I still believe, however, in the concept of "We the People." Rugged individualism that built this grand nation is far different from the signature of celebrity. And, it is often that celebrity has a debasing effect on a society. I often ask if there can truly be any positive lasting societal benefit derived from the narcissism that is very much in vogue. Yet, there is a lesson to be learned here. The best lessons in life are those things that we should not do. So in retrospect, I guess that our focus on celebrities—so characterized by their selfish desires, personal shortcomings, and failures—in a strange way empower those of us who are focused on purposeful selfless service.

Rather than selfish pursuits, I prefer to spend time with family, enjoying a barbecue, fireworks, and giving thanks to God for being an American—all blessings that "we" enjoy—and the opportunity given me to defend our nation's independence while serving the world community. I will also share with the children and young adults in our family that individual sacrifice yields benefits for all; society is blessed from altruism vice self-centeredness, and the rugged individualism that built this nation is far different from selfish individual pursuits often celebrated today.

FOR MANY, THE SIGNIFICANCE OF SEPTEMBER 11 HAS DIMINISHED

Everywhere that freedom stirs, let tyrants fear.
—George W. Bush

In the years following the tragic events of September 11, 2001, we have continued to ask ourselves as a nation: where do we stand? An obvious answer is that America stands united and determined, resilient and committed to protecting and defending our country from extremists who again would do us harm. Ideologically, this may be true, but with careful inspection, not all is what it should be. For many, selfish pursuits have distorted the images of the horrors from that day. Noble efforts have gone unrecognized, and political correctness has overtaken what needed be done. With so few Americans involved in the defense of our nation, many of our citizens think less of sacrifice, believing instead that their personal pursuits should be their focus rather than a collective effort by the citizenry. Over the years, support has waned, and blame has become a contradiction. For others, September 11 is no longer a day of reverence, but rather a nuisance as personal routine has been disrupted with programs of remembrance. With indifference, some of those among us make their way through the day without reflection. This should not be.

For instance, there are those who are not aware that jihadists were responsible for the deaths of thousands of American citizens that fateful day. Conspiracy theories and revisionist history perpetuated via the internet have inculcated misinformation and ignorance. For instance, an education system that seeks to blur the fault line underscoring Osama Bin Laden, Al-Qaeda, and the Taliban, who sheltered leaders and followers of Bin Laden's organization, serve only to obscure true events. I recently spoke with a twelve-year-old who believes that America's pursuit of those responsible is wrong. Lacking baseline knowledge of terrorist attacks dating back before their birth—events of that critical day and the years since—this teenager believes that what America has done is unnecessary and wasteful in resources. I often mention that our youth recognize antisocial celebrities and others who offer no social benefit, yet know nothing of true heroes who sacrifice so much and whose toil and blood benefit all Americans and the world community. Prominently displayed within our home are photos, plaques, and mementoes of the military service of our family elders, yet the attention of younger family members more often than occasionally centers on social networks where they themselves are the focal point.

With the days leading up to the yet another anniversary of that fateful day, I look to see the numbers of American flags displayed in advance. Remember the number of flags flown days after the attack? Remember the sentiments of patriotism, pride, and altruism? Remember the announcement that America was prepared to track down those responsible and bring them to justice? Recall the words of Pres. George W. Bush, who stated, "Time is passing. Yet, for the United States of America, there will be no forgetting September the 11th. We will remember every rescuer who died in honor. We will remember every family that lives in grief. We will remember the fire and ash, the last phone calls, the funerals of the children." In recognition of all who have served defending our nation, we must remember our military and their families, as well as the government employees and civil servants who have given so much. We must also continue to recognize that our enemies unceasingly conspire to do us harm. I do, however, feel a sense of a softening of our resolve. With political wrangling, finger pointing, an advancing secularization movement, and an apparent dichotomy of intent by those with whom we align, our enemies seek to capitalize on the internal acrimony and divisions that serve only to lessen our tenacity. It was and remains Al-Qaeda's intent to bleed and bankrupt our nation. Our enemies profit from America's internal discord due to negative images, false information, and a segment of the media bent on discrediting our noble effects.

With the approach of another anniversary of the 9-11 attacks, we must continue to pursue those who again would do us harm. We must continue to speak out against radicals and extremists and identify those who conspire to attack us from within as well as from the periphery. We must demonstrate the moral courage to take the fight forward while we strengthen our steadfastness to defend our nation and our way of life. With a voice of the majority, we must forward a message that we welcome discourse with all people while remaining united in purpose and determined to confront our enemies here and abroad. Our nation must not forget those who were taken from us on 9-11, nor must we forget those who have given their all in defense of our rights and freedom while recognizing those responsible and the root cause for their actions. Lastly, America must continue to commit its resources and treasure to assisting those who have been subjugated by tyranny and despair in lands where fanaticism swells and our enemies foster desires to conspire to attack our freedoms once again. With this we honor, remember, and we vow to redress.

TO MAKE A DIFFERENCE

I have had the privilege to be deployed numerous times during my career. Whether afloat or afield, these deployments have taken me far. Though the time away from family and friends has been difficult, I have managed. From each deployment, my experiences have varied, yet each deployment has been tremendously rewarding. Of course, there have been challenging times, with heartache and heartbreak associated with these deployments. For instance, I lost my brother while I was serving in Afghanistan in 2003. During a deployment in 2006, I lost my father; and a few months later, my father-in-law. In 2007, I lost my mother. I have lost friends who too served in Afghanistan: Americans, Coalition, and Afghan patriots. In retrospect and now looking forward, I realize the true blessing of being selected to serve and support national objectives while serving our Navy, our nation, and the world community.

But not all share my sentiments and positive outlook in life. I took note of a recent posting on a social network by an individual who, having served for twelve months in Afghanistan, looked back and denoted his disgust. I must admit that I often hear disdain from service members regarding deployments, time away from loved ones, and of course, personal deprivation and hardship. Such comments are disturbing to me, and I often wonder the reason for such comments from those serving in the military. Do we not swear to support and defend? Should we not anticipate the associated scarcities? Did we not volunteer for everything when swearing in at MEPS (Military Entrance Processing Station)? Are we not determined to redress the evil that at this moment plots to kill innocent Americans? So then, should we not expect to be asked to do those things others choose not to do? Surely to wear the uniform evokes pride in one's service. Yet, for some, they appear shamed by the service to which they serve, embarrassed of their uniform, though they expect, if not demand special recognition in every endeavor. Considering this individual's posting, did this individual not serve with great Americans and Coalition partners who too sacrificed their time at considerable peril? Did this individual not realize that his efforts aided in the democratization of a land torn apart by decades of conflict? Did this individual not benefit in some small way one single Afghan life and, in so doing, brightened the life of a person who may have known nothing but strife? Did this individual not realize that whatever the conditions, someone before endured greater hardships? Does this individual not serve in a military service that focuses on the personal well-being of all who serve? Does this individual not realize that by overcoming adversity, one becomes a better person, stronger, more tolerant, and certainly more appreciative of his good fortune as a benevolent American, who sacrificed much for the advancement of others?

In contrast, I know of an Afghan who recently was beset by tragedy who yet understands the ebb and flow of life. For what has been can be taken away in an instant. This Afghan also appreciates that with tomorrow, possibilities and blessings are to be found. This Afghan, though deeply affected personally and financially, remains steadfast in his belief that hard times, though they may be bitter, with time, determination, self-reliance, and a resilient faith yield a fruitful harvest. Perhaps this service member did not have the good fortune of meeting such a man as this Afghan that I know; for he, with all due consideration, believes himself blessed just to see a new day and thankful that from each experience in life he proceeds along life's journey on a proper path.

A RIGHT TIME FOR A WRONG DECISION

At some time or another, each of us has faced a point in life where a sound decision required our utmost attention; and though the time was right, we chose poorly. In so doing, with the decision made, we often rationalize our behavior as likely a personal indiscretion or to the point: "who'll know if I don't get caught," we may think, as a way of diminishing the wrong as a fleeting moment. The outcome of such a decision is a lessening of one's personal accord once firmly etched in their mind only to blur the definition of who they are, to ourselves, and to others. The lure of misadventure before long reels us in, and we pass the point where return is not possible, or so we think. It is here that regret and remorse lie before us like mire, that once we are beset, we eventually succumb, often overtaken by guilt. I often tell others that if you contemplate about what is wrong, then there is your answer! Nonetheless, we often dismiss our inner voice and plow on into an entanglement, only to sink into transgression.

Believe me, I articulate this from experience, and I am certainly qualified to speak from the heart with regard to this topic. I think it unnecessary to look for quotes of famous people to emphasize the point here. I have done many things wrong and done many wrong things in my life. At my age, I can certainly reflect upon the decisions that I once made that certainly went wide of the mark. I would be remiss, however, if I did not share with you that I shoulder burdens as others do.

Father and Mother World War II (1943)

Father and Mother Circa 2000

Paying my respects at my parents grave site

With my father as an infant

With my father as a small child

Baling hay

Prized bull

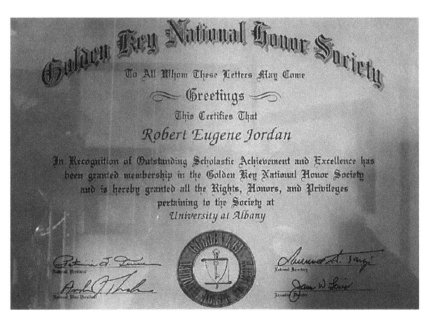

Golden Key National Honor Society

On the left, a photograph
taken near the end of Recruit training, Orlando, Florida, August
1993; and on the right, a photo of me while serving with the Joint
Intelligence Center, Pacific, Kami Seya, Japan, circa 1994.

As a teenager, I was involved in raising chickens and selling eggs in conjunction with delivering the weekly newspaper around the rural area of the Town of Esopus, New York. While attending Kingston High School, Kingston, New York, I was the president of the chapter of Future Farmers of America. After graduating from the Ulster County Community College, Stone Ridge, New York, 1979, I began to raise beef cattle, eventually farming approximately 150 acres in and around Saint Remy. The years of farming were transformative ones, as I learned many valuable lessons in life. I learned commitment, tenacity, and how blessed I was in facing eventual hardships and heartaches; success is possible through hard work, planning, and providence.

Having completed my bachelor's degree at the State University of New York at Albany, New York, December 1992, I was inducted into the Golden Key National Honor Society. With my academics completed, I decided to enlist into the United States Navy, entering the Delayed Entry Program, February 1993, and reported for duty at the US Navy Recruit Training Center, Orlando, Florida, June 28, 1993.

Aboard USS
Blueridge LCC
19, somewhere in
the South Pacific,
circa 1994.

Near the summit
of Mount Fuji,
central Honshu,
south-west
of Tokyo.

First Class
Petty Officer

Chief Petty
Officer

Senior Chief
Petty Officer

Chief Warrant Officer
in Afghanistan

As a Chief Warrant Officer serving aboard USS *Dwight D. Eisenhower* CVN 69, circa 2016.

Yet, though the burdens may be weighty, I manage to keep moving forward, having learned from past experiences and now contemplating my next move; for now is the time to make things right as I intend to follow a true bearing in life.

I am certain that you wonder how it is that these self-laden burdens are shouldered. Well, never one to miss an opportunity to offer a bit of counsel, I find it possible to do things once thought impossible by applying two principles: insistence and grace. No matter how insurmountable the obstacle, I know it can be overtaken, perhaps not by me alone, but by someone or for sure with a helping hand from a higher power. For instance, it has been stated that man has scaled the heights of Mount Everest, only to be surpassed in height by reaching the moon, yet man has looked beyond into distant galaxies. Man has traveled to the bottom of the ocean to discover things thought unimaginable, yet entered into the innermost depths of that which cannot be seen: a molecule. Man has hypothesized, imagined, and created that which next year will be obsolete. Man's ingenuity is propelled by insistence, a longing to see farther, to learn more, and to answer the age-old question, "How far is beyond?" Given insistence, the answers will eventually come.

Now, what of this principle known as grace? I refer to spiritual grace, divine intervention versus the secular view of just plain luck. I can recall years ago; I was insistent on doing the wrong thing. Fortunately, grace intervened, and today I live to tell about it. Perhaps it's a guardian—a heavenly over watch—but my departure from the wrong way in life came not a moment too soon. Some might state that the outcome was nothing more than a random occurrence. I, however, believe that though I had forsaken the right way, I found myself back on track, unscathed and renewed not because I was lucky, but rather because of an influence bigger than myself and my intentions. Now, my friends, that's grace!

I know of those who are hampered by indecision, wrong choices, and perhaps misery: those who are hurt and perhaps thought broken. You may ask, "How then to fix this?" My friends, I prescribe to you: first, insist in finding a better way in life; and second, grace, a thankful recognition for the divine benevolence for enabling you to learn from your mistakes and move forward in the right direction. Believe that the best decision comes at the very best of times.

WHAT WILL YOU OFFER THE NEW YEAR?

January 01, 2012

It is often a part of every New Year's observance that we think about what's in store for us. We ask, "What will the days ahead yield for me?" Will it be fame, fortune, more money, what else could be of benefit? Of course, we hope for the best and, over time, realize that our desires are as likely to materialize as it is when we play the lottery in hopes of instant riches. We would be better off saving the dollar then passing it across the counter for just one more fast-cash lottery ticket. Knowing the changes are so slight, we'll continue to forward our hopes of a life-changing wealth windfall. However, how many winners become selfish or self-centered, focusing on themselves materialistically rather than realizing that an opportunity to benefit others in tremendous ways can be had for the cost of a dollar. So too it is when we exclaim, "Happy New Year!" at the striking of midnight on New Year's Eve; do we not look inward, in the hope that with all that might be is selfishly ours and ours alone? Should we reconsider the Happy New Year for those we do not know and hope that the lives of others may benefit from a premium of wealth and happiness? The answer is, of course, yes! This is a revolutionary way of thinking, thinking of others before self, hoping for the betterment of others, and truly hoping for a Happy New Year for those outside our communal sphere. Imagine the impact such thinking would have for the New Year! Knowing the chances of striking it rich, we willingly push the dollar forward in order to grab that winning ticket, yet we ignore the homeless and hungry outside of the convenience store whose wish it is that someone would show a little compassion and offer them a mere dollar. How often do we dismiss such a person thought wretched, yet literally throw money away on a get-rich-quick scheme?

My family often comments about the fact that I seldom take advantage of a parking spot especially close to an entrance of a store. Possibly, there is an elder individual who would benefit from a parking spot closer to the entrance. Learning from past transgressions, I seek out service opportunities to benefit others. For instance, I frequent the gym regularly, and do not mind the extra physical activity of parking farther from the entrance, thus providing a space for another who might benefit from it more. I have observed people jockeying for position in order to get as close as possible to the gym's entrance; though they have presumably come to the gym with the objective of becoming physically exhausted, they do not consider the extra benefit the additional distance would provide. But of course, there is much more to happiness than parking spots.

What will make for a New Year of happiness? Certainly, the champagne will run dry, the festive hats and noisemakers will be tossed in the trash, and there will be days to follow that do not offer celebration. First off, we are intrinsically capable of caring for ourselves. We will make our lives comfortable, and we will likely not go hungry, though all of us pledge to lose a few pounds! As for me, I will do with less so that I can offer more to others. I will provide to those, thus enabling a better life. I will donate more of my money to charity so that others will not go hungry. I will continue to educate myself so that I can educate others. I will practice my faith so I can offer others a better person. The things that I will do cost me little, but they will hopefully pay immeasurable dividends to others. I will sacrifice more and push myself in order to make a better way in the world for others: the nameless, the homeless, the impoverished, the less fortunate, those who suffer under tyrannical rule and offer others the best in me.

You may ask, "But, sir, wouldn't you want to take a chance on instant riches, instant retirement, perhaps a sports car, fame, and influence?" The best way to convey my answer is to put my sentiments to paper and forward them without chance of retraction. I would rather work for something, toil long without the certainty of success, all for the opportunity of setting an example for others. I think it should be etched in our psyche that we should produce something through creative means, being empowered by sacrifice and hardships, rewarded by hard work, and benefit those who then choose to follow our lead. Rather than ponder what the New Year has in store for me, I concentrate on what I have to offer the New Year in the service of others for the benefit of community and country. Through my service, the joy of happiness is fostered by the potential for another person's delight in the days ahead.

THE ESCALATING WAR OF WORDS

We are all familiar with the old adage that "the squeaky wheel that gets the grease," and indeed, it is volume that gets the attention of an audience—whether intended or not. To overpower an opponent through vociferous rants seems to be the standard of the day. But there is a difference between what is said and that which is heard. And, different people hear different parts of speech, which of course is at times troubling. Lewis Carroll impressed upon his readers that "you should say what you mean, and mean what you say!" Yet, today, often what is said is stated to inflict a point of view that is sharp and cuts to the heart of the matter. Principled debate has long since degraded into personal attacks and mudslinging, focused on humiliating an opponent through supposition and speculation and, with an upturn in tone, rudeness and obscenity. Tolerance has been supplanted by small-mindedness and spirited discussion superseded by vulgarity and crudity. It has also been said, "History repeats itself." This, I believe, is true as today the political tone is reminiscent of the late 1960s. In fact, I see social, racial, and political similarities today as was the case during the run up to the 1968 presidential elections. Protesters, malcontents, and anarchists shout their agendas with contempt while the disenfranchised follow, as a growing mob seizes the opportunity to turn frustrations into acts of violence. However, their message is lost, as opposing sides are infused into a volatile environment. Similar to lint on a fine suit, it is the fringe that is noticed most during times as these.

These are troubling times indeed. Focusing internally, however, would lead to isolationism, so we must also focus on world events as once-veiled threats are today proclaimed as outright challenges to our national objectives and global security. With the Middle East moving ever closer to the precipice, it will require that cool heads prevail, yet an essential resolve is necessary to counter claims and circumstances of divergent ideologies that no longer engage in clandestine affairs.

Chest thumping and saber rattling must be measured when dealing with tyrants whose demagoguery foretell of intention rather than supposition. History has shown that irrational purpose fused with religious conviction has produced diabolical aspirations. Recently, the Iranians foretold the capability of launching long-range ballistic missiles capable of striking American assets within the Middle East, Southwest Asia, and Europe. With the Strait of Hormuz threatened and the media full of speculation concerning an Israeli strike of an Iranian nuclear facility, what is needed most is resolve, conviction, and a constant expression of our will, of our capability, without raising the tenor of our voice, without blinking or foretelling our hand. What we need most are leaders who are statesmen, who are articulate, and who evoke a persona of resolve void of unfounded emotion. We need leaders who inspire rather than segregate people between camps. Most of all, our country needs to become one nation rather than a muddle of divergent views that cause internal strife, a blurring of our national image, and a sullying of our national ensign. Of all words that need be said in unison is our Pledge of Allegiance and demonstrations of national unity rather than defilement of our national heritage.

Take, for instance, the Super Bowl. No other sporting match captivates a greater world audience. Estimates of over 100 million viewers worldwide watch this football game annually. "America the Beautiful" and "The Star-Spangled Banner" are sung before a world audience that salutes our country with honor and passion. Still, the half-time show, which was sexually suggestive—and for some, repulsive, and even for those less modest, a loutish display—seizes the moment. In response, the media will dismiss offensive gestures as nothing more than artistic expression and by today's standard commonplace. Yet, another football player, whose outward display of his faith, has been mocked and in the media criticized; his faith, reverence, and his personal beliefs will be repeatedly disparaged. The dichotomy here is as apparent as it is divisive. It is my belief that what is needed today is national civility, upholding of moral values and standards, and a portrayal of an American identity that rightly stands on its own without saying a word.

THE AFTERMATH OF
ANOTHER DEPLOYMENT

As I write this, I have been preparing to be redeployed after spending several months in Afghanistan. Throughout this period of my life, I have again learned many valuable lessons. This deployment represents my fourth tour of duty in Afghanistan. During these past months, I have seen many improvements, most notably the furtherance of the Afghan government and the Afghan Security Forces. I have seen children attending schools, orphanages improved, and I have seen many Afghans inspired by fledging prosperity, perhaps shifting away from decades of dependency. Over the years, Afghans have personally expressed their gratitude to me as a member of the American military. I have mentored and assisted them with the hope that I have made life better for those Afghans with whom I have interacted. I have seen abject poverty, sickness, hopelessness, and death. I have seen cruelty and observed the struggle for survival. Yet, with the countless amounts of time, money, and blood spent on their behalf, why do so many Afghans remain ambivalent to America and all that has been done to build a nation, not for the United States, but rather for the Afghan people? This question has perplexed me. I submit there are many more reasons than will be included in the following paragraphs. I will tender my thoughts concerning what disturbs my sleep, what causes me distress, yet inspires me to do more and causes me to willingly offer again my service in Afghanistan.

As I am neither an intellectual nor a pundit, my rationale will be elementary. With the promise of a new beginning, modernity, and a better way in life, why is our enemy still so determined? This is the core question. I believe that our enemies detest modernity: perhaps not for a select few, but for their underlings who are kept down, manipulated, and coerced to reject a better way. Recall how Osama Bin Laden enjoyed the benefit of a computer in his lair, yet still believed that for the masses, education is useless and a gateway to

154

"radical" vices. In Afghanistan, the agrarian subsistence and nomadic lifestyle is embedded. Lacking a worldview, and for those who remain illiterate, they are easily manipulated and simply coerced. Given the number of schools burned, teachers murdered, and the continued subjugation of women in rural areas, my elementary line of thought stands on its own as well as noted in the press more than occasionally. It is a part of the world where a father whose children are sick will turn to the Americans for assistance in his time of need. However, this same man, if found out by the Taliban, will be persecuted for turning to the infidels for help.

With war, mistakes will occur, and tragedy will surely strike. When they do, the rabble will vehemently cry, "Death to America!" Images of flag burnings and chants of "Death to the infidel" are broadcast around the world. Yet, when the Taliban coerces an unfortunate young man to become a suicide bomber and target innocent Afghans, where is the outrage? And, often chided as invaders, occupiers, crusaders, America is often cited as imposing its will upon the Afghan people. I have been in and out of Afghanistan for nearly ten years, and I have not seen anyone forced to forsake their religion. Yet, if an Afghan perhaps chooses to accept Christianity, this person faces death, likely by stoning, for exercising free will.

A question that I routinely ponder is, "Why do our enemies hate America so?" I believe the basis is religion and our freedom to exercise free will that enrages our enemies. As Americans, we have unlimited possibilities, choices, and opportunities. We are so blessed, and it is because of our good fortune that we are hated. It is when a mistake is made—perhaps by an exercise of free will—which our enemies are quick to rally against. It is because of free will that some among us choose to display the worst in us. Greed, zealous pride, disrespect, and xenophobic behavior that when displayed, these behaviors disgrace others, driving them not from the direction of our lead, but rather in disgust, compel them into the arms of those who will manipulate and sensitize them to perform heinous acts.

One last thought. I also think that our enemies also hate the fact that Americans admit to our faults, and receiving reprimand, and are so punished by the rule of law. Our enemies are quick to fault us, but their vengeful reciprocity is sanctioned through an ideology that accepts dehumanizing punishment as ordained. In no way do I suggest that Afghans are the enemy. On the contrary, I have met phenomenal Afghans who are willing to fight their interior battles, sacrifice for others, and make life better not just individually, but also for their fellow countrymen. These Afghan men and women are true heroes, who serve selflessly, with distinction, overcoming fanaticism, with the hope that slowly modernity will benefit all.

With the United States and the Afghan Strategic Partnership Agreement signed on May 1, 2012, the United States affirmed its commitment to the Afghan people and to the continued pursuit of Al-Qaeda. This historic partnership declared that the United States will not abandon the people of Afghanistan. Perhaps, in retrospect, US policymakers reflected on the hasty American departure following the former Soviet Union's egress from Afghanistan, February 1989. Concerned about their future, the Afghan people will see their armed forces facing a determined insurgency backed by regional menacing influences. With the commitment of resources from the United States for another decade, the Afghan people will decide their future and the fate of their national identity with the aid of the American people. Certainly, the Strategic Partnership Agreement will not eliminate the endemic problems that Afghans face. The partnership will, however, foster an appreciation for the United States on behalf of its citizenry while the Afghans meet adversity and attain solutions to endemic problems that have plagued their country for many decades.

Reflecting upon our own shores, should we consider a renewed social partnership with one another? Since returning from Afghanistan, I have observed a measurable difference in the outlook of individuals that I often observe. There is a noticeable lack of patience, discourteousness, and an undercurrent of irritation among many individuals. Perhaps this social indifference can be blamed on social indoctrination, a sense of entitlement, or self-centeredness? Nonetheless, there appears to be a growing social acrimony and discord. Impatience, insolence, and disrespect are evident. Is life so fast paced that the blowing of horns, shouting, and vulgarity are considered conventional? Perhaps with age and experience, and being blessed by good fortune, I find such behavior objectionable. Perhaps it is the media indoctrination of crudeness, brutality, and debasement that so many incorporate these behaviors in their social exchanges. Today it is hip to demean someone, laugh at their mistakes, and snicker at their misfortunes. Yet, a social pact based on concern, empathy, and altruism is considered by many of our youth as dull and unrealistic.

However, many among us truly consider reality shows as culturally authentic and representative of suitable social values. I also notice that rather than a "pull yourself up" attitude, a narcissistic approach is becoming more conspicuous. I often speak with young adults who expect what is "rightly theirs" because they deserve it vice because they have earned it. Perhaps with age, an altruistic social concern, and a dismissal of youthful selfishness becomes self-evident. What is needed now, however, is a social treaty redefining conservative principles of hard work, sacrifice, economy, and selflessness, where our focus is turned outward away from shortsightedness and reckless behavior to an affirmation of a social convention based on prudence, tolerance, temperance, and humanity. The ideals of military service can be directed communally with the ideals of selflessness, sacrifice, and for the good of all, resonating throughout society. As we pledge to take a stand and enable others to see and lift themselves, appreciate and emulate our military cultural norms, society as a whole benefits. As military men and women, we understand our role as American ambassadors abroad. I believe that the apparent cultural shift away from civility, morality, and compassion requires that we serve our communities as societal envoys, whose actions and good heartedness are desirable behaviors for our fellow citizens to emulate. Establish a partnered agreement with your neighbors, with those known, and for those unbeknownst to you, and there will be a dynamic shift in our community and our relations among one another.

THE RELEVANCE, SIGNIFICANCE, AND LINKAGE OF EVENTS

I recently took the opportunity to once again travel to the place of my childhood in upstate New York. Given world events, my military service, and family responsibilities, I do not often visit the quaint little village of Saint Remy. Though it meant driving sixteen hours' roundtrip, I felt compelled to visit my mother and father. This visit would take me not to our home, which was sold a few years ago, but rather to the cemetery to pay my respects and offer thanks for all that my parents offered me. Over the years, I have written a good deal about my parents and how they continue to inspire me. As I stood beside my father's grave, I realized that the next day was Father's Day, and in my hand a flag was held, which would be placed on his veteran's marker. It was then I also realized that only a few days ago our nation celebrated Flag Day. Given the relationship of the days, it was only fitting that I would visit my father's grave, reminisce, and with tearful eyes personally thank my father for his love and encouragement.

As I entered the cemetery, I realized the relevance, significance, and linkage of the events of this day. My father remains my hero and the man I hope most to emulate. I serve our nation due to the influence that my father's military service had upon me. Though he passed away during one of my deployments over a decade ago, not a day goes by that I realize how very fortunate I have been to receive his love, guidance, and direction. In fact, memorabilia from his World War II service is on display in my home, and I often offer in conversation memories of my father to friends and family. Yet, of all the things my father taught me, it was that I should find the time to do what is necessary. My father would often tell me, "Butch, you've got to make time to do what is right." So it was that I balanced family obligations and traveled to visit his resting place.

As I stood before the graves of my mother and father, I reflected upon my upbringing and the experiences that shaped the man who I am today. I also ventured about the cemetery to locate the graves of other family members. Reflecting upon my boyhood, I spent the summers working at the cemetery, moving and trimming about the gravestones, all for $1.25 an hour. I recalled my uncle, the cemetery caretaker, as he meticulously dug the graves of those to be interred. I recalled the times I would bring my Sunday school class to the cemetery to honor the veterans and place American flags on their graves. And, I recalled the challenges faced as my young friends would dare one another to enter the cemetery after dark and anticipate ghostly encounters that perchance would materialize. Standing before the grave of my father, I recalled as a youngster there before me I looked upon gravestones with my mother and father's names etched and their birthdates scribed without however an end date. I do recall the eerie feeling as a boy looking upon the eventual graves of my parents. And, I recall my father telling me, "This is where we'll always be found." Prophetic were my father's words, as this is where from time to time as a grown man I would return to visit with him and reflect upon my childhood and the many blessings bestowed upon me. Wishing him Happy Father's Day, perhaps I felt a slight grasp upon my hand, and it was once again I realized that I was not alone in this quiet place. Although my father passed away, his presence remains ever close at my side and his influence ever-present in my life.

LOOKING BACK ON
INDEPENDENCE DAY

An army of principles can penetrate
where an army of soldiers cannot.
                                        —Thomas Paine

For many people, the true meaning and origin of our Independence Day has been diminished by that of nothing more than an early summer holiday of lesser significance. The courage, labor, and toil that resulted in the Declaration of Independence has become perceived as less momentous over time. We take for granted the origins of our great nation, as national pride appears to have waned.

Recently, I was involved in a discussion with a friend who was convinced that the Constitution of the United States was ratified on July 04, 1776, rather than September 17, 1787. How quickly we forget. Over the years, the platform from which the founding fathers stood has become faint. The debates, the resolutions, the negotiations, and statesmanship have long been forgotten. The image of the founders at the Continental Congress in Philadelphia may be etched in our minds. However, the debates between and the trepidation expressed by some no longer resonates through our collective identity. Replaced by sales hawkers, rebate offers, and stuff that we do not need but now we must have, only to be taken for granted shortly thereafter, so too has become the relevance of Independence Day for many among us.

For instance, I often pass through the Great Bridge area of Chesapeake, Virginia. Along the road is a small sign that marks the area of historical significance as the site of the Battle of Great Bridge, whereby the Continental Army and colonial militia routed the British who then retreated to Norfolk. Historians refer to the Battle of Great Bridge as the second Bunker Hill, but today, other than the small road marker, the historic area is now identified by a strip mall. Looking back, I refer to an event that is indicative of the time, as General George Washington, having been notified of the signing of the declaration, ordered a copy be sent to him in New York City to be read to his troops so that they would know exactly what many among them would die for. The intent was to advise Washington's soldiers of what they would stand for rather than what they would retreat from.

Looking back on my earlier life, Independence Day was the highpoint of the summer. Black Cat brand firecrackers, sparklers, and plastic-wrapped smoke bombs were necessities. A family cook-out, and perhaps a trip to Kingston to watch the fireworks display, were the order of the day. But of all, it was our nation's bicentennial celebration that I in recollection warmly remember. The patriotic parade, the feeling of unity, of pride, and the youthful wonderment visited my thoughts when harkening back to 1976. At seventeen, I recall realizing that I was historically positioned to witness the bicentennial as I honored the past, realized I was immersed in a place of history, while I hoped for a future, not just my own, but rather for my community. What would the future hold, and what would I offer my community for the privilege of being among its residents? I believe it was then I realized that I was emerging from my adolescence and thinking in terms much broader than myself. And, it was then that I gained an affinity with our nation that continues to inspire me today.

When we allow ourselves to forget the lessons of history while focusing on singular pursuits and selfish desires, our nation will falter. An inspection of school curriculum, a decline in social mores, and the dependency on government institutions rather than as intended a self-determined populace working in concert in support of the government, it becomes very clear that there has been a demonstrative cultural shift. Evident is the fact that a good part of our general public considers the conveyance of a multitude of "rights" as an essential role of government. Some, too, have dismissed a culture that espouses life, liberty, and the pursuit of happiness as the God-given rights of man. Not as the founders intended, a good part of our society has become dependent upon government rather than the citizenry holding government accountable for its inaction. Looking back to 1776 and the close of the Constitutional Convention, when asked if what was created was a republic or a monarchy, Benjamin Franklin prophetically stated, "A Republic, if you can keep it." The founding fathers entrusted in the citizenry of the newly founded United States of America to keep it as intended. Although the founding fathers surely believed that the document would be amended over time, the Declaration of Independence stands as a concerted endeavor to form a nation as providence intended. We must not dismiss the original intent of the founders as we strive to refine this fortunate nation. Yet, as Thomas Jefferson stated, "All tyranny needs to gain a foothold is for people of good conscience to remain silent."

DIFFICULT TIMES INDEED

We live in difficult times. Political uncertainty, divisiveness, uncertain monetary policies, bankruptcies, the threat of lone wolves, and international terrorism causes many to hunker down, erect fence lines, and prepare for the apocalypse. Bombarded by the bluster of pundits and partisan pulpits, a weary citizenry can turn to selfishness while focusing on self-preservation. Rising personal concerns and threats to our nation, some among us may wring their hands, browbeat, and simply put their head into the sand. When cynicism is on the rise, optimism fades—for some perhaps, but not me.

I recently was involved in a discussion concerning the apparent demise of Western civilization. The participants of the discussion foretold the complete economic collapse and social ruin of our society. Forwarded were sentiments concerning the purchase and stockpiling of gold, silver, spices, and essential food stuffs, first aid, disinfectants, and ammunition in order to barter and swap essential needs between those prepared for catastrophe while making ready to defend themselves from disorder, a roving mob, and I suspect some believe even a few zombies. Yes, times are tough, but we're Americans! We've marched on through times that were then also troubling, with daunting challenges, and what appeared to obstacles insurmountable. Americans have slogged through the mire, accepting the contest as testimony to who we are rather than allowing a collective fatalism as a last will and testament.

Of course, it is prudent to be prepared, but wrong to believe that all is lost. Face it; only the rich can afford to buy gold nowadays! If not for the future, what, then, do you prepare for when all is lost? What is needed most are those who consider not what can be done for themselves alone, but rather what must be prepared for the betterment of our nation. We need good people to involve themselves as social advocates and members of community councils, to stand before their constituents and move an agenda that values social accomplishment vice personal enrichment achieved through underhandedness, political favor, ethical indebtedness, and moral debasement. We must accept that part of us is lost when one of us loses his way.

Consider the following excerpt from Richard Loseby, author of *Blue Is the Colour of Heaven: A Journey into Afghanistan*, who wrote about his adventure walking through a war zone, "Everything that was my future I concentrated upon, for the future is a wonderful thing to behold when the present is so threatening." I reflect upon a wayward man on the street corner, holding a cardboard sign noting that the end times were upon us. He proclaimed that the pounding of apocalyptic hooves were steadily growing louder, and with the fast-approaching horsemen, though unspeakable horror accompanied, he voiced his concerns over the din of traffic. Though his world was falling in on itself and his voice rang out, he did so with eyes closed, for he failed to see that all things adapt or fall extinct.

What is needed nowadays is for good people to open their eyes and their minds, setting aside one-sidedness and reexamining the meaning of public service. For many, public service has become a means to personal enrichment at the expense of those they represent, often forgetting that the term "We the People" is the greater sum of those affiliated with a representative party. Like a seedling taking root on the face of a precipice, a snail heading upward affixed to a ten-story window, or the miracle that life is and continues to be, it is time to accept that enough is not so, as there is so much more that can be, only if we believe in ourselves again. I believe that our days are far from dark, and what is needed is for the citizenry to step off in a new direction for a better America and for the betterment of all Americans. Find solace in the words of Ralph Waldo Emerson, who wrote, "Most of the shadows of this life are caused by our standing in our own sunshine." Americans, brighter days exist once we see through that which clouds our vision, our judgment, and our eternal optimism by casting off doubt and believing again in our divine abilities.

THE ASCENSION OF AN AMERICAN HERO

September 04, 2012

It suddenly struck me that that tiny pea,
pretty and blue, was the Earth. I put up my
thumb and shut one eye, and my thumb
blotted out the planet Earth. I didn't feel
like a giant. I felt very, very small.
— Neil Armstrong

I was ten years old when Neil Armstrong stepped foot upon the moon. I watched the grainy images with fascination, and never again would I look at the moon as I did the night before the lunar landing. I recall wondering what amount of courage it took Neil Armstrong to make his way down the ladder of the lunar module, taking step where no man had been before. As a young man, Neil Armstrong would be among other men that I would call a hero. As I grew older, Neil Armstrong would remain prominent among those few men who would inspire me.

Years later, while I would walk the pastures of a farm that I once rented, I would look to the night's sky. The farm was situated in a secluded valley, and the stars above would be so pronounced. As I walked along the darkened pastures in search of my small herd of cattle, I would ponder the issues of the day and look to the heavens and realize how very small I was and smaller still were my problems. As I grew older, my boyhood dreams of becoming an astronaut, a professional baseball player, a motocross champion, or a lawyer would wane. I realized that perhaps it was the celebrity that inter-

165

ested me more than the aforementioned title. And, even with big dreams, I realized the smallness of a person's statue when compared to the heavens.

Despite the dreams of my youth, over time, I realized that many of my youthful aspirations never would materialize. For instance, as a child, I had dreamed of being an astronaut; but as an adult, I realized that I lacked the formal education during my high school years necessary for such an endeavor. Choosing to forgo chemistry, calculus, and physics, I graduated high school with a vocational diploma. As for becoming a professional athlete, as an adolescent and a teenager, I did play baseball in various leagues, did play on championship teams, was selected to play on an all-star team, and even hit a grand-slam homerun; but as I approached my twentieth birthday, I realized that other ambitions were foremost than baseball. As for me becoming a champion motocross cyclist, I think one too many falls caused me to rethink that enterprise. I did, however, raise beef cattle and cash crops; and I guess looking back, I was marginally successful. But as I grew older, I realized what I was meant to do and then dedicated myself unreservedly in that direction. I returned to school and, yes, graduated from university and then enlisted in the Navy.

I realized that I was meant to dedicate my life to selfless service in the service of others. As a youngster, I thought about becoming a minister. Perhaps in a way, my dreams of the ministry have been realized. I also recognized that my youthful fantasies of fame and fortune were perhaps capricious at best. In my youth, though others with superior intellect, abilities, and talent would achieve their own success, I realized that although there were others, perhaps better able, smarter, or more gifted than I, I could in fact achieve something no other person could. I realized that on my own volition and determination, I could become simply a better man, a man selfless in his pursuits, with an intent to better humanity, to give of myself, offering the best in me to those loved, known to and unbeknownst to me. My father once told me, "Butch, though the days may be short, you've got to make the time." You see, time is precious; and though easily squandered on selfish interests, what you make out of the time given should be beneficial to many others than yourself.

And, it is here that I return to Neil Armstrong and what I learned from him. One should be noble, yet quiet. While greatness for some is measured in fame, a great man shelves fame as he walks upon the world. Notably, a humble man always stands taller than a man who stands on a platform whose foundation is rooted in vanity. Neil Armstrong was a quiet hero, the first man truly to do that which captivated the world that July evening back in 1969. Yet, the measure of the man he was and shall always be is defined by his modesty, humility, and gratitude to others that made it possible to step foot upon the moon and "take one giant leap for mankind." Neil Armstrong remains a hero, one who was reluctant to title himself and never comfortable with the title given. How often today do we admire celebrities and their narcissistic pursuits while our attention is drawn from others whose altruism is sincere, unconditional, and without stardom? A true measure of greatness is determined by modesty rather than conceit, by being thankful for an opportunity to achieve distinction rather than projecting one's arrogance. Truly, Neil Armstrong was such a man.

> The important achievement of Apollo was demonstrating that humanity is not forever chained to this planet, and our visions go rather further than that and our opportunities are unlimited. (Neil Armstrong)

NOVEMBER'S RITE OF PASSAGE

Much has been said about November elections. Pundits and politicians will state their strident positions, acrimony will build, and ideological tensions will grow. With constituents bombarded by campaign ads, robopolls, and governmental gridlock, voter ambivalence and distancing from the political process broadens. Creative statistics and political spin saturate the evening news. For some members of the electorate, party affiliation, favor, and personal image will be deciding factors. Of course, economics and national security linked to world events, and a candidate's platform should be taken into account. However, many among us remain uninformed; and frankly, others feel disheartened and disenfranchised. Hollow political promises and detached and disingenuous elected officials perched in lofty positions who extend themselves through a handshake often expect a handout via campaign contributions rather than demanding personal accountability of themselves. Strong sentiments true, but not directed at any one politician or party. Rather, my opinions are directed at the reader in the hope that you will exercise your right to determine our nation's future direction through political competency, honesty, and qualification by delivering your rightful vote.

I find it interesting that in reviewing the presidential elections that I have witnessed, the central themes revolve around the economy and national security. In fact, my first vote cast for a presidential candidate was during a time when our embassy was attacked, American soil desecrated, Americans taken hostage, the Middle East in turmoil, and America in recession measured by the misery index. The year was 1980. Again, our nation faces economic uncertainty; and with the Middle East facing chaos, once more Iran at the center of the turmoil, the war in Afghanistan, pursuit of the remnants of the Islamic State, and divisive social issues at home, the time is now to exercise our constitutional right to cast a vote for candidates that pledge to work tirelessly for their constituency. It is today as relevant as it was when colonial revolutionary Thomas Paine wrote, "Those who want to reap the benefits of this great nation must bear the fatigue of supporting it." But by doing nothing, surely what results is drawing our nation asunder. When one detaches from the process, an opportunity to support a great nation is lost.

I sense a debilitating popular apathy and a growing dependency on government. I also take note of campaign positions directed singly vice at the constituency. What can be done for "you" and are "you" better off are themes that I find troublesome. Among us are those who have accepted and anticipate a government that is the guarantor and outlet of all things. Yet, such a government is stifling to personal growth and fosters dependence. Many among us are disenfranchised concerning the political process, yet are beneficiaries of a government they are dependent upon. I believe in rugged individualism. I believe that I am the maker of my own way in life. I believe that through my life's experience, I have improved the man that I once was. I believe in hard work and sacrifice, and I believe that as I succeed, I will better society. I believe that our government is a guarantor of inalienable rights from which I am enlivened to succeed. And, I believe that awarded the right to govern, the members of our government must be held accountable by the very people who elected them. It is with a deeply felt unease—at times anxiety—about our nation that I write.

Respectfully I submit that many of our politicians have been disingenuous. It is now the time for specifics, sacrifice, national pride, and inclusion of all constituents. As the debt continues to climb at nearly three million dollars each minute and millions of Americans receiving food stamps, with 1 in 6 Americans living in poverty, home foreclosures on the rise, personal debt climbing, and personal income stagnant, now is the time for "We the People" to determine "our" fate as a republic. Some may consider these words disrespectful, divisive, or directed at one political group; perhaps others will believe such discontent is exclusively derived from disenchantment. I submit that it is not a racial thing, but rather it is certainly a thing of color—the colors of Old Glory! My hope and my words are about "the red, the white, and the blue." For today, our colors are faded. The time is now to choose the best among us, perhaps the new guard, and demand professional and ethical accountability. It is time for our choice to determine the future for our families, our community, and our nation. Detachment from the political process will lead to our further decline; our involvement in the process will determine a course that will lead to a better way. Consider the words of Alexander Hamilton, who wrote, "A share in the sovereignty of the state, which is exercised by the citizens at large, in voting at elections is one of the most important rights of the subject, and in a republic ought to stand foremost in the estimation of the law." Exercise your right wisely through education, preparation, and pride.

WIN, LOSE, OR DRAW, NOBLE MUST BE THE DESIGN OF OUR EFFORTS

November 01, 2012

Finding myself in Afghanistan for yet another tour of duty, I do so unreservedly and with the hope of making a difference. This being my fifth deployment to Afghanistan, and during my previous deployments, I have seen both improvements and setbacks. I have experienced the reward of accomplishment and have learned of friends killed in action. I have seen joy expressed by Afghans in receipt of the benevolence of the American people, and I have seen outrage directed at us, often spurred on by civic leaders who have ingratiated themselves through political relations with the same government that they rail against.

What is evident here is a dichotomy of senses, between good and bad, and between common and the extraordinary. Recently, I was involved in a conversation concerning the outcome of our nation's longest war. I was asked my opinion if I thought we would win this war. I thought for some time and again realized the dichotomy of the senses. I remember the aftermath of September 2001. I was eager to get in on the ground and redress the evil that was done to us: to avenge the deaths of Americans and to win decisively. Over the course of the next decade, I realized as many among me have that the decisive win would be elusive. Rather, involved in a counterinsurgency, the battle plan was two-pronged dealing with enemies while attempting to provide stabilization, a foundation of governance, and a realization of a semblance of civil rights to a population that had been downtrodden by tyrants.

As the years passed, victories would come on the battlefield, but the way ahead for stabilization, growth, and civil rights would be a difficult path to travel. It appeared to me that the dichotomy between principles of community and thinking communally were and often overtaken by corruption and collusion, which hinged upon gainful personal pursuits. I see myself as a good man: humble and giving, a man of principle, and a man extending myself beyond the next step. I have been raised to be such a man, and through trial and tribulation, I have refined myself to adhere to the principles of temperance and benevolence, offering more of myself, often at my own expense.

I often wonder what the Afghan sees in me. Am I nothing more than another foreigner, another uniform, another flag, temporarily providing assistance, yet only to move on, feeling good about the offering, yet unaware of the plight of the Afghan who must quickly consume or hide that which was given, only to face retribution from another whose flag it matters not, but whose retort will be harsh and to the quick? I hope that what the Afghan sees in me is a caring heart of a man who is of a different faith, a man who holds the impoverished in his thoughts and prayers and who is prepared to give his life to battle back an insurgency bent on subjugation, repression, and domination.

Responding to the question of winning, I offered, "Win, lose, or draw, noble must be the design of our efforts." This is what I tell those whom I am charged to lead. This is what I have told my family. This is how I trust my granddaughter, when talking about me to her grandchildren, will recount what her "Papa" did for the people of Afghanistan during the long war. In retrospect, I measure the time lost over these years that has been taken away from my family and granddaughter, only to realize the blessing of the time spent in defense of them. I have given up this time so that my granddaughter may live without fear and thus be granted a life of prosperity. May she always know that in sacrifice, benevolence is forwarded to others: those known and unbeknownst, of different races, of different cultures, and of different faiths. With this in mind, noble too will be her efforts.

A TIME TO STEP FORWARD
AND COMMIT

My father once told me, "Butch, if you're going to move forward, take a big step!" I am sure that the theme of this memo will become clear, and I hope that my words may inspire others to follow along. Another election come and gone: no social upheaval, no revolution, and a return to some semblance of civility. The United States buffered by reason remains intact as pundits, politicians, and psychics are again proven wrong. The outcome of the election proved to be a clear victory for some, while for others, a stunning defeat.

We can hope that a new spirit of cooperation springs from the acrimony of just weeks ago. Many among us are happy with the results; others are disappointed. Still, we continue to move forward as America has done since 1789, refining and amending the Constitution for the benefit of all. But what of reality and what awaits a nation during times as these?

Our nation is perched upon a "fiscal cliff"; for some, the reality of being stymied, perhaps lost due to the woes of unemployment, the uninsured, the have-nots, cry out. Thousands petition for a better way, disappointed with our elected officials, who it seems apparently care more for their party than the people they represent and often smugly shrug off critique by those from the underclass. With such an unsatisfactory record, incumbents retain the privilege of seats awarded them by a constituency to whom they are appointed to answer, yet nevertheless for some seldom hear, often dismissing the dissonance as nothing than banter from the fringe.

I have sworn to support and defend the Constitution of the United States and obey the orders of those appointed over me. I have done so for nearly twenty-six years and will continue to do so. I am honored to serve our Navy, our nation, and the world community. As I ponder the design of life beyond the military, I can write with confidence that I plan to continue public service. It is appropriate that

I submit my agenda. I ponder if I should seek public office, volunteering to dedicate myself to the perils of political life. My concern is not unfounded, as our country will face unprecedented vulnerability in the years ahead. With steadfast commitment, our country truly needs leaders who are focused on preserving the social foundations while building a future whereby those elected will faithfully hold themselves and their associates responsible. We need leaders whose integrity is judged not by backroom kowtowing, but rather by the fulfillment of public pledges of servitude to the electorate, who are always accountable to the people and whose word is a bond to be honored.

With much family trepidation, I contemplate entering the political realm, promising the electorate that I will sacrifice on behalf of those who have elected me to truly do so. I believe it best to forgo the trappings of the underside of the political environment where shadowy brokers influence and corrupt even the freshest of minds. I believe it should be public record when a lobbyist crosses the threshold of an elected official's office. As a public record, gifts, perks, influence, subterfuge will be duly noted and dutifully refused! I believe that those who enter public service should do so knowing that the true reward is in fact one's service, not perk or inflated stature. I also believe that many an elected official have lost a sense of public accountability, rather submitting to the will and whim of corporations, media moguls, and supplicants of special interests.

I began writing these monthly memos years ago, and these memos represent service contracts defining the man I am and that which I believe in. These memos are public record, having been forwarded to countless service members and civilians around the globe. I have done so knowing and expecting to be held accountable for my words, my behavior, and my beliefs. I trust that this memo in particular will serve as an instrument of personal scrutiny in the years to come. For I am but a humble servant, and perhaps one day I may serve constituents as I have done so throughout my naval career. My political, personal, and spiritual beliefs will differ from those that will resoundingly oppose me, and I shall do my best to deflect certain spiteful attacks. Yet, I will offer a decent, compassionate, loyal, and dedicated man who will continue to sacrifice on their behalf. Though I shall face rebuke and scorn, I will not forsake those whom I serve. I have defined myself in such a way during my military service, freely extending my hand to those who wish and would do me harm. Appropriately referenced, said Ronald Reagan, "If we love our country, we should also love our countrymen." I would give of myself selflessly and to the best of my abilities, intent on benefiting all who appointed me to serve.

WHAT IS HAPPENING TO OUR NATION

January 01, 2013

Today, our nation is again divided at polar ends. Tragedy all too often further defines the division between opposing viewpoints. Well intended by some, political opportunists will often rally around a tragedy for their own cause. As a nation mourns another senseless act of mayhem, the rancor only widens the breach between us. I believe that an investigation must focus on the deeply entrenched motives behind such events rather than concentrate on the means to which the perpetrator chose to carry out his delusions. I also believe that our focus must not be solely on the perpetrator, but rather on our society as a whole. As a nation, we must forgo the conflicting acrimony directed at the opposition in order to one-up a political opponent, seeking rather to unify by first addressing the root cause of a deteriorating moral social environment and identifying those who are at risk of causing such harm to innocent people.

The idea here is to realize that a better way individually, communally, and socially must first be realized and embraced. All too often, we seek to remedy tragedy through political advantage. The debate on gun control versus Second Amendment rights further fuel the social enmity. Rather than defining the root cause of such behavior, we are quick to blame. However, I believe that the fault is in the system itself. How a person can live and function undetected and with circumstances that should spur a response from parents, friends, and colleagues is a point seldom made. There are telltale signs that define the fracture of common sense that should have been the cause of alarm that go unheeded. Is it apathy? Is it the lack of a social consciousness? Is it civil liberties contorted to prevent reasonable and responsible action from being taken? Have we so internalized our lives that we do not notice the troubles of our neighbors? Have we lost a sense of community?

I think so. We no longer care for our neighbor, as we seek to shield ourselves from communal involvement. Our sense of community is enlivened only after tragedy happens, while the sense of kinship dissipates soon after the memorials fade and flowers wither. As we soon forget, it is this that is a perpetuation of a tragedy. People seldom just spontaneously erupt into a fit of rage. Rather, long before, present are telltale signs—festering emotions, perhaps an inward turn, or a noticeable malady—and these things should be noted so that preventative measures can be taken before tragedy strikes. Even still, people bent on heinous acts will use what they can to inflict injury on others and themselves. As best as we have, we have tried to mandate morality, yet some among us still act with depravity. The degree to which antisocial behavior is glamorized in today's society is a reflection of our ambivalence.

Antisocial behavior is ultimately punished, but what of those who did not act to forestall the escalation of the destructive actions? This is a cause-and-effect relationship. Yet, with societal decomposition and the hands-off approach of civil authorities, caustic behaviors will continue to fragment the foundation of our society. I advocate that those of faith should practice it. For those who are not congregational, think communally. We must forgo our divergent interests and political agendas and rally around one flag. We must consider our neighbors to be an extension of family, offering care and consideration to those particularly at risk. We must offer care to those less fortunate, and we must not ignore the pleas of those who have been overcome, stricken, or disadvantaged. In an attempt to become a pluralist society, the hyphen represents the divide that separates us. Divergent interests and opposing agendas today offer little more than disharmony. Quick to blame rather than identify a solution at its base lends itself to a quick assembly, only to define the breach wider still. Rather than subdivisions of dissonance and divergence, it will be through communities of inclusion and concurrence that we can protect each other, forgoing trepidation, choosing not to shutter our lives and ignore the pleas of others.

WHAT WILL BECOME OF YOU?

For many, February is a time when the winter doldrums are at their weightiest. New Year's resolutions have been forgotten or dismissed, and the bleakness of the winter months drags on; the world is cold and gray, and lifestyle sedentary.

Even still, time marches on. New life stirs beneath the frozen earth; the days grow longer, the sun stronger, and the temperatures warmer. For me, February is the month of renewal and for resolutions. It is the month of leap years. It is a month where we prepare for spring—such as spring ahead, move forward at a rapid pace. It is a time of turning the corner and making ready for the days ahead. Yes, there will be hardships still: another blast of arctic cold, perhaps one last snowstorm as Ole Man Winter goes out like a lion, but nonetheless inconveniences only, for the season of rejuvenation is but a few weeks away.

February is a time to reconsider the way ahead, think about the year past, and plan to succeed in the ventures of our lives. What will become of you? Are you prepared for what awaits? I remember my father once asked me, "Butch, will you one day be blindsided by the unexpected?" I thought about this and wondered, "Heck, could I anticipate the unknown?" Then I realized that I had answered my own question! So to this day, I ponder what will become of me, what I will offer others as a testament to my life's legacy, and will I one day be remembered by those unbeknownst to me? At first thought, one might answer the question as if an unknown. I prefer to confirm that my actions herald the appropriate response, and I trust you too will answer similarly when pondering what will become of you.

I often tell Sailors that every day is an evaluation and innumerable eyes perceive every action. What one does, in every detail, is being observed and remembered by individuals likely outside of our own field of view. Hold your allies close, but keep an eye on those unaligned for they are the ones who will inevitably surprise you, at times shock you, with anecdotes about you that you hoped to forget.

You've got to be at your best and make your actions count for the good of others. With such limited time on this earth, we must focus more on others than on ourselves. Seldom do people remember with favor a selfish man.

"Blessed is the man who turns away from self-interest and in giving to others realizes a common existence, yet an extraordinary life," it is said. What will become of you? Will you be remembered for your benevolence, or shunned for your self-centeredness? Perhaps at my age, which I confirm is far past midlife, I ponder the mistakes of my youth, the things that I shouldn't have done, and the things that I am ashamed of. Although I can't undo the past, I can commit to redefining myself as a better person, a compassionate and understanding man, whose work is not designed to brick me apart from the world, but perhaps to build bridges in order to reach those in need.

I worry that when my earthly time is over, I will only be remembered by the closest of family. Given a few years, that memory too shall fade. My concern is that perhaps I squandered opportunities to make a lasting impression on the lives of many. There are those who might believe I may desire fame or fortune, perhaps even celebrity. These are but mere material things, which as with age also diminish. A dear friend once told me, "A person's good name is worth more than precious jewels." I believe that money, fame, and material items are fleeting. I ask you to join me in considering a thought that often occupies my mind: "Are you happy in life having less? If you're happy with less 'stuff,' perhaps you hold considerable spiritual wealth!" I have known others who were wealthy, yet unhappy, who focused their desires on material items, expensive and ostentatious, and of course in the real sense hold little value. As I plan for my later years, I am committed to giving more of myself in the service of others. I am confident that I will know nothing of fortune, of fame, and of celebrity. I am convinced that there shall be no windfall, no social step up. I am positive that my life will be simple and likely best described as ordinary. Yet, I am poised to offer the best in me in the service of others, benefitting lives I shall not count, nor know, yet I trust who will one day think of the man who gave of himself to benefit those unbeknownst to him.

WHY ARE YOU HERE?

Reflecting upon yet another deployment nearly complete and the light visible at the end of the tunnel—perhaps I should apply an Afghan reference, the Salang tunnel—I again ponder as I have done four previous tours of duty: "Why are you here?" I will answer honestly and from the heart. I will assure the reader that the words to follow will not be a political rant. Since arriving in Afghanistan nearly a decade ago, I can write sincerely that I have asked myself, "Why are we here?" and at times pointedly I've asked others, "Why are you here?" Times have been tough, the separation long from family and loved ones. I've missed the death of a brother and my father due to being on deployments. I've spent countless hours worried about those I hold dear, and I have lost a friend who was killed in action. I have seen Afghans who have accepted our benevolence and then strike out against a compassionate hand, burn the flag that they once welcomed, and mock our dearly held values. I have seen many people come and go, as I too have been seen. Even still, I volunteered to return to Afghanistan in order to serve a fifth and final tour of duty.

Friends, those with whom I serve and others I serve have asked, "Why would you again return?" Given the uncertainties, the perils, where anything can happen, and considering the sacrifices, my decision to return again and again has come without long deliberation. Some have told me that my decision is a selfish one, as I am only concerned about the reward and award of service in Afghanistan. My answer will be elaborated further, yet my terse response to such a statement, a statement I've heard more than a few times is this: "My decision to serve yet again in Afghanistan is, of course, done so in order to serve you!" My family has been tremendously supportive, as we have weathered many difficult times while I have been far from home. Providing guidance, and I trust an example for the children of our extended family, I hope that they have learned that there is much more to life than that which can be held, that there are many ignored who deserve our attention, and that we must step forward in the service of others, for the richness of our offering may have at first glance little monetary meaning, but to change a life of one who is unbeknownst to you, know that nothing can compare to.

I have been approached by more than a few Afghans over the years who have asked, "Why are you here?" I have been accused of being an invader, providing benefit to the wealthy and men of influence, enriching myself at the expense of others; believe me, I have heard much worse. I have been accused of being an unbeliever, a hedonist, a violator of women, and just another who seeks to dominate the poor and uneducated. I take every opportunity to share my perspective, thoughtfully answering their questions. I tell the Afghan that I am a man of faith, who holds them and their families in my prayers. I tell the Afghan I am a temperate man who does not consume alcohol or use tobacco products. I tell the Afghan I am concerned about human rights and enabling men and women the opportunity to provide better for themselves, their families, their community, and their country. And, I tell the Afghan that I pray that my actions liberate those who have known such pain and anguish, poverty and ruin. For these reasons, I have served to provide a better way for their lives.

As I plan the years ahead, I hope to continue serving publicly. In so doing, I will serve my fellow Americans and the world community. Having spent ten years in and out of Afghanistan, I cannot forsake the people who have endured so much and who seek a better life. Political brinkmanship on a world stage will certainly run its course with Afghanistan as the field of play. With the inevitable political wrangling, social upheaval, and uncertainty about their future that the Afghans feel today, they deserve a voice of one who has broken bread with them and shared much with a people as intriguing as their long history.

The years ahead will not be easy ones. There will be internal strife as Afghanistan seeks to again define its sovereignty and perhaps a national identity. Our relationship with the people of Afghanistan must be an enduring one as they strive for the obtainment of their peace and prosperity. To quote noted journalist David Brinkley, "A successful man is one who can lay a firm foundation with the bricks others have thrown at him." At times, it is far better to counter with righteous intention than it is to cast yet another stone.

WHAT I HAVE LEARNED?

April 30, 2013

I've experienced much during my time in the military. Looking back, I'm having difficulty remembering things I've already forgotten! Nevertheless, I recall that I've traveled to many lands and have been in places where I couldn't have imagined what life would be like. I have been amazed by the environments and the stark contrasts of locations, all the while shocked by the abject poverty. I've extended myself to the poor and have been deeply troubled that I could do nothing more as the convoy I was riding in passed by those who knew only misery. I have been ridiculed, and I have been praised. False bravado has been matched with an ingrained hatred for what I represent.

Many expressionless faces have I looked upon; hopeless and hapless were they, though their joy was expressed through toothless smiles as they welcomed the most meager of offerings. People have greeted me with extended arms and hugs of affection, when the falsities of others revealed dark intentions. Tears have been shed, and outcries calling for my demise have been heard. Accepting that tragedy is inevitable, still, when a good friend was killed, I too questioned, why am I here? Then there are fellow countrymen who oppose our noble effort: who test our resolve, and who seek to discredit what we do, and what we in our own right embody. It follows that I serve, sworn to support and defend those who in our country oppose me. Considering all aspects, I have been blessed to have been in the company of patriots, many of whose sacrifices are incomprehensible and from whom I learned much.

Yes, the years are behind me, yet what I have learned will enable me for the years ahead and permit me to be a better man as I continue to serve publicly. Our experiences in life establish a foothold to

183

take another step forward. It has been said that every perception is stored within our memory. If so, why can't I recall my cellular phone number! With all those moments stored, some things are better off forgotten. Nonetheless, we are who we are because of these events in life. Each time I return home from deployment, I clearly see a less-united America. The division, the discordant political rancor, the apparent degenerative social dialogue, and the lack of respectful discourse are shockingly evident. Our society has become increasingly narcissistic, confusing privileges with inalienable rights, which in turn has led to an environment of selfishness. Conversation tinged with profanity is the norm, educational standards are diminishing, and with revisionism on the rise, the fabric of our nation is being slowly torn apart from growing internal divergent interests.

However, even in the most difficult of situations, perhaps the opportunity for humanity is ever-present. We must seize the opportunity to better ourselves in order to improve society. Today, the status quo appears to be measured in diminished returns. I for one expect better from those with whom I interact. As I present what I hope is an example to follow, not without flaw, but rather contrite and one whose faith is foremost, thereby leading me on a pilgrimage through life, I ask others to follow.

My father once told me, "Butch, it is best to leave behind something in this world other than a grave marker, for all possessions are in the end trivial, yet your actions are fundamental to preserving who you were long after you are gone." What have I learned? I have learned that in war, there are countless opportunities for kindness. And, as I return home, I am prepared to extend myself further to benefit the community writ large, for there are countless opportunities to serve, lives to touch, with the hope that I can effect a positive change.

THE TRUE FACE OF EVIL

June 05, 2013

The mere thought of being subjugated, the loss of inalienable rights, and living in fear strengthens my obligation to combat those who are bent on the use of terror. A recent political narrative revealed a declaration pronouncing an end to the war on terrorism as it was revealed that Al-Qaeda has been decimated. Yet, an event in 2013 in London, England, whereby Lee Rigby, an army veteran, was murdered in Woolwich, revealed to me a turning point in the mindset of extremism and defines the true face of evil.

Having committed the heinous act, the perpetrators remained at the scene to engage the responders. However, the postattack diatribe captured on camera that defined their murderous intent served as a chilling postscript to the butchery. With bloodied hands, one particular perpetrator professed justification for his actions. Accounts of witnesses revealed that the two attackers were spurred along, shouting "Allah Hu Akbar!" Later, it was learned that the men have had jihadist aspirations and one of the pair attempted some time ago to join the Somalia-based terrorist group Al-Shabaab. Clearly defined, this act of savagery illustrates the mindset of two deranged individuals. Moreover, the incident implicates an emboldened enemy focused on implanting fear among the populace while a wider agenda of fanaticism espouses the establishment of an Islamic caliphate.

Over the years, I have spoken with Afghan Muslims who were surprised at what they learned. Learning that religious tolerance and social acceptance of all faiths remain fundamental in the United States, the Afghans with whom I interacted were astonished. Commonly, these individuals subscribed to the notion of my supposed intolerance and persecution of Muslims. I recall speaking to a group of teenaged males who were orphaned at various ages and who believed that all Christians harbored a hatred for Muslims, and they thought that their questioning would reveal similar sentiments in me. They were, of course, surprised to learn of the compassion with which I provided them and the benevolence of the United States. Learning these things, they readily accepted them, reassured that the offering came without prophesizing, and that accepting such generosity was not the behavior of an apostate. As time passed, these reluctant Afghans learned that I was neither a crusader nor an occupier, not one who voiced a prophetic word, but rather one whose actions provided an example of kindheartedness and grace unbeknownst to them.

However, this is only one such example. The ideal of compassion to win the hearts and minds will not change the fanaticism ensconced within the minds of those who would become homicide bombers or within the hearts of those who would decapitate another human being while professing the act sanctioned by their god. Such individuals are the enemies of humanity. The reader need review the sectarian violence pitting Islamists against Muslims and the targeting of Christians, international relief agencies, and individuals working with Non-Governmental Organizations. While America continues to aid and assist for the betterment of the impoverished, our enemies ignore the plight of their own people.

Given this, why are we still hated? Certainly, those charismatic espouse hatred to those who are perhaps illiterate and unworldly; those who detest modernity; those who seek to subjugate through the corruption of sacred teachings; those who are xenophobic, disenfranchised, or prefer not to enfranchise themselves; those who are socially isolated, vengeful, whose twisted yet pliable logic is easily manipulated, inculcating hatred of the West and in particular the United States. Perhaps it is because we are clever, resourceful, and charitable? Perhaps it is our competitive nature of eating or the immorality of celebrity that causes such disdain? In a simplistic sense, perhaps it is a matter of resentment and irrationality that serve as the impetus for inhumanity.

It cannot be known for certain—but still, something must be done. A two-fold approach is necessary to attempt to instill an enlightened view of the benevolence of our nation while we continue to offer the best of America to the world community. We must also seek out those that again would do us harm for they choose to be our enemy. And, always, we must remain vigilant in our defense of our nation as we take the offense in order to further identify the true face of evil, demonstrating our resiliency to combat fanaticism.

TRUTH, JUSTICE, AND
THE AMERICAN WAY

One need not be a superhero, but rather a good and just citizen to hold dear and pursue the motto, "For Truth, Justice, and the American Way!"

As a child, Superman was larger than life. George Reeves would don the suit and cape and battle evildoers justly though without malice. George Reeves's character, Clark Kent, was a role model to follow. He was bright, articulate, a gentleman and a hero. My childhood friends competed to be Superman as our fantasy role playing mimicked the television exploits that we eagerly watched in grainy black-and-white. So it was the innocence of our youth. Over the years, the exploits of Superman have been remade with the marvel of special effects and stunning graphics, and so Superman has changed. Yet, the message as professed resounds as an incontrovertible reality, that truth, justice, and the American way has it seems as of late become jaded by egoism, selfishness, and political correctness, though I find the term "political correctness" to be an antithesis of what is in fact current or correct. Take, for instance, the ongoing political scandals and congressional inquiries whereby the axiom of truth, justice, and the American way is indeed being scrutinized due to questionable actions and deeds. My intent here is to look beyond the mire of the current political situation and embrace the principle that has become cliché to some, perhaps contradicted by others, yet vigilantly maintained by those who wear the fabric of our nation. Superman the fantasy, yet there are superheroes among us to be sure.

I grew up in different times. Of course, there were controversies and social upheavals as the Vietnam War raged. However, a real hero remained true as my confidant, my mentor, and a standard bearer to follow. My hero was my father who taught me much. I am me because of him, and within me he remains. My father taught me to be honest, hardworking—a caregiver, a protector, and patriot. Though my view of the world differs from my father's as I have traveled to many foreign lands, what remains a constant is that there truly is no place like home. My father also taught me to stand firm on the convictions that lifted me up, be not afraid however to take a chance at a new endeavor for life is short and opportunities fleeting. Over my years, it has become necessary to rely upon my father's teachings. And, as I look upon my father's photograph, I am proud to see myself in his eyes. My father was an ordinary man, a simple man, yet he was to me my hero—real, whose firm grasp, whose smile, and whose wit enabled me through times of trouble, yesterday and today.

My father also prepared me for my military experience and political aims that I believe I will focus upon after my military career ends. The lessons learned will enable me to pursue life with virtue and enable me to shoulder increased burden and surmount daunting challenges. There are others too who are heroes. As a military, we are held to a higher professional, ethical, and moral standard, where character is one's signature, where rank does not overshadow the proper path, and where individual pursuits remain secondary to the needs of others. We are a mighty force, yet we are benevolent. We truly sacrifice in the face of adversity, and we volunteer for what will ultimately take us from our loving families. We are accepting and obedient. We are fair and encouraging, expecting the very best in ourselves to enable others. Maintaining high standards of conduct, we demand that all pursue excellence. And, we are accountable to ourselves, our political leaders, and to the community. We do not make excuses when we fall short of the mark, and we address those that do with punitive actions designed as corrective measures based on precedence.

Though we may hold divergent personal views, we are unified by a love of country and reverence for our flag. Perhaps those who point fingers at the military should look inward and through self-analysis calculate if they too hold such high standards. And, when seeking true heroes, our critics need only look to the military as exemplars of public service and follow those who truly espouse truth, justice, and the American way.

TO EMPOWER CHANGE, FIRST EMBOLDEN SELF

As recent events have illustrated, these are complex times in which we live. With answers being sought, intellectual machinations seems to produce more hypotheticals than true remedy. Divergent cause and effect, blame and outcome, supposition and revision often stoke further dissent. Political advantage and financial reward tend to mire still the episode better resolved through legal recourse though often considered by some as capitulation. One may ask, "Then what is one to do when trouble is present?" Though the first reaction may be to retort with reprisal, the best recourse is one that presents an uncharacteristic portrayal of civility and charity. To empower change, first embolden self through discourse vice dissent. Aren't we quick to lash out against unpopular decisions of which are truly outside of our control? Such dissent seems only to fuel the disharmony that separates two camps. What is called for is in fact a sense of first reconciliation while we identify and remedy the endemic problems as defined. Paradigms of personal integrity, dignity, and goodwill are today discounted as civil disobedience is provoked. How long can a fire be stoked before the embers fade to ash? With considerable effort expelled and momentum lost, a positive outcome is likely fleeting. Yet, learned men often spur dissent, encouraging rancor and further civil unrest. Taking to heart the words of Dr. Martin Luther King Jr., "Darkness cannot drive out darkness; only light can do that. Hate cannot drive out hate; only love can do that." Yet, how true are the words of American singer-songwriter and musician, John Haitt: "It's always the last one in who's in a hurry to try and slam the door in the next one's face." Dialogue focused on resolution of fundamental wrongs within our society such as poverty, illiteracy, dependency, and moral decline—although for some best left alone—must be examined. Through inquiry, only then will change occur.

True, the first to influence such discussions may very well be construed as provoking. Yet, in unison with leaders from both camps, so inclined will harmony result from the persistent acrimony often voiced today. This is a burden that all shoulders must share: blind to color, with hands extended to clasp the palm of another though by some thought foreign, Americans all! Political, social, and spiritual leaders must first identify the root causes behind those who fail to gain momentum in striving to improve their lives, thus improving the collective society. We are endowed with the gifts of learning, adapting, understanding, and appreciating our current standing in life, and as Americans, we continually seek to improve our lives and the opportunities of future generations. Still, there are those of each race and from each class that fail to move forward. Dependency and a sense of entitlement have created a subservient class. Money alone is not the sole answer when applying a solution to that which plagues society. First and foremost, it is self-awareness that within each of us the solution begins. Self-amelioration is made possible when the displaced or downtrodden realize that personal destiny is self-emboldened and begins with believing in a higher power, believing in self, and with dignity and conscious that we are righteous platforms to enable goodness for all. How often it is that a right is applied as a remedy to an issue?

As Benjamin Franklin wrote, "The Constitution only gives people the right to pursue happiness. You have to catch it yourself." Personal pursuits pursuant to good order and discipline, embracing toil and tribulation, will likely remedy every issue; the contradiction, however, serves only to widen the breach between those who have and those that do not. Segregation of racial communities—at times communally self-imposed—serves only to divide society into divergent classes. America must embrace that we are but one community. We must see not the color of skin as what makes us different but rather the compassion within our hearts that unites all colors. We must work a defining resolution and address a pressing singular agenda rather than attempt to balance a myriad of political issues. Furthermore, we in good faith must act to aid and assist those among us to devise and develop for themselves the means to better their existence that in turn will unify society and lessen dissolution and discord within our community. To empower change, first embolden self through faith, hope, and charity as benevolence extended to all will soften the heart made hardened by injustice and imbalance.

WHAT IS AMERICAN EXCEPTIONALISM?

Much has been written and more said about American exceptionalism. Recently, America has been maligned and denigrated as politicians, both foreign and domestic, pundit and media types, and those disenfranchised have rebuffed and rebuked our great nation. For centuries, America has been hailed as the greatest nation on the face of the earth. For some, envy is a powerful emotion, which blurs their vision and obstructs their reason. Yet, for those whose bitterness has transformed their perceptions of our nation as maniacal and oppressive, they fail to salute the benevolence of America, as we respond when called upon to support and defend, and provide assistance and relief as only American ingenuity and perseverance permit.

As Americans, we welcome diversity, realizing that although different, and at times opposing, our collective identity is unifying. People of all faiths and those who do not believe consider themselves Americans. We do not dominate, force compliance, subjugate, or imprison those who voice reasonable dissent. Adherence to the law for safety's sake affords civility to an embracing citizenry. For those who are unlawful, punishment is just, and redemption is freely offered to those who wish to rejoin society. The American criminal justice system is based on constitutional precedence. We hold dear the ability to speak our minds, though we also accept that not all speech be granted an audience. Americans are open-minded and live side by side as neighbors. With unparalleled opportunity, the ability to elevate personal social status through education and entrepreneurship are hallmarks of America. We are judgmental of ourselves and welcome debate, and through debate we fend off tyranny, thereby preserving the union and our constitutional republic. We expect and demand accountability from our elected officials for they serve the citizenry. We hold dear our liberty, and the constituency stands ready to challenge those who would deny or repeal it. As Thomas Jefferson stated, "When the people fear the government, there is tyranny. When the government fears the people, there is liberty."

Americans must not relinquish the swiftness to admonish our elected officials who forget or forsake those they serve. And, we reprove without fearing governmental retaliation. America is a free and open society: expressive and rooted in individualism, with members of each generation at times engaged in ideological movements running contrary to established norms. Yet, this is what Americans prize: the freedom to pursue the freedoms of self-interest, expression, and assembly. Though others may consider our interests as selfish pursuits, no other nation is as munificent. And, it is this unique dichotomy against which our adversaries rail.

I recently visited the site of the September 11 memorial, where I came to the conclusion that there is no better place to witness all that is great with America. It is hallowed ground in the heart of Manhattan—quiet, reflective, and peaceful. From around the world, they come to pay homage to the lost and to feel American. Foreign languages, differing religions, divergent peoples, all gaze into the memorial pools and look to the sky as the Freedom Tower stands as a testament to the American spirit.

On that September morning, when the world watched as thousands of our citizens were murdered, as a nation we united, paid homage to the victims, and determined to exact justice, vowing to pursue Al-Qaeda and those affiliated. Yet, the justice was a measured response while also pursuing a noble effort to free the Afghan people from the oppressiveness of the Taliban regime. The attempt at nation building has yet to play out. From our efforts though, the Afghan people are now poised to determine their own destiny. Again, America proved its exceptionalism by offering its treasure—the men and women of our military—and billions of dollars, pledging to remain a partner as the Afghans build a nation from the established foundation as they believe best for themselves. Over the past decades and as recent world events prove, our enemies are determined to again do us harm. They may hit us and hit us hard, but we will rebuild bigger and stronger, remaining a nation indivisible and always prepared to redress the evil done upon us! And, in Lower Manhattan at the September 11 memorial, it is here that we all look to the heavens and realize yet again that America is truly exceptional.

RALLY 'ROUND THE FLAG!

We are faced with troubling times indeed. Yet, reflecting upon the words of the American revolutionary Thomas Paine, "These are the times that try men's souls." Rather than hand-wringing and browbeating, these are days when those so inclined stand among their fellow countrymen prepared to reconcile the tribulations of the day. Volunteers are needed to move others forward in a direction right for all.

All too often, selfishness and private gain spur individuals into public service. Perhaps cloaked in humanity—later to be revealed as partisan opportunism—personal behaviors of certain individuals contradict civic-mindedness. With much to do and many who are in need, it is apparent that now more than ever, volunteers are required. Given the need to serve selflessly while redressing political stalemate, needed are those perhaps reluctant yet willing who pledge as servants while offering their best at a time when all appears mired in controversy and gamesmanship. Needed are those who are committed to service, who stand ready to support and defend, who are perhaps of meager means, yet espouse to better society rather than enrich themselves.

Ours is a great nation, prosperous and benevolent. And, the fabric of our nation is recognized as a symbol of freedom, liberty, and unparalleled opportunity. Our flag stands for who we are and what we represent to others: a generous nation, compassionate, lawful, and empathic. Photographed countless times after devastation has passed, our tattered flag stands iconic and stoic in true splendor. Now is a time to rally! Good people are needed to do great things. Required are those who look upon the formidable and, seeing no easy way, press onward on behalf of others to fulfill dreams of a nation. Rather than run off, the first step must be well placed to assume the burden of leadership. Each step forward must be measured, and each milepost keenly sighted. Those that choose to stand up must be unreservedly committed to the daunting task. Our military service enables us, for we have gone into the fray, anticipating difficulty and peril but proceeding with accomplishment as a focal point. Through it all, service members persevere while taking great pride in the service of others. We believe in ourselves, and we have faith in those with whom we serve. We offer our lives so that others may live. It is our vocational ethos that has molded our service into an enviable paradigm.

Needed are volunteers willing to move forward while others remain ambivalent. Needed are those who seek repointing the foundation of our nation, not imposing their will upon others, but willing to do their best for the benefit of those who are contradictory. Required are faith-filled volunteers who step forward not with jackboots, but rather, having pulled themselves up from their bootstraps, present an enviable example for others to emulate. Uniquely, service personnel volunteer for the unknown and accept jeopardy for the advancement of society and the defense of liberty. It is without hubris that we stand before our countrymen as humbled servants to those who revere us, to those who are equivocal, and by some, we are disparaged. We have reluctantly accepted praise, and we have tolerated being spat upon by some of our countrymen. Yet, we serve one and all, sacrificing as we do so others may prosper.

Because of our military service, we are prepared for future public service. We have accepted the burdens and acquired a greater appreciation for our nation as we've fulfilled national objectives. Now is the time when further service is in high demand. We must again rally 'round the flag for the advancement of a constituency. Consider the words of Daniel Webster, a leading American statesman and former US senator: "May this be your calling, your destiny! Let it be borne on the flag under which we rally in every exigency, that we have one country, one constitution, one destiny." With goodness in our hearts and with admirable virtue, now is the time to rally for America!

I AM A FORTUNATE SON

November 26, 2013

These are days of Thanksgiving. Tradition stands, and the holiday feast planned, a bountiful table to be enjoyed, and blessings to be counted—yes, these are days of Thanksgiving. I often reflect on my youth, my family, and the holiday shared with loved ones. Years past, while we patiently waited to partake of fresh turkey and all the fixings, I recall being seated in our family home watching football as aromas of spices and warm fruit wafted through the rooms. But first, grace was to be said, and it was so that we as a family would recount our blessings, good health, and fortune as yet another year passed.

Fondly reflecting upon my early years, and as I grew older, vacant were the loved ones who passed; and as the feast seemed somewhat less grand, our fortunes remained ever-present. Thinking of days gone by, I recall the turbulent times of the 1960s and early '70s. I remember members of our village and the church congregation, the prayers for service members far from home, and the quiet dismay over the political atmosphere. I recall the antiwar sentiment, the protest movement, and civil unrest. I also recall an antiwar anthem about those fortunate and those perhaps not so who were sent to war. Made famous by John Fogerty, a telling line of one such anthem declared, "Some folks inherit star spangled eyes; ooh, they send you down to war; Lord, and when you ask them, how much should we give? Ooh, they only answer More! More! More!"

Through these times, I looked to my father who would tell me, "Butch, the true measure of a man is not in his size, but by the amount he gives of himself." My father instilled in me that if I should be asked to serve, then I should answer the call rightly, quietly going forward rather than vociferously protesting against one's duty. Over the years, my father's advice resonated, and having dedicated my commitment to our nation and our Navy, I have been rewarded with the opportunity to serve five tours of duty in Afghanistan and around the world. With each day of thanksgiving, I realize that from it all, I truly have been a fortunate son.

The month of November holds another day of significance. The nineteenth of November marks the anniversary of the Gettysburg Address. On that Thursday afternoon and before the quiet crowd, President Lincoln commemorated the service of the soldiers who served and died on the nearby battlefield. The Civil War far from over, it was yet fitting that the reinternment of the dead be done with veneration. In keeping with this day, Lincoln's immortal words resonate: "From these honored dead we take increased devotion to that cause for which they gave the last full measure of devotion—that we here highly resolve that these dead shall not have died in vain—that this nation, under God, shall have a new birth of freedom—and that government of the people, by the people, for the people, shall not perish from the earth."

Coincidentally, a distant relative of mine who fought at Gettysburg, serving with the Union Third Corps and the 120th New York, wrote a letter to his family describing the numerous regimental and company casualties sustained on the second of July 1863. The letter was written to his brother on the thirteenth of July 1863, noting, "I am alive and well and where we are, we are looking for another fight soon and it may be today." It was this letter and others like it written by Abram Osterhout that instilled in me the will to serve and not shy from awaiting perils. With war well beyond the horizon, I have been blessed to serve with the finest Americans and true patriots. In the past, I have been far from home, and though it has always been difficult being far off from those I love, I have been honored to serve with those whose commitment has motivated me. When gathered around the table anticipating this year's holiday meal—having missed more than a few Thanksgivings due to being deployed—I will offer praise as I reflect upon the blessings of years past and those who have influenced me as a boy and the man that I am today, and I will give thanks as I truly am a fortunate son.

WHAT GIFT ARE YOU PRESENTING?

Once again, the joyous time of the year is upon us: times of good cheer, when friends and family exchange gifts and share an eagerness for glad tidings during the approaching New Year. Several times throughout my naval career, I have been abroad during the holidays. Being far from those I love and often unable to offer the physical gift of the latest gadget or trendy device, I pledged that I would do my best to offer a gift that would not be set aside, packed away, or soon forgotten. I pledged to offer the best in me for my family, far from my side but especially close at heart.

Try as I did, I have, however, been at times unsuccessful, presenting less than my best. Though my lofty aspirations, though obtainable, were at times not always achieved, I've done my best to realize that often my faults and not circumstance failed those I had hoped to have benefited. During these times, I have turned to my faith in order to offer those in my life a better man: a man of strengthened character, a man of tolerance, a man of temperance, and a man that perhaps others might aspire to follow. I am not infallible, and as I grow older, my flaws are quite clear to me. What is also apparent is the way and means to improve the man I am.

Though much has changed over the years, it is from my youth that I draw upon the lessons taught to me by my mother and father and others from that special hometown that even today harkens me back to a simpler time, a time of innocence, and an era much different than today. Though I have transformed over the years, the principles of faith have remained constant and define who I am while enabling me to better myself. And, with the New Year and intended resolutions, I pledge to be a better man for those I love, those I lead, and those I serve and serve with.

Yet, who really is the man who writes these words; perhaps easily put to paper, but what of true intent? Provided here are a few lines to offer the reader a narrative of who I am. I am imperfect, I am damaged, and I am a sinner. Realizing my faults, I acknowledge my sins. I am not a pious man, but rather a man whose faith guides me along my life's journey. I have learned tolerance and acceptance of those whose behavior and beliefs may be contrary to my own. I believe that we are all created equally in the image of our maker. It is free will and its exercise, which then determines the path we take. Striving to be a better man, I employ tolerance and acceptance of those whose choices differ from my own. There has been much rancor voiced in the media of late citing religious beliefs, the right of free speech, the lack of civility, and a good measure of intolerance. Needed is a voice of reason advocating inclusion rather than derision.

For instance, accepting differences within us all, yet not condoning behaviors that are contrary to one's faith, it would be far better to offer kindness than scorn. Several years before I enlisted in the Navy, a friend and coworker was hospitalized with AIDS HIV. Shunned by others and considered a pariah by many, he was dying alone and in need of compassion. I visited my friend shortly before he died. Although I did not condone his personal lifestyle, he remained a friend and very much in need of my support. When I came to his bedside, I found him so weakened by suffering that he could barely move. Yet, as we talked, he extended a hand and clasped with mine as we prayed.

Perhaps another would have denied him this intimate contact, but my faith enabled me to extend myself to another in a time of need. As I have sinned, I have been forgiven. And so, I offer those who have chosen a different path, a man less judgmental, and a man tolerant and considerate. During this holiday season and in the coming year, I will offer my best to those I love and to those I serve. I believe in mercy and grace and the power of faith. It is inevitable that I will falter and disappoint myself and perhaps those I care for. Yet, with faith, I can return to a proper path and offer myself as a better man: one who is compassionate, empathetic, and a man resolute in his determination to selflessly serve others.

So then, what am I gifting? Neither token nor trinket; I will, however, present a limitless heart for the New Year. In prayer, I wish for the reader and their loved ones many blessings.

WHAT DOES DISAPPOINT OFFER?

Recently, a young Sailor asked me to write a memo concerning overcoming moments of disappointment. I can write with authority that this is a topic that I certainly appreciate. Over the years, I've disappointed myself, my family, and those I am charged to lead. At times, falling short of the mark has encumbered me while exacting a heavy toll. Surely, many disappointments in my life have been made opaque by the years gone by. Still, they linger in my mind, paradoxically defining who I am.

What have I chosen to do about them? Rather than dwell on defeat, I remember most the remedy! Rather than recall the despair, I recollect the discovery of a previously undefined inner strength. What of this inner strength? With each burden comes the occasion to accept one's faults caused by personal failings or happenstance and redefine yourself. Not focusing on ourselves, please consider the burdens of others. In so doing, while realizing that others whose trials have disappointed, we can offer a helping hand. It is while accepting the burdens of others that we are made better. Moving past guilt, shame, and letdown, we begin to heal. Realizing that by looking beyond ourselves burdens are lessened, and so it is that we are remade with a bigger heart and broadened shoulders. Stronger, yet sensitive to the needs of others, we are better from the opportunity that was borne from disappointment.

From one whose strength is undeniable, consider Arnold Schwarzenegger who addressed both disappointment and resolve, stating, "Strength does not come from winning. Your struggles develop your strengths. When you go through hardships and decide not to surrender, that is strength." Consider the number of times that Mr. Olympia was unable to lift just a few ounces more than the previous lift, and yet he persevered to overcome the once-thought-insurmountable differences that very well could have forestalled his career! During my life, I've been challenged by many disappointments.

What I've relied upon to refocus my attention has been my trust in faith. Though temporarily distressed, I have moved forward as faith has been my guide. As I have been made better through adversity, I've been readied to accept the burdens of others. And so stronger, yet not lost to the problems of others, through my faith, I stand prepared to aid and assist those who are overwhelmed and put upon.

I've also learned that perseverance enables success from past setbacks. And, from these hindrances, I'm rightly prepared for the inevitable success as a result of commitment, confidence, and grit. Consider still the conclusion of the Winter Olympics, where both winners and losers have been defined. From my youth, I recall the mantra of ABC Sports and the signature Olympic television commercial as famed commentator Jim McKay defined "the thrill of victory and the agony of defeat." Consider that Olympians practice for years and compete in regional and national events, only later making their way to the world stage as precursors to the Olympics. Consider the hours spent in training, dealing with injuries, and securing financing for travel. Consider the personal commitment and the individual sacrifices. Consider then the mere moments of the Olympic competition that may yield no medal and may perhaps even result in physical injury and the subsequent emotional pain. Consider, too, speed skater Dan Jansen, who was favored to win the gold medal in the 1988 Winter Olympics, but only hours before competing learned of his sister's death. Overcome by grief, Dan Jansen fell twice during competitions and returned home without a medal in hand. It would be six long years, countless hours of training, and numerous training events to follow, but Jansen was undaunted and, in the 1994 Olympics, went on to win the gold medal and set a world record for speed. Truly, these are the moments that define one's mettle.

Over the years, I've learned many valuable lessons. I've learned that a better man is prepared to excel when events might otherwise debilitate. Ask yourself, "How often can we be crushed by the weight of guilt?" More often, we can be weighed down by remorse as a result of temporary matters. Then again, taking to a knee and with a bit of invocation, I find that I can shoulder the burden; and with a deep breath and a focused effort, my spirit is uplifted and I am remade spiritually while being healed emotionally. As a grandfather, I know that my little grandgirl will ultimately face life's disappointments. To her, these events can easily though temporarily hamper. Yet, as with all things, time has a way of easing one's burden. As I cannot prevent all things detrimental from occurring, and perhaps I shouldn't, considering the eventual stubble and inevitable tumble, what my past experiences offer is the knowledge, the empathy, and my heart's tendering to my granddaughter who will enviably look to her "papa" for guidance and encouragement. So what does disappoint offer? From our experiences to those in need, offer them always your very best.

THE JOURNEY INTO THE UNKNOWN

From time to time, I have been approached by one junior to me and asked to write a memo concerning decisions and the inexplicable. I often tell Sailors there is much that awaits them in the unknown. With quizzical looks, they wonder how then to plan for that which is mysterious, perhaps the unexpected. My retort to them is not unwitting abandon, but rather determined preparation to meet the inevitable open-mindedly and wholeheartedly. One must be prepared to meet the challenges that certainly wait, for it is destiny that will be revealed along life's progress to the one who is prepared to look in the right direction. Having served with the Navy for more than two decades, the place I find myself has not been without failure or without risk; I must admit there have been times when I have been hapless, though always hopeful. Life has at times been hard, but far from impossible. Trying periods yes, yet perseverance rewarded; I've offered to serve where others would not and perhaps inevitably I was best suited. With the unknown before me, I've trusted those that determined the place of my service; all the while it was my faith that eased uncertainty.

My decision to join into the service of our nation was made with considerable thought. Once determined, my life's progress was set forward into the extraordinary, and I've learned that the power of decision once made yields a personal mark etched onto the path ahead, serving as a road marking for others to follow. I've also learned the following: indecision drives nothing, and motivation—although the fuel of determination—yields little without the first perpetual step forward. Yet, capricious advance often leads one in the wrong direction. Plans less rigid are those of mastery. Flexibility, adeptness, and foresight are elements of decision that afford answers to a questioning soul.

To journey into the unknown, one must prepare to be at one's best. While preparing to meet the challenges that ultimately will be confronted, while not knowing specifically what awaits, service members must ready themselves physically, emotionally, and spiritually. Rather than undertaken blindly, the journey must be observed with eyes wide open. Consequently, as we grow to adulthood, we put away youthful notions and focus on the future. Certainly, deciding to join the military is clearly a matter of consequence. I often tell Sailors that much will be asked of them and they must be prepared to answer the call to arms, for when it comes, indecision must not be revisited. A truly defined commitment is required, perhaps later refined, yet decisions must always be resolutely intent on faithful service.

Consider the words of Theodore Roosevelt, who wrote, "In any moment of decision the best thing you can do is the right thing, the next best thing is the wrong thing, and the worst thing you can do is nothing." From time to time, Sailors have asked me to describe the toughest decision that I've made during my military career. In retrospect, the toughest decision was determining the right time to enter the military. Embarking upon a new life into the unknown, leaving family and friends, a well-paying job, and the comforts of home, at thirty-four years of age, entering basic training was in fact without reluctance, as my commitment was firm on that late June morning over twenty-six years ago.

My career has been tremendously rewarding. Although the past has not been without difficulty, hardship, or at times heartache, the naval service has truly been gratifying beyond imagination. I have learned much about distant lands and unfamiliar cultures while serving with the finest individuals who have shaped me into the man that I am today: a better man for those I love and for those to whom I serve, at the best of my abilities, selflessly and decisively.

THE PROMISE OF OPPORTUNITY

My father would often tell me, "Butch, take an opportunity before it's out of reach!" Having been blessed with countless opportunities and proper decisions, my father's words resound to this day. I must admit, however, that on several occasions, my choices were contrary to the right path while at other times I failed to achieve what I could have. In retrospect, though, I've done okay. And, it is because of my current station in life that I am able and prepared to share with others my good fortune.

Truly, over the years, incalculable blessings have been bestowed upon me. Having been born to wonderful parents, who worked hard and sacrificed, they planned for the future while forgoing excess in order to provide for the immediate. My parents taught me many a lesson that I would practice in my adult years. I was blessed to have my parents as their guidance afforded me a foundation that has enabled me a rewarding life, which importantly affords me opportunities to reward others through personal sacrifice and the richness of compassion. I also consider the detractor who might take to task my words. One might ask, "What do you know of poverty, squalor, or a life without opportunity?" In response, I would offer, "I am blessed to know little of it as it is because of unprecedented opportunities that in return I hope to benevolently share with those who have not yet seized their own."

Whether you live in opulence or you were raised in poverty, one finds that in life there are countless and divergent possibilities presented to us all. Is it not possible to squander away a fortune yet set aside a treasure? In both circumstances, choices determined and paths chosen govern the opportunities that present themselves. For instance, my wife and I live within our means; we debate the purchases of those things not absolutely necessary, and while saving for our future, we consider the needs of our family and the educational opportunities for our granddaughter. We share our good fortune with family and offer donations to charitable causes. We truly live the good life. Yet, our family overseas knows all too well poverty, hunger, and disease while being weighed down mostly by uncertainty. Sharing our blessings, we have extended to family the opportunity to immigrate to America. Although a long process, one fraught with delay and disappointment, it has ultimately proven successful as family members have made the long trek while joyfully accepting the promise of opportunity that American citizenship will provide.

We know that opportunity does not guarantee success. Yet, with faith, dedication, and a plan to succeed, success is much more than possible. Considering our family and the herculean effort to bring about lifesaving change, it is fitting that I cite John Quincy Adams who aptly stated, "Patience and perseverance have a magical effect before which difficulties disappear and obstacles vanish." Consider the following: the promise of opportunity enables an individual to establish benchmarks in order to measure individual success. And, here lies the promise: that sacrifice, perseverance, and providence offers hope with every opportunity. And, with each endeavor, we measure the way ahead and focus on the finish. We then must be resolute in our commitment while realizing that with every undertaking there exists occasions where our own actions benefit others. And, with every prospect lies the opportunity to selflessly serve others, benefiting those whose current station pits them against the elements. Therefore, the promise of opportunity richly enables the disadvantaged. As we are social stewards, this should be your promise in the service of others: share with others your personal advantage and give of yourself as your sacrifice will enrich their lives and future generations. Whether your life's station is inherent or begotten, it is the assurance of selfless service and the blessing of reciprocity that enables the lives of others and truly fosters the promise of opportunity.

FOCUS ON THE HORIZON
FOR BETTER DAYS

The days ahead will be difficult, and not without struggle. Accordingly, plan for a tough advance and for the inevitable to be confronted. The path ahead will be trying, testing individual resolve and the unity of the collective. From political division, economic uncertainty, and looming threats, the task of moving forward appears daunting indeed. Current events are enough to make your head spin! Yet, to live in isolation, believing oneself to be insulated from trouble will not, as history has taught, keep peace both within and buffered from peril abroad. As stated by Franklin D. Roosevelt, "Our national determination to keep free of foreign wars and foreign entanglements cannot prevent us from feeling deep concern when ideals and principles that we have cherished are challenged." It also appears evident that the more one knows, the more apparent the division among us. Faced with such uncertainty, now is not the time to ignore the troubles of our communities or of the world. Rather, the time is now for spirited social and political engagement. The divisions within must be addressed by those who must pledge to deter personnel and financial advantage, thereby serving the citizenry altruistically, free of vice and corruption, and void of scandal. Such are the things that weigh us down and pull asunder. When pursuing progress, selflessness will bridge the divide vice self-regard that only broadens the gulf. As servants of our nation, the opportunities before us will inevitably define us. From the decay of our inner cities, violence, and betrayal, to economic disparity and yes, political theater, to addressing dangers from both within and overseas, military men and women offer a paradigm of service, sacrifice, personal advancement, and obtainment through a code of conduct and an ethos of benevolence. As military members, our service is defined by offering a better way, lending a hand in fellowship while enriching others through experience as a life fulfilled through vocation. Henry Wadsworth Longfellow wrote that "the life of a man consists not in seeing visions and in dreaming dreams, but in active charity and in willing service." Still, we are resilient, prepared to answer the call to arms and defend that which we hold dear while giving of ourselves for others, whereas the evils perpetrated against us are redressed, we offer liberty to those who know only of tyrants. For those who look beyond their own experience and who desire more for others rather than for themselves, military men and women readily offer the above-noted enviable traits while being prepared and willing to tackle the issues that divide us.

I often speak with groups of young men and women who at times are struggling with acclimating to military life, some homesick, some challenged by academics, others not prepared for the rigors of a lifestyle that demands an individual standard and compliance to uniformity. Though not insurmountable, for some, this can still appear to be a tough slough. At times, Sailors focus upon themselves rather than upon those that they serve with and those to whom they serve. Some consider military service benefits as entitlements while others are discouraged by the events that include the treatment of veterans by administrators and bureaucrats. My balanced discussions focus upon social issues, unemployment, and not becoming socially and politically disenfranchised. Some wonder if they are strong enough, steady enough, and prepared to continue into the unknown vice return to a life familiar though perhaps a life without promise or a life lived contrary to social values and norms. My advice is this: focus on the horizon for better days. Plan to walk a difficult path with those who will guide and direct, selected to prepare others to meet life's challenges, united with a purpose to selflessly serve others, bettering themselves through a shared experience, and yes, in part competitive, though designed to fulfill the desires of those who long to serve their fellow Americans and members of the world community. As my father would tell me, "Butch, if you focus on the horizon, you'll soon see how close it truly is." Believe me, better days will be found at your focal point!

THE COMING STORM

June 30, 2014

As a beacon of hope, America represents a land of promise, where individuals are enabled to encourage the divine rights of life, liberty, and the pursuit of happiness. America signifies an earthly place where lives are enriched, lives healed, and where opportunities abound. People long to step foot upon our shores as it is here that benevolence, compassion, and tolerance are social standards, where the rule of law and common sense deters tyranny, where the common man has a voice, and where the people hold the power for political change without fear of reprisal.

During the run up to the 1980 presidential election, Ronald Reagan voiced the infamous comment that truly defines our nation: "A troubled and afflicted mankind looks to us, pleading for us to keep our rendezvous with destiny; that we will uphold the principles of self-reliance, self-discipline, morality, and, above all, responsible liberty for every individual that we will become that shining city on a hill." Today, America remains a bastion of freedom, opportunity, equality, and independence. Though troubles exist, tendered are timely beneficial solutions that profit society.

As we look inward upon this, our remarkable constitutional republic, there on the horizon looms a coming storm. This tempest is seeded as an Islamist movement emerging across Europe, the Levant region, Asia, and Africa. The emerging caliphate is a threat that must be addressed as it threatens those upon whom it focuses. The rise of Islamism must be seen as an ominous threat that has engulfed wide swaths of geography as the violent movement revealed a campaign based upon subjugation, intolerance, and brutality. Forced conversions, rape, enslavement, and butchery are the touchstones of this violent movement. A common thread that binds the movement

210

is the castigation of America. Extreme are their ideas, radical their beliefs, intolerant of equality are they. They publicize the injustices and the vices of America though we champion unparalleled opportunity, religious tolerance, liberty, charity, and goodwill.

Above all else, I believe that what antagonizes adherents of the Islamist ideology most is that our flag proudly waves not with spiteful intent but rather in spite of their best efforts to pull asunder. Islamists threaten our American way, burn our flag, and target our citizenry. Through our extension of an olive branch, Islamists will in retort offer a barbed vine designed to tear at the heart of our magnanimity and, as a noose, subjugate the weak, yoke them with despair, and throttle the nonconformist. As a nation, we must acknowledge that this malevolent movement has threatened our way of life.

Considering America as a beacon of hope, reflect upon a lighthouse as a representation of our great nation. Over the centuries, the piercing light of a lighthouse offers hope to those in peril, guiding them ashore while as a beacon, directing mariners in peril to a site of tranquility where relief awaits. As a navigational beacon, seafarers are alerted to outcroppings of rocks or shallows, where many before have run aground, being swallowed up by the sea. The analogy is clear as the lighthouse represents an invitation to all in peril, yet to those that would scheme to do us harm, the rocks and shallows represent the defense against menacing threats. There are those who are disenfranchised and others whose self-imposed societal alienation serve others who look to attack us both from abroad and from within. Recently, an American man detonated a suicide vest worn in Syria. It is known that there are others like him that fight alongside Islamist forces in the Levant region. To prepare for the coming storm, as a nation united in purpose and destined to protect our legacy of munificence, we must extend the hand of diplomacy through authoritative discourse. At the same time, we must also emulate Theodore Roosevelt, who stated on September 2, 1901, that we must recommit our collective to "speak softly, and carry a big stick."

A MORAL COMPASS: THE RIGHT DIRECTION AND THE WAY AHEAD

As leaders, our persona is constantly on display. Your uniform surely conceals the outer skin, but not your inner self. As a leader, you hold an enviable position based on knowledge and experience. Yet, you must know that envy is a powerful emotion. As a leader, you must subscribe to conduct that is at all times becoming. If you fail to adhere to this subscription, those you are charged to lead will in turn venture down the wrong path. As a leader, you establish a paradigm that others strive to emulate. In you, they must see themselves. Your conduct must be unquestionable. In all that you do, your behavior defines the person you are.

You must not allow yourself to fall victim to selfish pursuits. Yes, they may derive you temporary benefit; but for the long term, such as life should be, those things transitory hardly stand the test of time. As you set the example for others to follow, you must be versatile and multidimensional without being overly complex. You must be resilient and always ready to answer the call. You must believe in yourself. And, in the face of adversity, when eyes are upon you, you must not waver. This is the burden of leadership. In tough times, those you are charged to lead will keenly focus upon your ability to shoulder the burden. There will be some that will expect you to fail, others hope, and yes, others still will conspire to see you fall short. You may bend, but you shall not break. Understand and accept that doing your best to do that which is right will be the harder course than not.

Remember too that being unsuccessful does not have to yield failure; only when you fail to refine and amend your actions will you fail for certain. Experience is based not only on success, for the best lessons in life are those things that should not be repeated. Leadership is truly a measure of experience, of overcoming adversity and seeing your way through difficult times. Your conduct must continually be refined and advanced. Selfishness must be put aside and selflessness must prevail for the benefit of those you lead. Think broadly, ponder ways to rally others, accept that you are to serve them, and believe that your success is really their achievement.

Know too that we all miss the mark from time to time. Yet, from those experiences, additional challenges will unfold that test your mettle and enable you to refine past shortcomings. I often tell Sailors that for the past fifteen years, my sleep has frequently been less than sound. I am haunted not by the things that I have done or the events that I have lived through, but troubled am I by the things that I could have done and the things that I should have accomplished. I have failed along my journey, though I continued onward. Times have been trying and not at all easy. There have been detours and certainly more than the occasional bump in the road. Yet, I have been privileged to serve with the finest among us, sacrificed, and toiled while others have outdone me, outperformed me, while guiding me in the right direction. For this I am thankful. It is because of them that during times when I have lost my footing that I kept a keen focus on the way ahead. For all the rewards bestowed upon me, I am grateful to those who have mentored me, guided me, and led me forward.

Finally, as a leader, respect your moral compass and others will follow in the right direction. Your obligations to financial, ethical, personal and professional commitments are tantamount to good order and discipline and define who you are personally and professionally. There are those you serve and then there are others unfamiliar. Though you may not perceive them, the unacquainted observe your actions, listen to your speech, evaluate your behaviors, and emulate your actions. Being responsive and responsible, we must maintain a proper course, steadfast, and determined to do what is expected without being demanded. As you proceed along life's path, know that well-placed plans must remain transportable. Life holds many surprises. We must be accepting of change, rallying the strength to overcome that which may appear daunting while believing in ourselves and those who support us. Unexpected changes, diversions, and at times, disappointment must not be viewed as insurmountable. Rather, the ability to remain focused on achievements while overcoming impediments will yield true rewards in life. Consider the following: It is far better to pay forward than to pay back. Be at your best in all that you do, give of yourself to others so that they may benefit not in your name but rather for the name of those they care for. A moral compass and a true course will surely yield the proper direction to follow in life.

SELFLESSNESS IS THE BONDING ELEMENT OF SOCIAL UNITY

The nightly news on television of late is fixated on recent events that include racial strife and social injustice. The viewer takes in the violence, the rancor, and the surreal multicolored haze of tear gas illuminated by emergency vehicle lighting. Vigils and candlelight gatherings are marred by hoodlums bent on looting, violence, and self-reward. The focus shifted, the spotlight shines upon the debasement of American culture. Reluctance and ambivalence have befallen many who perceive the events as the way life is, while for some, the violence and reprisal the way it must be. The viewer can take in the spectacle, change the channel, or turn a blind eye. Yet, for others, the two-block area of Ferguson, Missouri, during the early days of August 2014 represents a much wider divide. Opportunists quick to seize the moment interject their own brand of carny with the hope of soliciting funds fueled by the emotionally charged atmosphere that they themselves stoke. Ironically, some whose celebrity and who purportedly stand for justice turned tragedy into profit-making "cents" from the situation fuel by racism and revenge.

The tragic death of a young man, troubled, perhaps wayward, confused, longing; whose behaviors and choices must be a part of the calculus to determine this heartrending outcome. To be determined appropriate or excessive, the reaction by the police officer will be established as justice will be done. Yet, with the outcome, there will be those that will not accept the determination of the legal system and only view it as further evidence of the true sightlessness of an approach to justice that has in their minds perpetuated further humiliation. Of course, this view is distorted for and by some, while the fabric of our nation is torn a bit more by those who do seek reprisal through violence. As answers are sought to address the issues that plague the inner city, and as Ferguson, Missouri, has shown, the divisions that exist in the heartland, solutions are indeed present and appropriate actions ready to be embraced by those enabled to pursue a better way.

Answers can be freely obtained from nonpartisan clergy and unbiased community advocates, who address fundamental issues that deter individuals from stepping forward. Rather than venerate antisocial behaviors, the citizenry must esteem civility, morality, and common decency as obtainable goals. A sense of personal responsibility vice a sense of entitlement must be embraced. Mentors must stand up and step forward in order to provide enviable societal models. Forgoing malice and discouraging inflammatory rhetoric bent on spurring violence, a communal tone with reconciliation a focal point, beneficial is the movement that unifies through inclusion vice segregates through division. Required is an elevated sense of personal accountability, reliance upon faith, uplifting social morality, law abidance, and importantly, a welcoming of the richness of diversity, as we must also appreciate the fruitfulness of commonality as societal stewards.

Rather than focusing on the downward spiral of societal division, I truly believe that community leaders should look to our military as a model of inclusion, tolerance, and opportunity; a social model that rewards hard work, determination, perseverance, and selflessness. Rather than browbeat ourselves for wrongdoings, the military reports transgressions and works transparently to correct behaviors without turmoil or upheaval. Our collective ethos unifies rather than divides. Respectful and responsible are we as we serve those who may object, may disparage, and may criticize the very ones charged to protect their right of dissent. The military has been on the forefront of establishing, enacting, and reinforcing individual rights. The military rewards hard work and encourages personal and professional development, instilling the values of social order, compassion, empathy, and personal sacrifice, thereby enabling others to follow a proven path of service that benefits not only the military community, but the community writ large. Importantly, as members of the military we truly reward our nation and the citizenry of the greater society. Such is an enviable model indeed; such is the necessary model for Ferguson, Missouri.

WHAT MY GRANDDAUGHTER SEES

September 30, 2014

My life has truly been blessed. I have been granted the opportunity to build the foundation from which another's life will flourish. I know that my actions, beliefs, attitude, and benevolence will shape the life of another; one who looks to me, who really looks at me, in search of answers to the most pressing of life's problems, and one who believes in me to provide solutions to life's daunting dilemmas.

Now, you may ask, "How daunting can predicaments be for a three-year-old?" As her "papa," I appreciate that every issue faced by my granddaughter, to her may seem daunting; and in wiping away a tear or two, an opportunity presents itself to offer the very best in me for her. I know that each solution will exponentially affect her, and so it is my design that I be a positive force and always and in all ways provide a helpful remedy. For I pray that one day she will look to me not only for influence, but as an influential and larger-than-life benefactor, whose offerings of benevolence will influence her very own children one day. It will be tales of her papa that I hope she will talk about many years from today, and in many ways I hope she will emulate what her papa through his offerings taught her. As I share stories about my father with my granddaughter, I hope she'll share stories about me with her children, for these tales of yesteryear help shape future generations and so it is important that it be done.

Recently, my granddaughter took a bold step forward. Planning on one of life's pivotal moments, she did so after talking about this special occasion for several weeks. My granddaughter was resolute as she discussed with me her intentions and expectations. Now, you're probably thinking, "Intentions and expectations from a three-year-old?" Yes, conversations such as these we share, and I am always amazed at her ability to discuss such matters with her papa. So then, what my granddaughter sees is an opportunity to enrich her life, to meet new friends, and begin her education. And, with steadfast determination, she waited for the school bus to arrive. Eager to commence a new adventure, she stepped aboard confidently, without reluctance or experiencing departure anxiety; with her bright smile seen through the window, she blew a kiss to her mommy, and off she went to explore the unknown. Without a true understanding of time and distance, off she went, willingly and excitedly, emulating perhaps the cartoon adventurer Dora the Explorer on her personal quest. I often think about what my granddaughter sees: a life of adventure and of discovery, her world void of bigotry and racism, and free of need, living comfortably with endless opportunity, living safely and securely, knowing that her family is always near, holding her close to their hearts, a focal point in many of their lives.

My granddaughter sees her papa as a man who loves her and who provides her tales of adventure. Of course, some are fanciful, with humor infused; but all of these tales are to inspire and broaden her life's perspective. She knows of a far-off place called Afghanistan. And, as papa watches the evening news, she tracks with her finger the headline scroll that appears on the lower portion of the screen. What my granddaughter believes is being revealed are words detailing adventures of a mystical word. Exposed, yet unbeknownst to her, are the world's troubles causing her papa pause and alarm. Knowing Papa is captivated by the news, every so often does she observes a tear that appears in his eye as he views the troubling events of the world, the loss of one's innocence, or of tyranny's creep across a landscape once hard fought over. Heartwarmingly, my granddaughter views papa's flag flown from the front porch and now tells him that the flag is "our flag." And, at her young age, my granddaughter discerns the word *Navy* as it appears and is eager to wear a uniform similar to her papa's. What my little *Apo*, my dear granddaughter, sees is a world full of promise, though when moments visit her with a sting of a scrape or when a hurt appears overwhelming, or when things go bump in the night, what my granddaughter sees is I trust the very best in me, one who is there to comfort, there to protect, and there to inspire.

WITH THANKSGIVING, FORWARD THE BLESSINGS BESTOWED

With the arrival of a definitive change in the season, and with frost on the windows and the sting of a cold wind, we begin to hunker down for another long winter. As we reflect upon days gone by, and with the decreasing daylight, we enter a cycle of bundling up and shaking off the cold while thinking about longer days, the warmth of sunlight, and the rebirth of springtime many weeks away. Yet, there is that one day and that special meal that we anticipate each autumn. A bounty of food and good tidings, the warmth from the kitchen, and with family sat around the table, the patriarch with great care carves the aromatic focal point for those in attendance. With blessings before us and benefits shared by all, many of us count calories vice recount the blessings bestowed upon us.

At our table, hands are held and with heads bowed, I offer thanks and praise for that which we are about to receive while offering recognition for both blessings attained; and for our abilities and desire to offer the best of us to those in need. And, thankful must we be for the dedication to serve others both at home, within our communities, and around the world. It is because of our service that blessings will be conferred to those who are cold, who are sick and the infirm; to those who suffer under tyrannical rule; and to those who once were hopeless, it is the blessing of American benevolence extended through might and charity that we too must be thankful. Though the last Thursday of November is designated as a day to count one's blessings, enjoy our family and friends in feast and fellowship, it should also be a day where blessings are recounted as well as realizing that we must be prepared to offer our best to others in the months ahead.

There are many in need, many disadvantaged, others exploited, neglected, maligned. There are those who are victims and tormented; far beyond the media, outside the realm of social interest, out of sight

219

yet perhaps there are those in our own communities that are forgotten, forsaken, overlooked, perhaps shunned. Before us are opportunities to serve others and provide for those that are unable to care for themselves: the aged, those alone, those without, and many who are deprived of hope. As members of the military, we are prepared, willing, and able to respond as ordered to offer those in need deliverance from despair. In reflection of the days gone by, we must also give thanks for the prepared measures taken in anticipation of what may be demanded of the men and women serving in the military. Our efforts are a vocation of benefit while in the service of others. We have stepped forward having pledged to support and defend, and when ordered, enter the fray wherever humanity is threatened. We serve altruistically extending the compassion and generosity of our collective blessings to those who are mired in misfortune and to those who struggle to make a better way for their communities.

As veterans, we have sacrificed much, with separations from families and the consequential uncertainty and anxieties, and the inevitable personal change that results when those among us return from hostile environments. Thankful must we be for both the service opportunities presented us, and for the love and support from those who remain on the home front. And, thankful must we be for daring to state an oath that will take us into both quandary and quarrel, to places unbeknownst, to hostile environments abroad, in the defense of freedom while deterring fanaticism. As we give thanks and prepare to enjoy family, festivities, and football, we remain ready to defend our nation and the freedoms we hold while primed to oppose those whose extremism offer only a distorted view. In offering thanks and praise for what we have received, and in recognizing the merits of our preparedness, now is the time to make ready to address the unimaginable with the extraordinary, for it is far better to be prepared than to be making ready at a pivotal time in history.

IT'S GOOD TO GO BACK BEFORE MOVING FORWARD

When not deployed during the holidays, from time to time I would return to the place of my childhood to visit with friends, family, and reflect upon the past while counting my good fortune because of where and how I was raised. As with past visits, the long drive north provides hours of personal reflection. My thoughts wandering, I returned to my teenage years to relive events from a time far different from the present. Certainly, however, much has changed since my high school days, but what remains a constant is the upstate New York village of my upbringing. Even today, I reminisce about baseball, teenage pranks, and the group of friends that no longer reside there, fast cars, first experiences, and of all things, riding my bicycle down Main Street while sitting on the handlebars and pedaling backward—quite a sight and quite a feat for the young man with the uncombed hair, whom the neighbors certainly wondered as I did about what the future held in store for me.

Well, over the years, the trials and tribulations have both defined and enabled me. And, with each visit, I am reminded of the blessings bestowed upon me. There I learned that ambition is a rightful personal trait, where opportunities are presented as gifts to be cherished, and the outcome of these endeavors are to be forwarded on behalf of others. It is when I go back that I again appreciate who I once was and am grateful for the man that I've become. From my childhood, those years of wonder and of what the years held ready for me, for the daring things that I did, from the lessons learned and from the heartaches endured, it is because of those who have left an indelible mark upon me that I go back to bow my head in remembrance and offer thanks and praise for the man that those experiences have made. Every so often, it's good to go back before moving forward. As I move forward, I look to the future with hope and promise. Yet, there is much turmoil and strife throughout the world. Within our own country, there is social upheaval, dismay, and distrust. The news is full of disorder and demonstration with violence and division among members of our community. The exploitation of racial disharmony only serves to widen the cavity between elements of our citizenry. With the growing threat of radicalism spreading across the Middle East, Europe, and Africa, and with the threat of infiltration and insurrection within our borders, many may believe that the troubles experienced today will overtake us. Others among us remain oblivious to the coming storm. Though forecasts are evident, they go about their lives with abandon, self-centered, appearing self-absorbed in their daily activities; many among us have lost focus, hunkered down, while afraid or indifferent to the plight of others.

One might say, "Why go back when you should be readying to get out while the getting's good!" I shall not subscribe to such a notion. Now are times presented that require our very best with selflessness as the touchstone of our personal compact to those we are charged to serve. We must stand and offer our neighbors a healing hand, reconcile with members of our communities, and come together as cornerstones of the republic, strengthening the bond of union and turning away from those who interject corrosive rancor designed to tear us apart. We must pursue a merger of divergent views through civility and tolerance. And, with going back to the place where my parents lie at rest, I again pledge to do my best in my own home, in my community, for our nation; and whether I find myself abroad or afield, I will rightly offer my best in our nation's defense in order to thwart our enemies that seek to tear us down.

WHAT WE STAND FOR

February 10, 2015

Given recent events, a young man asked me, "What do jihadists stand for?" I thought about this question for a time and deliberated a bit that it was best rather than a one-sided answer citing the barbarous actions of those whose ideology corrupted their interpretation of their religion, I considered that my answer warranted a focus upon American ideals and a culture of benevolence when juxtaposed to a theocratic culture bent on ruthless tyranny. Then I was asked, "Why do they hate us?" Here, before me, was an opportunity to answer two questions defining the greatness of America and that for which we stand. As Americans and as members of the military, we are a diverse group with divergent views, attitudes, and beliefs. We look different; we speak differently; we are of different ethnicities, nationalities, and races; and we're defined along religious and political lines. We hold dear our diversity, and we Americans trumpet personal freedom and individualism.

Over the years of my military career, I've talked with foreign individuals who hold a very biased view of Americans. When told about the richness of our culture, these individuals are often astounded by the social and religious variety coupled with unprecedented personal opportunity that each American can individually pursue. Importantly, Americans cherish the ability to pursue their dreams with an entrepreneurial spirit. Yet, we recognize that though we pull ourselves up, we should not walk over others as we pursue our personal desires. We also recognize the rule of law and open-heartedly contribute to the well-being of those less fortunate. We are blessed, and we share our blessings not only with others at home but extend ourselves abroad. And, when we share our good fortune with others, we also extend ourselves to those who would denigrate us and often ungratefully accept that which we offer to those who are unable to provide for themselves. We assist others unreservedly because our collective conscience compels us to do that which is right. And, this is what we stand for!

I've thought long about the best way to further define what we stand for, and in so doing, I can define why our enemies conspire to again strike at our heart. To an enemy, it is a symbol, perhaps considered a mere piece of sewn fabric, perhaps easily torn and easier still ignited and trampled upon. For our enemies, this symbol has been distorted by the twisted influence roused by hate, irrationality, and greed. Our symbol has enlivened the desperate and encouraged the downtrodden, inspiring those facing defeat, and united those to rally in the face of indomitable odds. Many have given much while some have given themselves to encourage others to follow, to remain strong and purposeful, standing tall when others might stand down. What causes our adversaries such upset and stirs them to lash out against us is a piece of woven material, often faded, yet nonetheless causes those that oppose us the impetus to denounce America while at times assailing those who pledge allegiance to it. The symbol that defines us is that which they rail against. But why you may ask do our enemies rebuke all that which the symbol represents? It is because the symbol represents individual freedom, opportunity, and inalienable rights of life, liberty, and the pursuit of happiness! This symbol is our flag, that which we salute, that which adorns our uniforms, and that which proudly waves in the face of the enemy.

When asked what we Americans stand for, I answer the query this way: we stand where our flag stands! We stand and salute those who have shared our service, those who have fought back the ambitions of tyrants, and in recognition of those who have changed the world. Our flag represents the extraordinary efforts of ordinary Americans who, being inspired by the ideals of liberty, vowed to support and defend all that we hold dear. United to defend Old Glory at home and abroad, this is what we stand for!

DIRECT QUESTIONS, CANDID ANSWERS

As I often speak to Sailors about purposeful selfless service and ready them for their next assignment, one young Sailor recently asked me, "What lies ahead given the spreading terrorism throughout the world?" To the Sailor, I offered that what awaits is an extraordinary experience, the outcome very much to be determined by personal impact, tenacity, and perseverance.

The days and months ahead will be demanding, and there will be much to learn, where technical proficiency will be honed and one's reputation earned. Yet, there is much to realize about the world: a world where a reemergence of fascism on a grand scale exists that entwines theology, thus empowering the disenfranchised, emboldening the weak and those once exploited, and those driven by carnage to subscribe to a literal though corrupt ideology, one which seeks to reestablish a caliphate through prize and plunder, murder and mayhem. These are the enemies of humanity, who seek to swell their ranks through barbarity that empowers their followers and who seek through the use of terror and social media to rouse a campaign designed to instill popular fear, yet calculated to invoke retaliation that only stokes further the fires of fanaticism.

Responding to the Sailor's query and with no intent on alarmism—rather to instill the truth forthrightly—I offered, "What lies ahead is pure evil." The days and months before us will be as trying as they will be defining, and they will be fraught with peril. As military men and women, we must be prepared to sacrifice for the long term. These enemies will, through despicable acts, draw us in and relish their own demise as an end state fashioned by their own savagery. Prepared must we be to hasten their demise and put an end to their assault on humanity.

Yet, we must also be determined, committed for the long term, clearly defining the strategy for decisive military operations while planning an aftermath through political and social agendas, which champion opportunities of partnerships rather than outright nation building. The Islamic State is an apocalyptic cult whose enemies are apostates, Christians, Jews, and the undesirable, waging a true war on women and those who are deemed weak-willed and unwanted. To their enemies, they offer slavery or death. There is no negotiation nor rule of law to wit that will be abided as the Islamic State is bent on domination and savors death fashioned by its maniacal pursuit. The Islamic State has metastasized, merging jihadi affiliates whose demented objective continues to evolve around the globe. Hearing the pleas of those who turn to us to strike at the core of the extremism, we must be prepared to act definitively against the enemy of civilized people for they will not capitulate nor deny their desire of conquest.

Following a lengthy conversation, the Sailor then asked me, "What will then be asked of me?" I offered this Sailor that much will be asked of and from him. Importantly, I rhetorically offered, "What will you ask of yourself?" I further offered that what will be expected from those who don the fabric of our nation is at all times our very best. We must be prepared to be deployed in defense of our nation, offering hope to those who pray for salvation from those whose barbaric actions beget sorrow and, for many, death. We must be ready to leave our families for long periods of uncertainty and worry. Yet, our families will find solace in our contributions to eradicate this pandemic of savagery.

Though we will face peril, and many of us will serve in harm's way, we will remain vigilant, shouldering the burdens of those who serve on our right and to our left. Our actions will define that which was done for the following generations. Inevitably, there will be those lost from among our ranks; and though the sorrow felt will overshadow, it shall not become unconquerable, for our spirit is invincible, our intentions true, and our purpose resolute. Lastly, I remarked, "As the unimaginable awaits, you must be prepared to act extraordinarily in the service of others, both known and unbeknownst to you. Such is the definition of selfless service, and this will be how we will be defined, for steadfast must we be to change the course of history!"

A FLASH OF SPIRITUAL
ENLIGHTENMENT

Since September 11, 2001, I have been deployed numerous times in perilous environments with amazing patriots. I have seen the effects of fanaticism, and I have lost dear friends. I have questioned the adversarial motive and their agendas to gain a greater understanding of the indigenous mindset, diplomatic objectives, and political theater. Considering alarming current events and as further deployments await, my quest to balance personal and professional pursuits lead me to wonder more about the world while introspectively considering who I am and what my role might be in the lives of my family, my community, and the Navy.

With another birthday behind me and contemplating my future, I seek to balance occasional trepidation concerning the looming storm that due to my vocation I am aware of and to which others are oblivious. With personal interactions and observations, I often become concerned for the future of America. There are many among us whose narcissism and attempts to shutter their worldview place us all in jeopardy. With numerous ominous threats before us, ignorance of worldly matters is a measure of either arrogance or personal neglect. As an ardent follower of the news, I at times become dismayed by the events of our time. Both domestic and foreign trials can dampen one's spirit. With economic uncertainty, financial imbalances, racial tensions, and associative health risks due to my glycemic index, one can become overwhelmed when trying to keep pace along life's journey. Take, for instance, recent political events: partisan wrangling, deleted emails, and political indictments while trying to determine the right from being wronged; the spread of extremism throughout North Africa and the Levant region; conflict in the Ukraine; health emergencies throughout western Africa and the ever-expanding influence of narcoterrorism; perhaps an untenable nuclear deal, teetering economies, the threat of nuclear war—

together these matters coupled with the need for yet another eyeglass prescription can yield a sure bout of melancholy and buckle one's stance no matter how staunch one's posture. Yet, we must adjust our footing, buck up, and bear the weight, if not for ourselves, then for those who look to us as a paradigm of strength.

During times such as these, it is far better to lead and rally than submit to retreat, for in withdrawal we lose the esteem of those we are charged to lead and, in turn, they surely will lose their way. As leaders, we must remain stoic when faced with life's challenges, for as Henry A. Kissinger once stated, "The task of the leader is to get his people from where they are to where they have not been." And, in retreat, this is a place both leader and one's charges should not be. During times such as these, one can become consumed with grief and regret.

Such a time was the sad day that my mother-in-law passed, leaving our family devastated. With arrangements to be made and a family to care for, needed was a rallying force. What was necessary was a larger-than-life influence on the lives left distraught. Yet, what I received, and at just the right moment, was in fact a whisper that in turn was "a flash of spiritual enlightenment." During the funeral, I asked my granddaughter if she wanted to see her great-grandmother lying at rest, and she stated that she did. As we approached to pay our respects, my granddaughter did not exhibit trepidation. As I lifted her to my hip, and as she looked upon her great-grandmother, this little girl calmly whispered, "Papa, are we in heaven?" Now mind you, this little girl not yet four years old did not ask if her grandmother was in heaven, but rather if "we" were in heaven. Her words were far from simple musings of a child, but rather a profound statement, whereby my response to her was of course an affirmative. From this child's words came the realization that when tested and perhaps the way made tough, self-awareness exists in every moment with burdens uplifted in praise: not by the trumpeted volumes of angels, but rather at the volume of a child's whisper. Only, of course, if you listen! Now that's "a flash of spiritual enlightenment"!

WHAT IS NEEDED IS REASON

The time has come for reason. What we watch nightly is the civil denigration and the continued downturn of our society. Cities ablaze with racial disharmony, yet again striking a dissonant chord with political gamesmanship and social provocateurs, many among us turn away, focus myopically, and snap yet another selfie while the very foundation of our great nation is straining under the internal pressure of disunion, derision, and prejudice.

We see the inevitable volley of excess in retort, which results in the far-flung in order to redress injustice. The fallout yields a widening breach among two camps, and with the broadening gulf, each group risks further parting through ongoing disharmony. Reconcilers appear to be self-serving partisans who spiral to pull society downward. Without doubt, "what is needed is reason."

Theological fanatics inspired by slaughter and plunder, now claim responsibility for an attack within our borders. Not the first such attack against our citizenry and our liberties, they scheme to gain more of a foothold through social media, vowing to raise the black flag atop our governmental institutions. Yet, there are radicals among us who seek to challenge our beliefs by trampling upon Old Glory as their right though they wrong all who have served. Among us are those who fail to appreciate the blessings of opportunity though they are determined to incite riot, looting, and pillage, somehow empathizing with these foreign zealots. And, among us are those who will rally around the Constitution, citing its provisions while identifying with anarchists who would shred the Constitution at first opportunity.

During times such as these, what is needed is direction and leadership. With divergent interests, partisan pursuits lessen our collective focus. We must prioritize an agenda with national security at the forefront. With enemies at our borders, inroads left unchecked provide pathways for our enemies to encamp, plot, and strike. I

229

become heavyhearted as I ponder these societal ills. I worry as I see communal fractures appearing. For instance, I recently observed interviews with a group of young males from inner-city Baltimore, Maryland. These young males appeared socially and intellectually disadvantaged and presented themselves as disenfranchised wanderers in life. What they need is a vision, a purpose, the willingness to see the proper path before them, and the ability to follow that path. Many are hoodlums who take advantage of the system, disavow themselves from social norms and values of decency and respect, while prepared to strike out at any instance of self-perceived provocation. Crime and violence are popular touchstones that for all intents wall them off from the greater community. Needed is a seed to be planted, cultivated, though ahead may be a long hoe; with time and care, lives become productive, lives of mutual respect and of personal dignity emerge, and with care and nurture, can in fact bear fruit.

Faith-based community outreach programs, void of political agendas focused on the principles of self-worth and altruism, will turn a barren field into a harvest of bounty. Yet, members of society who reside on the fringe must believe that social conformity is healthy for the community writ large. They must see figures of authority as enviable examples rather than as icons of oppression. Still, they must believe in themselves and trust that personal integrity and responsibility, ethical behavior, education, compromise, conformity, family, fraternity, and faith will reward them personally, all being worth their toil. Members of the inner city must envision a life made fruitful through purposeful and selfless service rather than enriched through the spoils of illicit behaviors. They must embrace personal accountability, and through spirited mentorship enjoy lives made anew, productive, and socially compatible. Young people from within the inner city and those from rural america must disavow themselves of the drug and gang culture, embrace faith-based teachings, and believe in themselves while allowing themselves to be guided toward the good. They must likewise be empowered to pull themselves upward as social stewards rather than seeing themselves as victims of the system. They must realize that they control their respective destinies and present themselves as enviable paradigms of rightful and just behaviors, all the while revering our national ensign, the same cloth that many set ablaze and trampled underfoot.

DEFINING YOURSELF NOT BY THE OBVIOUS BUT RATHER BY THE POSSIBLE

Some will say, "Tragedy forestalls progress; reeling in retreat, we may go under." True, but on a pilgrim's progress, the way forward will be wrought with the apparent insurmountable and stubborn challenges. One may stumble and one may wonder, but if strength can be mustered, made better, stronger, refined, using one's mind and relying on one's heart, prevailing onward, one's efforts will yield to a triumph of the will. The way along life's journey will prove to be a test of intellect, ability, endurance, and faith. Linked, these attributes form an unshakable bond, enabling progress, perhaps at times without ease, making headway along one's determined course in life as an end state of ambition. Truer still, there are no guarantees in life; but with focus and grit, a positive trajectory is possible when we couple perseverance with altruism, serving selflessly for the betterment of society.

We are stronger than we believe, yet our vision can be made opaque by narcissism and self-idolization. When we look beyond ourselves, a world appears that enables personal growth through the service of others. A Sailor once asked me, "How far is beyond, and if life is beyond our line of sight, what can be seen?" A person is made complete when faith is incorporated into one's persona, for with faith, there exists a light in a dark world. In the words of Martin Luther, "Faith is permitting ourselves to be seized by the things we do not see." With faith, we pursue goals not blindly, but rather with purpose and resolve, enabling us to see the path ahead.

Recent events have shaken society and strained the fabric of our nation. Building tensions, economic malaise, acts of violence, and reactionary behaviors by individuals among our diverse cultural composition strain our social configuration. Quick to define these sociopathic acts, psychological maladies are often identified. Not to discredit the application of science or theorem, I believe that evil is among us and motivating individuals to act out against established norms and values. Yet, I know also that goodness is far mightier than wickedness. Though such heinous acts may strain social cohesion, it is goodness that will prevent our communities from being torn apart.

I further believe that we must define ourselves without the use of hyphens, rather believing that we are foremost united as Americans. We must forgo diverse causes and focus upon our national identity, recognizing that the true flag to revere is our Old Glory. Our enemies view our diversity as emblematic of fissures in our nation's foundation. Only with a unity of purpose, abiding by the rule of law, respecting authority, and embracing a united identity as Americans can we shore up and repoint the foundation of our nation. Considering the immortal words of Abraham Lincoln, who stated, "A house divided against itself cannot stand"; this profound sentiment must resound today for among us are people listening to both delusion and derision.

Concerned about the future, a Sailor recently asked me, "Sir, given the economic uncertainties, what currency must I hold, and how should I invest?" The discussion centered upon our military ethos of service, integrity, and respect. I told this Sailor, "The best currency to hold is one's technological and tactical skillsets, maintaining proficiency in expanding technical applications in an ever-demanding environment. With this, you will invest in yourself—and when you do, your service will pay dividends forward to shipmates, the Navy, the nation, and the world community." All too often we lose focus while at other times we focus on the obvious; relatively few are the times that we choose to focus on the possibilities, though. Why? Because hard work, sacrifice, perseverance, and the likely temporary setback stalls the progress of many when it is easier to seek quick dividends for oneself. National policies often become deferred due to divergent interests and past grievances, distrust, or discord. By investing in ourselves in order to pay dividends forward, thereby benefiting not a select group or an alliance among dissenters, rather, we must put aside the hyphen and see our efforts advancing a united republic: "One nation, under God, with liberty, and justice for all" for all Americans. Furthermore, we must forgo finger pointing and barbed comments and extend a compassionate hand; for we are Americans who must be united by nationalistic pride by a focused ambition and altruism, dedicated to lifting up this great nation as our citizenry believes again in the unprecedented possibilities.

A COMPARATIVE OF CONVERSION

July 27, 2015

It is far better to offer an olive branch than a vine of thorns. I often enter into discussion concerning events of the world and the difficulties that we as a nation and world community face. Broached are topics concerning economics, politics and religion, and the growing threats that we face. Discussions will inevitably shift to the increasingly savage attacks perpetrated by the radical elements fueled by theology and hate.

When we examine the stark differences between "us" and "them," it is apparent that the fanatical ideology of those who subscribe to the radical tenets is diametrically different to our own way of thinking and of living. We the People delight in life, focus on our future, see ourselves made better for our families, stand united to deliver a benevolent hand to those in need, give of ourselves to aid a neighbor, and unite as a community recognizing our differences. We are bound to rally and support one another for we are Americans.

Enemies of humanity worship death. They see the here and now as bleak. Militaristic are they, bent on punishment, savagery, and enslavement. Our enemy disparages rivals, demonizes dissent, and through fear dictates over those who fall under its dark shadow. They are a blood cult, which through viciousness seek to impose its ideology upon those who see advantage in a gaining storm. Their mantra is "convert or die."

Our refrain is "convert and thrive"! But do we demand theological conversion? Do we crucify those that reject an olive branch? Of course not! Convert? Yes, to a humanistic view of tolerance, inclusion, and incorporation, the right to pursue one's passion in life, all the while accepting ideological differences. Through open-minded cultural assimilation, we offer the blessings of America, whereby each of the citizenry is free to love and live, worship by choice, and pursue their dreams.

We the People subscribe to the rule of law; while accepting our flaws we accept that through amendment of behaviors as it is with the law.

We the People will define a better way of jurisprudence and life for all amicably.

We the People value truthfulness while our enemies honor deceitfulness when dealing with those who subscribe to a different theology.

We the People are fair, and as we honor our Judeo-Christian heritage, we believe in the tenets of life, liberty, and the pursuit of happiness; the right to worship as we choose; the right to assemble with the knowing that the US Constitution provides for our collective and individual rights. Because We the People are so blessed, we shall not be overtaken by tyrants, nor yoked by despots, and live according to our choices as we live for the betterment and benefit of society.

We the People decide our own destiny, not through armed conflict and brutality, but rather through a peaceful revolution; we vote and thus we empower those to serve the greater good of our society while willing to aid and assist those who endure the burden of totalitarians.

We the People believe in a noble effort and offer our enemies a pathway to modernity and prosperity. And, though our enemy seeks to discredit us and seek to exploit us, rational people know in their hearts that our way is a better path, a pathway to personal prosperity, where compassion and dignity and equal rights for all define unprecedented opportunity.

This is why Islamists seek to pull asunder and seek to raise the black flag, demand that we bow down, command that we convert or die. These jihadists offer empowerment to those who advocate death and despair, demands submission, reject constitutional law, and fuel their blood lust on the suffering of the weak and those they deem undesirable, which includes those of their faith who do not subscribe to violent extremism. Our military is focused upon rules of engagement, limiting needless casualties, while offering quarter to the enemy who are no longer combatants. Our military will sacrifice themselves for others so that others can live. Islamists are focused on the suffering of innocents and a maniacal fascination with death.

Above all, and in comparison, what radical Islam cannot offer is that which We the People freely offer all: hope and humanity, charity and optimism, as we extend a bounty of blessings. And, rather than the wicked nightmare, "We the People" extend the American dream.

LIFE IN THE BALANCE

I am often asked about the way to keep all that life presents in balance. It's interesting that those younger than I should do that, as the older I get, the more visibly pronounced my gait is when I walk! Yet, to be asked for advice on the life of another is truly a blessing. I take not lightly the confidence they hold in me by those who experience troubles. Sailors will ask me how I handled stressors in life, how when times become overwhelming, when the lives of others were lost, and life seemed impossible did I manage to overcome, bear the weight, see the horizon, and keep moving forward. These Sailors are often taken aback by the one-word answer received. Believing that perhaps a long-winded rejoin is about to commence, they receive the word: faith!

It is as if a puzzle is about to be solved, expressions change, and an epiphany occurs, for the Sailors comprehend the meaning, yet long for more. I offer that with faith comes strength; with faith, a life off-kilter can be righted, vison cleared, strength enhanced, and those things once thought improbable can be obtained. Faith is the inner voice, the inner strength, the belief that one can step off in a different direction to obtain a new goal, to be made better, sturdier, resilient, and with faith become one whom others look to, to guide them, to lead them, to in fact make lives better.

All this emerges when we cast off self-doubt, uncertainty, complacency, and denial, that by our own doing we can be remade, enriched, and prosper, becoming more giving, loving, and compassionate, all when we believe. Yet, at times the way ahead is uncertain, and we may be unsure. In the words of Martin Luther King Jr., "Faith is taking the first step even when you don't see the whole staircase." As a boy, there were times when fear caused me to do those things contrary because they were easy, as before me my anxiety was lessened because I could see that which presented a temporary goal.

What I failed to see was the right course. Being afraid of the unknown, my fear caused me pause. For instance, being afraid of the dark and believing something lurked in my darkened bedroom, my grandmother would tell me, "If you're afraid of the dark, just close your eyes and go right in. You'll never see what's there!" Knowing the right way, which demanded more of me, I often chose immediate satisfaction.

Over the years and enduring trial and tribulation, I have become both stronger and wiser and, with a reliance of faith, believe that I am ready for what awaits in life. And, with faith, I know that I have been made better, more resilient, and thus prepared to stand before those under my charge and lead them in the right direction. As we age, the burden of our daily lives increases. Considering the stress of one's job, family responsibilities, social obligations, financial debts, and the inevitable unforeseen, our lives can become offset. We come to look upon life as a lever where perhaps a loved one's failing health, an unexpected expense, or ever-changing ambitions of children, or possibly a crisis in midlife results in a broadened staff of life. So then, what about the necessary fulcrum? How do we right a life off-kilter?

It is faith that enables the proper balance to our burdens. It is faith that permits people to overcome addictions, repair relationships, and soften a hardened heart. It is faith that enables people to surmount the insurmountable. It is faith that enables the stricken to be healed. It is faith that spurs people along when matters weigh them down and with doubt having blurred one's vision; it is faith that enables us to see clearly. And, when times are overwhelming and we are heavily burdened, when we are haunted by the past, and we think that the only way is to end it all, there is another way, a better way before you. For some, the war fought is far from over. Though far from past battles, their fight continues to draw them in. Faith empowers a belief in a finer day.

Once hopeless, the hapless remade, and from the dark, there is light. Faith heals a hardened heart. Faith enables one to breathe the freshness of a new day and, once transformed, extend a hand to a brother or sister in need.

AFTER ALL, NOT SO MUCH

With the change of the seasons, we again welcome a waning of daylight, cooler temperatures, and the fall foliage, children returning to school, football season under way, and of course, political theater to amuse us. We go about our days perhaps just as we did last year at this time. Settled into our routine, we seldom notice what is taking place around us. We work, we return home, we run errands, we help with homework, and we are creatures of habit. We're quick to notice a gray hair or a new wrinkle but seldom do we notice that extra five pounds; and if we do, we're quick to find the sweatpants, not to engage in cardiovascular routine, but rather find comfort as we settle down for another supersized bowl of ice cream!

Yes, I too am guilty of this. Quick to point to the faults of others, we seldom look at ourselves with such a critical eye. We go about our daily lives without sighting the peripherals. Are we so entranced by our own lives as to overlook the obvious? I tell my granddaughter, "As you observe the world before you and around you, there is much more to see than what you sight with your own eyes." Presented here are questions that puzzle me daily and perhaps due to events, such as the commencement of the election cycle or the recent blood moon that caused me concern. Why are we so passionate about "our" teams of sport, yet so ambivalent to the needs of homeless in our own communities? Why do we focus on the lives of celebrity, yet overlook the needs of our veterans, where reportedly 300,000 have died waiting for treatment and twenty-two veterans commit suicide each day? Why is that we expect others to behave in accordance with what is vogue, yet excoriate those who are called upon to live a life of devotion to faith? Why do we pay good money to watch the debasement of society depicted in film yet turn away or dismiss the actual savage events with ridicule? Why do we, a society of liberty, dismiss a radical theology that espouses the subjugation of its people and teaches that the rule of law is subservient, yet ridicule those who speak out against it as bigots and xenophobic? Why do we dismiss the persecution of members of faith leading to humanitarian crises yet fail to recognize when a life truly begins? Why have we dismissed that which identifies us as Americans with a border that is breached daily often in plain sight? Why have we become so polarized on issues, yet there is little outcry as the Pledge of Allegiance is altered? Why have many among us become so narcissistic as to focus on self rather than selflessly serve others? Why do many among us identify with celebrity, their vulgarity, and those who desecrate the symbol of a country that offers unprecedented opportunity, and quick are they to derail the principles of our great nation, a nation that affords the ways and means to achieve and prosper? And, yes, why do drivers in Virginia who know that a red traffic signal means STOP dismiss it all, knowing what is right, what is safe, and what the law is!

In the words of the immortal Yogi Berra, "You can observe a lot by just watching!" Yet, why are so many among us blind to their surroundings? What is needed is a reformation and a reaffirmation of our nation's guiding principles. We must consider ourselves as Americans—yes, a compassionate nation, yet a nation where the rule of law applies to all whether you consider your home your kingdom or your city a sanctuary. We must consider an ethos of sincerity, forgoing greed and corruption. For no greater personal reward comes from your entrepreneurial spirit than having earned it "the hard way," thereby setting the enviable example for others to emulate.

We must accept that along life's progress, we will inevitably fail; our struggle problematic, yet with ambition, determination, and resolve, the struggle is conquerable. With faith, one's pilgrimage through life must be considered as not a singular event. As we navigate the trials and travails in life, our actions are seen by many. We then are afforded a chance to present a paradigm for others to emulate. With faith, with patriotism, compassion, and a true sense of purposeful and selfless civic duty, our efforts and obligations will yield a society that finds favor in who we are vice mired with envy and selfishness.

RECONSIDERING TWO QUESTIONS

Several years ago, I authored a memorandum titled, "Two Questions to Ask Yourself." Over the course of my career, I have been asked a myriad of questions by Sailors considering the way ahead. Often, Sailors hope to learn of their role in the Navy, associated travel and exotic ports of call, specific experiences, and related service opportunities. They expect to be told of the adventure, the encounters, and the benefits, and not of the perils and pitfalls. My conversations will always concentrate on the unforeseen rather than the empirical benefits that will certainly befall them. I tell them that their goals are often shortsighted and they must sharply focus on the "blurred object." In the Navy, goals like targets are far off; and at this early point in their careers, what awaits them is unimaginable. This, of course, is a quandary for many, as they must consider the possibilities long before reality materializes. More often than occasionally, Sailors have asked me two specific questions that cause me to delve deeply in retrospection. And, at my age reflecting upon years gone by, my memory too seems to focus upon a "blurred object"!

Provided are the two questions that I am often asked. The first: "Given your career, do you hold any regrets?" My answer today, as it was several years ago, is a resounding "Yes, I do." I regret at times not working hard enough, not working longer into the night, and remaining at rest when others woke, at times being selfish and occasionally not thinking of others while focused on myself rather than concentrating on the needs of those I was charged to lead. My goodness, have I not exposed personal inconsistencies and shortcomings? Yes, of course I have. Yet, know that because of those times that I have fallen short of what I expected of myself, it is what I do today that inspires me to do more. In fact, the purpose of this memo is to forward a personal contract to many denoting my sentiments of service, how to serve others, and for whom do I serve. I hold to the notion that if I lose my focus, someone will surely remind me of what I have written, that which I have embraced, and declare me less the man that I profess to be. In time, I surely would rather be remembered for the effort expended to achieve than that which I could have achieved but thought better not to apply myself. Yet, the one great regret that I hold is that my parents were not able to see me as I am today, which prompts the ideal that one must always be at their best for life is fleeting.

The second question was, "Given your religious beliefs, how do you justify what you do in support of the global war?" My answer as it was and as it remains today: "Those who are enemies do not have to be!" Those who conspire to again do us harm, to once more slaughter the innocent, to cripple America and then revel in the agony that their conspiracy wreaks have acknowledged that they are the enemy of our nation. Because of their actions, they must be dealt with accordingly. We are a peace-loving people who champion the rights of all people. America has extended the benevolence of her people to those who were once our enemies. We seek not to incorporate those who differ intrinsically from us but rather to enable the poor, disadvantaged, and the needy while assisting fledgling governments in defining for themselves a better way of coexistence. The enemy of America, once no longer able to carry the fight, is assured that they will receive the care and kindness that America provides for its own. We hold true to the doctrine of war, yet we also subscribe to the laws of armed conflict. Radicals, extremists, and zealots seek to punish, cripple, and inflict merciless injury upon all Americans. The enemy of America employs a corrupt ideology while conspiring to impart fear in order to target those they wish only to further subjugate. Our enemies denounce America's Judeo-Christian heritage and mock adherence to the rule of law, yet are quick to cite constitutional provisions when it profits them. America employs a measured response seeking to end hostilities while incorporating the amelioration and emancipation of the indigenous who have suffered for all too long under the sway of enemies of humanity. My faith empowers and enables me to extend myself to those who welcome the deliverance that our benevolent efforts provide. My regret here is that I have yet to become "a man for all seasons" for those I love and for those I serve. Yet, this is one objective I trust that will always remain a daily focal point.

WHAT IS THIS BLURRED OBJECT?

November 25, 2015

Contained within the lines of last month's memo, I wrote about conversations with Sailors, the focus of which "will always concentrate on the unforeseen rather than the empirical benefits that will certainly befall them." I tell them that their goals are often short-sighted and that they must sharply focus on the "blurred object." Such is not a terminal statement, but rather one that I trust will stimulate further conversation. Often, I am directly asked to define the "blurred object" of my own focus. As each of us views life differently, we see things in our own way. We focus on our personal pursuits to satisfy our immediate needs. We look to the future and fantasize about a better life, a life of prestige, a life of obtainment, a life of satisfaction. Yet, with fantasy, we momentarily see life complete, though in reality many of us would never be satisfied as hedonism, greed, and consumption would spur us along without noticing the blessings as bestowed.

For many, the famed Rolling Stones lyrics rings true: "I can't get no satisfaction, 'cause I try, and I try, and I try, and I try." With fantasy, we do not see the labor, sacrifice, and inevitable failure, the doubt and the hope, and the herculean effort necessary to reach this state of blissful fulfilment. For many, the blurred object is in fact the journey rather than the end state of their desires. Reflecting on political theater from a few years ago, a prominent figure stated, "We have to sign the bill to see what's in it." I can think of no better example akin to a "blurred object"!

At times, life is like a toothache. When the pangs of pain throb, we put off, we attempt to ignore, we seek momentary relief, and we chew on the other side. Yet, the longer the delay, the greater the decay! For many, the dentist is the blurred object. Long before I entered the military service, the local dentist that I sought relief from was parallel to Orin Scrivello, the sadistic dentist as portrayed in the movie, *Little Shop of Horrors*. Believe me, to this date, that dentist is no blurred object!

In response to a young Sailor who pointedly asked, "Sir, so tell me what's your blurred object?" I told the Sailor this: my blurred object is my legacy in life. For this reason, I choose to focus on the processes along my journey, for with faith, the end state already is revealed to me. It is better to focus upon the day's journey, and in so doing, I'll walk the proper path. I am focused upon the present, being a better man for those I love and those I lead—faithful, determined, and committed to present an exemplary man through service and family obligations.

In life, however, there are matters that are neither blurred nor intangible. The real and ever-present threat from radicalism must be focused upon. Vicious hordes—using both technology and the media to forward their sinister methods of subjugation, persecution, and murder—recruit from among the disenfranchised and disillusioned youth. As Americans, we must sharpen our focus and resolve to detect, penetrate, and punish those who subscribe to a violent theocratic sect. Since September 2011, thousands of terrorist attacks have been reported from around the world. These assaults have killed hundreds and wounded far many more. What of those who have been brutalized through heinous acts of physical and psychological measures yet remain hidden from the world? Do we truly know the numbers of children forced into sexual servitude or as child soldiers manipulated into bondage? Do we know the numbers of forced religious conversions or the number of crucifixions? These statistics continue to mount. People cry out for they have been forsaken—not by their faith, but by those who have turned a blind eye! With the political reluctance for expanding the role of our armed forces combating this new form of fascism and its affiliates, all of whom are enemies of humanity, I am confident that from within our highly skilled and determined armed forces, members are unreservedly prepared to commit to directly engaging this dreadful enemy. With the United States leading the effort, I am equally confident that a formidable and sizeable international force would be rallied. This force would emerge to take the fight forward to those who scheme and conspire. Lest we forget, we defeated the Third Reich and the Japanese Empire through the use of overwhelming military might and political resolve. Again, the battle cry emerges: "Let's roll." Our force has sworn to uphold and defend against all enemies both foreign and domestic. Extremist bands have perpetrated attacks within and beyond our borders. Committed to service, I for one am neither ashamed of my beliefs nor afraid, for I am a follower of my faith and a servant to those who are in need. Poised to defend and dispatch those who chant "convert or die," I will not be yoked by tyrants, and I will cast of the chains that would otherwise weigh me down. I am sharply focused on what awaits in life, and though I may not yet be able to see beyond, my faith enables me to proclaim, "Follow me!"

A YEAR IN REVIEW

January 07, 2016

Over the past year, I have written numerous memoranda addressing pressing social issues and human behaviors interwoven with patriotic themes. I have written about confronting terrorism while offering my personal views concerning faith and family, spiritual enlightenment, and rightful and just conduct. And, I've defined the focal point of "the blurred object." Admittedly, I have experienced a faithful awakening and have experienced a multitude of blessings this past year.

I have also noted societal matters that have sparked violence, at times spurred along by provocateurs and anarchists. I have witnessed those among us who are misguided, becoming increasingly narcissistic and petty, those who forgo pulling themselves up by their bootstraps but rather wait idle for another to put their boots on for them. Of course, a metaphor, yet many among us have opted for government intervention and assistance rather than inculcating the rewarding principle of hard work and embracing an entrepreneurial ethos. Over the past months, I have been overjoyed by what I've seen and experienced in my life yet, at times, saddened by perhaps my parochial view. So, I have committed to reading at least a book a month, advancing academic interests while fostering a worldly maturity in order to appreciate the indigenous mindset, while beginning to strategize postmilitary pursuits of continued public service, eager to continue to serve, yet not getting too far beyond tomorrow and recalling what my father would from time to time tell me, "Butch, if you prefer extraordinary vision, you must keep an eye on the path ahead and watch where you're going." In retrospection, I enjoyed many high points with family this past year and, of course, time spent with my granddaughter. I watched with amazement as she continued to broaden the way she views the world. Yet, unbeknownst to her, I've observed citizens act contrary to reason and strike out at society. With cities ablaze and racism and bigotry exposed, I recall my youth during the tumultuous 1960s and hope that our nation does not recoil to days of similar political and social unrest. As a nation, we must embrace in totality, "We the People." United in purpose, we must rejoin those on the fringe, perhaps outcasts, while addressing those who purposefully seek to pull asunder.

For instance, I recently attended a holiday gathering where the festive atmosphere included karaoke. During the evening, a young man took microphone in hand and interjected racial slurs and profane verbiage that to the ethnic assemblage, of which I was in the minority, should have involved disdain, but garnered no negative response. Though a sign of the times, I was saddened that no elder rebuked the young man. Coincidently, the day after Christmas, I found myself in a convenience store where I observed a patron insulting the cashier during a one-sided heated exchange concerning a rightful free cup of coffee! After several minutes of reprimand, the patron departed, only to drive away in a late-model foreign coupe! So much for a time of peace on earth and goodwill to all! With dysfunctional political machines and their favor for theater, with political correctness meant to realign through emotional wrangling, with the enemies of humanity conspiring here and abroad, with members of all faiths persecuted while those who trespass are afforded sanctuary and not prosecuted, when human rights activists fail to speak out against extremism and world leaders purport to take the moral high ground, while extremists slaughter those they determine to be inferior, it is the downtrodden, the weak, and those considered inferior, who are subjected to inhumanity.

As revisionists seek to distort the history of our republic, I affirm my pledge to support and defend; and following my life's path, the guiding tenets being love, faith, and hope, I am lifted up, enabled to serve with compassion those here and abroad. In so doing, I think of the victims and consider their families and seek justice for the weak. This has been a year that has deeply troubled me. With social upheaval, racial tension, the surge of fanaticism, and attacks on the homeland, I ponder the future while thinking about those among us who are touched by tragedy. In times of trouble, I rally personal convictions and consider the daunting burdens faced by our leaders. May they sharpen their focus on the true root cause of our suffering and determine the best course to address tragedy while redressing the enemies of humanity and the evil perpetrated against us. Given the year in review, we can hope for an end to partisan political games-manship as those in our communities and our nation remain in our thoughts and, for those so inclined, in prayer. Considering ourselves as "We the People," let it be that we find ourselves empowered to better the days ahead as we resolve to rejoin as one nation united.

LIFTED UP BY MY UPBRINGING

Blessed was I having been raised in a loving home and being spiritually nurtured, I yearned to emulate righteous familial examples. Acquiring an entrepreneurial spirit, a good education, and employment opportunities, a deep-rooted patriotic ethos enabled me. My mother sought spiritual enlightenment for me as I accompanied her to different houses of worship. And, because of my upbringing, later in life I would teach Sunday school at the church for which to this day I continue to hold a deep affinity. My father instilled in me a conservative political sense. I was taught that the rule of law was in place to hold society together while our faith acted as moral cohesion, though with a definitive separation of church and state.

Through my years of trial and tribulation and my journeys that took me to many foreign lands, this conjoined balance between law and religion properly guided me. Coupled with a patriotic sense as an exemplar of selfless service, I have extended the benevolence of America while offering the best in me to those whose needs remain greater than my own. I learned that as Americans, we are a proud lot. As circumstance dictates, we forward assistance both at home and abroad. America is seen as many things to many people. Some see America as a beacon of hope; others whose vision made opaque by contempt see America through hate-filled eyes. Most accept American values; others are determined to undermine.

Over the years, I have been taught that Judaism, Christianity, and Islam can be traced back to Abraham. Each espouses divine tenets of human behaviors that forward and define their respective societies. Over the centuries, reasonableness and reformation have transformed particular communities of faith, championing inclusion and tolerance, science and technology, all the while accepting modernity. Americans welcome change that enriches their lives, broadens outlook, and enlivens our societies while the tenets of our respective faiths remain foundational in times of change, providing guideposts as we make progress along our individual pilgrimage. During the course of our lives, we mature, are socialized, become educated, and become worldly, all the while adhering to societal norms as we assimilate and become members of a collective society. Members of my own family have immigrated to America for a better life. Though the assimilation is not easy, with the help of family, the rule of law, and the tenets of faith, they acquiesce; and within time, family members become productive and resourceful, respectful of their new home, culture, and social scene. As I was taught, they too accept both the rule of law while relying on their faith. The overarching theme is, of course, "do onto others as you would have them do unto you." Following the tenets of faith and the rule of law, there will be, however, no vengeful reciprocity against the one who transgresses against them. In an era of political transformation and certainly political theater, the news of the day is often highlighted by headlines of war and terror, the flow of migrants seeking refuge, and the scourge of extremism. News reports of waves of migrants longing for asylum have focused upon the cruelty left behind, the hardships of the journey, and the hopes and dreams for a better life. Coming to America has been the dream of countless immigrants who in return fabricated every sector of our society, ultimately building America as Franklin D. Roosevelt penned the "Arsenal of Democracy." The transformative experience from both a personal and societal sense is evident as the American dream became a reality.

Our America is not a utopia. We have lived through our own turbulent times. There have been injustices, there have been inequities and racism, and xenophobia has plagued our society. Still, the founding fathers enacted the Declaration of Independence to rebuke tyrannical rule. Americans ratified the Bill of Rights and abolished slavery while championing both human and civil rights as America welcomed immigrants who likewise desired to realize their dreams of a better life. Considering American attributes and the unprecedented opportunities, why then are there those whose hatred is so malignant that they scheme to kill innocent citizens and people of faith? Why then are there those who rail against our constitutional republic and the rule of law? Why do some wish to retreat into enclaves where hatred, misogyny, homophobia, and dehumanization become infectious while advocating a vengeful ideology that has yet to be reformed? Rather than assimilation, why do some rally with vicious intent bent on debasing society rather than transforming themselves? Intemperate zealotry is a malignancy that requires immediate and acute handling in order to effect eradication. Military action may isolate this plague; it will, however, take concerted governmental and faith-based initiatives to effect needed reformative remedies in order to influence change that will morally, ethically, and spiritually change the mindset of those most at risk of radicalization by an ideology of venomous hate.

LOOKING AHEAD, MOVING FORWARD!

Having completed yet another deployment spending seven months at sea, I returned home and renewed my dedication to put my thoughts to paper. As I returned home and with the election season over, I find myself recommitted to forwarding my thoughts, ever mindful of not becoming overly strident or partisan in the opinions that are conveyed. Over the past months, controversy begot controversy, and a downturn spiral of decorum resulted. With political one-sidedness intensifying, the social divide during the 2016 elections truly defined the divisiveness that permeates our society. I spent many hours reading books authored by spiritual leaders, academics, and individuals whose unique experiences truly elevated my understanding of the misfortunes of the world. Having served multiple tours of duty in combat environments since September 2001, I have been compelled to know more of my enemy beyond the cursory "us versus them" mindset. During discussions that often became debates, I presented findings and facts. Inconceivable to some while to others my thoughts were determined to be phobic, yet presented as indisputable specifics, my quest to enlighten has been personally rewarding. As advocates for social justice obscured the realities of a determined enemy, a utopia based upon inclusion and unity comprised the acceptance of unreasonable risks as their visionless movement became the hallmark of a campaign. The ideals of utopia masked the realities of our enemy's intolerance, tyranny, and inconceivable brutality while they rallied for the downfall of democratic societies and foundational doctrines based upon inalienable rights.

As a boy and later as a young man, I've witnessed episodes of social upheaval and seminal events that included political assassinations, the Vietnam War, men walking on the moon and an aerospace tragedy, the end of the Cold War, the Gulf War, the rise of transnational terrorist groups, and the tragedy that occurred on September 11, 2001. I have witnessed political shifts and cultural leanings. I've observed both acceptance and intolerance. And, I've seen the benefit of technology and how it can be misused. From Watergate to WikiLeaks, from a grainy black-and-white television to streaming videos, much has changed over the years. Recently, though, there has been a cultural shift where patriotism is considered antagonistic, where once favored flag waving became a symbol of enmity, and revered heroes stand down rather than standing tall; where positions of authority are now considered symbols of oppression and where criminal behavior is seen as vogue, peaceful dissent has morphed into making space for lawbreakers to loot and burn, all the while readily shifting situational blame to that of privilege rather than that of partisan collusion. Much has changed, but the words of my father remain constant. He once told me, "Butch, have no regrets when looking back and great optimism when looking forward, for those things you dread in your past, may they remain behind you as you enthusiastically consider what with favor awaits."

With the New Year and as we look forward, may we as a nation move in the right direction. I pray that the rancor of the past does not accompany us in the coming months. May our nation find social, political, and economic renewal, and may we consider the rule of law with original intent. We must not waver, holding with certainty that illicit activity must not be sanctioned and that our sanctuary must be as secure as its borders. May we view the unfortunate with respect rather than disdain, and may we fulfill the founding principle of liberty and justice of all yet holding true to that which is regulated by law. And, with a determined resolve, may we focus on countering the evils perpetrated by fanatics whose beliefs are contrary to humankind and with a determined offensive counter their persecutions both here and aboard.

LIFE'S PRECARIOUS MOMENTS

Life is full of precarious moments. As we navigate through life, we face many ups and downs, heartache and heartbreak, tumult and turmoil. How we manage the stress of each day defines us. Yet, we don't do it alone, as there are many who observe our travels and depend upon us to find solutions. As we move forward, others will follow; and as we forge ahead, there will be those who will be rallied to take upon themselves to follow and to eventually surpass. Though achievement may be rich, what defines the travel is the travails overcome along the way.

Years ago while serving in Afghanistan, we were convoying along a hazardous route heading to Kabul when I noticed a group of men involved in demining. These men, who accepted the task to locate and mark landmines for removal, were assigned a plot of ground marked with red and white stones, where they formed a line abreast moving ever so slightly ahead, probing the ground with a nylon dowel. Once the landmine was identified, the location was marked and the individual then continued moving forward. Wearing a helmet, face shield, and ballistic vest, these men sit on the ground inching forward ever so slowly.

A daunting endeavor, estimates cite well over 600,000 mines laid over decades of war throughout Afghanistan. I have seen movies that depict a soldier who stepped on a mine and, suddenly realizing the threatening position, contemplates what to do next. For many, I presume what comes next is prayer as antipersonnel mines are designed to maim. Over the years of service, I have seen many locals in Afghanistan who have been victims of landmines. Of all ages, hobbling on crutches or by wheeled cart, their wounds truly never heal. Yet, considering the service of the demining personnel, I can think of no more a precarious position than to realize that you are perhaps sitting on a landmine. Certainly, this is an occupation with little room for error!

Surely not diminishing individuals involved in demining efforts, each of us will from time to time find ourselves in precarious situations and smack dab in an occasional emotional minefield. It has been said, "Life marches on" and so must we. At best, we strive to keep lockstep along the way, yet we must be aware of where we place the next step. There will be impediments, there will be obstacles, and there will be challenges along the way. Yes, there will be hazards that could cause the loss of life or limb. With a sharpened focus and committed resolve, however, continuing onward while experiencing upheavals and collapse that test our mettle and try our resolve, our progress forward will define our pledge to defend and our compassion to those in need. As we move forward, it is essential that we cannot lose sight of others. As we advance, we forge a way ahead for those that will follow. For those who admire us, we must do so with professionalism, with dignity, and with kindness. For those who choose to be our enemies, we must dispatch our might rightly and justly; and for those who choose to lay down their arms, we will enable for them a better way, a pathway defined by our goodwill, consideration, and kindheartedness in order to redefine from those once disadvantaged a fruitful life.

Along our path, we must maintain a sharp focus. All too often, when being impatient, we outpace ourselves and at times lose our way. At other times, we may consider and follow a shortcut that causes us to become lost. There is a difference between a shortcut and a detour, however. A detour is designed to return us to our original trek. A shortcut may lead us to a dead end. Often, Sailors will ask me about the proper way. Young Sailors are habitually impatient and want immediate results. I tell them, "Life's achievements do not occur by the flick of a switch." Life is defined by self-reliance, persistence, tenacity, overcoming disappointment, and moving ahead beyond failure. It is uncomfortable for many and distressing for some to embrace failure as a necessity in defining self. True, failure can be embarrassing, disappointing, and at times especially painful. Some say, "So what, that's life, get on with it!" In life, we all define ourselves by our misfortune, as it is what others remember most. Some will taunt you and others will ridicule you because of it. Yet, because of one's faith and resilience, far more will salute you for overcoming and ultimately succeeding as you set an enviable example of navigating through life's inevitable minefields with grace.

THE NEED FOR DIRECTION

How often do we ask one another, "How's it going?" without offering the time to sit and listen to a lengthy reply? Terse questions habitually demand brief answers. As we navigate our personal day-to-day journey, we have life's calculus on our minds. And, as we swipe the next screen on our smartphones, we focus our attention to the plight of another on a four-inch display rather than what lay before us in the expanse of life. Some may ask, "What's going on?" Do we really expect in-depth analysis, or accept as customary "get to the point" and move on? We're caught in a cycle of work, errands, play, and daily demands that yield at the end of the day most interactions in recollection to be faint. We move forward, but do we make progress?

The answer is of course yes, as we move along to another day in the journey of life albeit likely indistinct with many personal interactions unclear: overlooked and often dismissed, perhaps an extended hand pushed aside rather than embraced or possibly an essential act of kindness disregarded, while those in need were unjustly dismissed. As life offers unprecedented service opportunities, we often ignore the occasion to present the best in ourselves to those who need our better nature. Bothered by the needs of others, compassion is negated where it is at times needed most. Life requires careful planning, and as we reckon for ourselves, we often employ the skill of others. We should not, however, demand from our advisers the course that our lives will take. Having sought guidance, take ownership of life, and step forward knowing that your efforts are of your own design. Viewing life with an entrepreneurial spirit, we pull ourselves up to another station.

As you do, presented is another question to ponder: are you not obligated to bring others forward? Yet, we are not sheep that follow one ahead, even as those forward are falling from a precipice. The need to plan accordingly should be evident; though considering life's journey before us, we do not know how far beyond the inevitable exists. And, as we make our way, the need for shepherding is unmistakable. As written by German philosopher Martin Heidegger, "The human being is not the lord of beings, but the shepherd of being." As we advance and plan ahead, it is with faith that we entrust our way into the unknown and for many the unimaginable. As leaders, then, being purposefully proactive, shepherd those under your charge; for there are wolves circling the pack. Here, then, is the question that we should be asking ourselves and others: "Where are you going?"

As we go, we can see only so far. It is often said, "To the horizon, twelve miles; with elevation, somewhat farther." What lies beyond is the unknown. Often, Sailors ask for advice concerning their careers, and of course I formulate my answer based on what is known and how I made my way, albeit during an earlier and less complicated time. As I provide guidance, I offer with optimism that the best way to look beyond when crafting a plan is to consider taking the high ground to see afar. And, with faith, we are inspired to plan well ahead; with hope, we can see the journey through. With complex matters to be faced today, surely we need less wringing of hands and more hope, less diversion, and more devotion. Rather than our focus being self-centered, we should be attentive to purposeful selfless service that rewards others.

Occasionally, I've met young men and women who are hapless and others who appear void of hope. Looking for inclusion, recognition, and gain, attempting to suppress past transgressions, often they look to the wrong people or places for relief and benefit. The path to success is before them; though the way is hard, consuming, and at times wrought with peril, the route to personal success has been etched by those who have rightly gone before. I offer Sailors the following: "Where are you going?" From the outset, plan ahead with a sharpened focus—although be it colorblind—void of bias, accept the advice and counsel of those successful and who will prepare for you a proper way to attain success. Choose your mentors carefully, and heed their advice and counsel. In return, I offer a simple truth: if you sharpen your focus and step rightly forward, work hard and with patience, sacrifice, and commitment, then conviction and hope will reward you and get you where you're going. With a course plotted, tread headlong into the unknown faithfully and always in the right direction.

BUILDING UPON YOUR
PERSONAL CORNERSTONE

That which stands is enabled by a foundation, and that which is infirm cannot stand for very long. Each of us has been raised in a particular way and shaped by our circumstance: by our parents, our adolescent trials and tribulations, our schooling, and social interactions. Influences both good and bad, success and misfortune, what we rally around, and those things we avoid define the people that we are. As we mature and reach adulthood, we are defined by all that has been in our lives. Our identities are an amalgam of the personalities who have directly influenced us and those whom we wished to be. Some begin their adult journey in life sooner than others while circumstance—perhaps good fortune and at times tragedy—nudge us forward. At a particular point in life, we leave behind childish ways and accept what life holds in store. We dwell on the past while setting plans for the future. Life requires each of us to be vocationally astute as we build a life day by day. Like a mason who places a single brick one atop another, what results is an architecturally greater sum of its parts. Yet, there is much more to a finished structure than brick alone; much of what reinforces the entirety of the construction is seldom seen. Regardless of the enormity of the structure, it is the foundation that reinforces the whole; most importantly, it is the cornerstone upon which all else rests.

Sailors often ask me about my career and my rise through the ranks. Recently, a Sailor asked me at a forum to describe how I navigated my career to that of a Master Chief Petty Officer. I surprised this Sailor as I attributed my success less on my intelligence but directly to my commitment to serve selflessly, my commitment to volunteer for the tough assignment, and my commitment to readily accept orders that perhaps others reel from. Though we are all different, with different ideals and norms, our aspirations are similar. Each of us strives for success. As the Navy is a mixture of divergent individuals, disparate values must be aligned, and polarized beliefs, morals, and principles united. Tenets of sacrifice, resolve, and united effort may be foreign to those who have been tainted through narcissism and selfish pursuits. Each Sailor must be transformed and enlightened through a proven process that enables an individual to look beyond themselves. United in purpose, invested in the service of others, and with a sharpened focus, each Sailor learns that they are a necessary and valued asset; and unified in uniform, we defend all that our citizenry holds dear. It is the legacy of those who have gone before and those who serve today that provides for an establishment of service from which the new accession Sailor measures their personal best efforts. As Sailors, our foundation is our core values: Honor, Courage, and Commitment.

As a boy, I was blessed with loving parents who provided for all of my needs. I grew up in a wonderful place that shaped me. I was influenced mostly by my father who taught me much, and as a boy, I wanted to be him. My father would tell me, "Without a foundation you'll never stand, and in life you must stand firm." What I learned from my father is the foundation that I stand upon today. Throughout my life, it has been the faith in the Father that has been the cornerstone of my life's foundation. And, in life, as we venture far, we will eventually return to our roots. As we grow older, the breadth of who we are expands. With life comes joy, woe, good times, bad times, times of elation, and days of sorrow. We will be tested by circumstance and by happenstance. We soon realize that things will not always go according to our design. Life is hard and not without dilemma or drama. We will be rattled and we will be shaken, perhaps to our very core. A certainty in life, heartaches will befall us. And, in life, there are no guarantees. There are many eventualities in life, yet only one certain inevitability. Life is defined by the way in which you live it.

As we age, we assume greater familial and financial responsibilities. We must balance all that life offers as we steadily make our way through it. With the demands of military service, stability is essential as it brings certainty during uncertain times. Over the years, I have endured my share of challenges and I have withstood the eventual storm due to the foundation laid in my youth. In reflection, the words of my father resound today: "Without a foundation you'll never stand, and in life you must stand firm." Yet, what upholds my personal foundation is a cornerstone based upon my faith. As you build upon your personal foundation, ensure that your footing is firm and that your faith is strong; and as you face all that is in store, resilience will reward those who seek your counsel and whom you are charged to lead.

"COURAGE IS FOUND IN
UNLIKELY PLACES"

Days of divisiveness are upon us. The rancor and bitterness that is spewed forth is not easily ignored, and for many readily accepted as truth. In my life, I have seen much, though I must admit that these are truly days that discourage me. Often some say, "How did we get here and where did this come from?" The lack of awareness and analytical thinking is the systemic cause of the malaise in which we find ourselves. Many accept hypotheticals because often what they are told is forwarded by celebrities, marketers, and partisans. Many more accept the vulgar rants of late-night personalities and strident political figures that by virtue of luck and happenstance are in a position to promulgate their opinionated narratives as fact. The "us versus them" mentality has overtaken reason. There exists a breach between rival factions that threatens to widen by the day.

But what must be done to prevent an irrevocable chasm from developing? Not much can be seen by those who bury their heads in the sand. Needed is a unifying vision, coupled with analytical thought, and an end to the dismantling of a civil society. My father would tell me, "Butch, bootstraps are meant to be pulled up by the wearer." Today, however, many among us expect to have their boots both polished and pulled on by someone else. Yet, while hard work and entrepreneurialism, sacrifice, toil, and labor are increasingly considered outdated, chauvinistic, and even systemically unfair, the result is a lessening of standards and trophies for everyone. I believe that as a nation we must realign our national priorities and impede the onslaught of disunion brought about by power-hungry and fast-talking carny barkers in thousand-dollar suits and unruly hooligans with masked faces. If we do not, the cultural tone of intolerance, insolence, and crudeness will only continue to increase. Needed are those among us who wish to serve selflessly and with compassion, those who are focused on the needs of others. Needed today are individuals whose intent is to serve purposefully, forgoing personal advantage. Strident polarity must be overcome with a focus and embracing inclusion—recognizing differences while encouraging a union of civility.

All too often, subscription to radical ideals that demonize opposition and label those whose perceived challenge as being phobic are quick to debase, demoralize, and marginalize. As Americans, we must rally to merge divergent views rather than segregate through intimidation and delegitimization of our opposition. It takes courage to rightly stand where others might back away and in so doing define oneself as a leader whereby character, integrity, and humbleness become influential standards for others to emulate. And, it is our youth who are the most influenced by the behaviors of others.

Recently I enjoyed school lunch with my granddaughter. As her class approached the cafeteria, I could see all eyes looking at my uniform. I could see that my granddaughter beamed with pride as her papa waited for her. As she approached, I took note of a message inscribed on her shirt: "Courage is found in unlikely places." First penned by English professor and poet J. R. R. Tolkien, the phrase is a resounding reminder of what is needed today to realign and inspire individuals to a proper path. Courage is synonymous with strength, and both personal attributes are instinctual within an individual. Courage and strength define character and are essential traits of a leader. Many may ponder if they can muster the requisite courage and strength when defining situations demand. From my experiences in life, both courage and strength must be developed over time—and yet it is likely that there will be seminal moments when we truly learn the depth and breadth of each.

Such defining moments are opportunities to stand tall in the face of adversity and convey with dignity and decorum perhaps in an unpopular position. In the immortal words of American revolutionary Thomas Paine, "These are the times that try men's souls." Certainly given today's acrimonious political and social environment, where antisocial and lewd behavior and vulgar speech have become common and where subversive propaganda is no longer whispered in back rooms but forwarded throughout social networks, where destructive behaviors are celebrated, and where violence is considered obligatory personal expressions, where disrespect for authority is vogue, and where the rule of law is refuted by elected officials who once affirmed to uphold the very laws that they so overtly repudiate, the act of finger pointing must be superseded by a welcoming extension of a hand in order to reunite, reinvigorate, and move forward in the right direction. In these days, leadership based on faith, hope, dignity, and respect—where courage and strength, joined through compassion and an agenda of graciousness—is absolutely necessary. It is vitally important that youthful eyes, which so often see only a troubled world, may be able to look to the previous generation for an example of rightful and just behavior, defining a fitting pathway in life to follow. Yes, "courage is found in unlikely places." May courage be found within you as you answer the call to selfless and purposeful service to our nation while establishing a leadership paradigm for future generations!

WHAT SHANE CAN TEACH US

June 28, 2017

In life, we often reflect upon our youth and the special moments that shaped the adults that we are today. And, reflect I did, as I recently attended my granddaughter's kindergarten promotion ceremony. While seated in the cafeteria proudly looking at her on the stage, I harkened back to a time when I was seated in the cafeteria of the Port Ewen Elementary School many years ago, where for a special treat the entire school assembled to watch the Academy Award-winning movie and classic western tale *Shane* (1954). That day was over half a century past, and as a young boy, I was captivated by the story of Shane as portrayed by actor Alan Ladd.

Having recalled this memory, I ordered the movie later that weekend, and my granddaughter and I watched as *Shane* once again taught many life lessons. This is a quintessential western, where good people are subjected to intimidation by bad men, only to later be saved by a quiet man who steps forward to rectify the wrongs perpetrated against those outnumbered and outgunned. From the movie, we learn that selflessness transcends servitude, where the defense of the weak enables strength, and humbleness begets humanity. Shane represents the timeless hero whose toil benefits others without fanfare as a modest, quiet professional who, having saved the day, slips off in the distance without the trappings of celebrity.

When people are victimized and terror reigns, when people forced from their lands become exiles by those whose perverted focus on personal gain benefits villains at the expense of the frail, when cries for justice pierce the darkness and examples are made of others through wreckage and murder, in all these times, the oppressed look to a savior, the one who will right the wrongs and redress grievances while offering reason and rationale to the downtrodden, only resorting to a clinched fist when it becomes essential for self-preservation. What Shane teaches us is that at times it is best to stand tall, showing strength in silence, and when mocked, to not turn away as bad men humiliate. There will be those who seek to learn that a good man's incremental approach to righting wrongs is in fact one step along a pilgrimage that defines an individual's strength as others whose hopes, which rest often upon emotion rather than reason, to see a liberator rather than a sacrificial lamb.

There are times in life that are pivotal in defining if we stand rightly or turn and retreat. Often, we stand not singly but in the company of others who long to be shepherded. Yet, when push comes to shove, many will stand down. At times like these, when all seems lost, one from among the group will stand firm when others falter. And, what is it that drives a person forward to tread where others will not? It is a longing to do what needs be done in the service of others that results in the extraordinary. Resilience is found in faith, and it is faith that enables us to do that which others reel from. It is during times of tribulation that both who we are and how others see us is defined. At times however, those who support us as we champion them will forsake us and turn away in doubt, and while some before turning will scorn us, mock and perhaps condemn. Disappointment in life is inevitable, yet trust in humanity cannot waver. We must accept that those we serve are fickle and will, when opportunity or necessities exist, forsake the course and turn to those who will provide immediate remedy albeit contrary to the long term.

In life, we all stand before crossroads that lead in different directions. We often confuse opportunity as an advance forward without careful introspection. It need be noted that a new path may lead the traveler into an abyss. What Shane teaches us is that each day, we define who we are. Setting the example of strong leadership, during uncertain times, others will look to us for guidance.

In life, you undoubtedly will stand judged by others who are unwilling to stand by your side. Understand that time is a continuum that we often fail to appreciate. Instant gratification, satisfaction, and reward not forthcoming, dissatisfaction results and waver ensues. When all is failing, we must rely on faith in one who will carry the day. When bad men prey upon the weak, as bad men perpetrate violence upon the feeble, when people are turned out and must fend for themselves against a punishing world, there will be one among us who will stand up while others recoil. Yet, there will be a moment that when rallied, the weak will follow one who will defend them from harm. I trust Shane will teach you many valuable lessons in life as you serve selflessly, defending the freedoms that all hold dear. Having answered the call to service, the world is a precarious place, as extremist ideologies are permeating civil societies. May you be such a person as Shane and be a righteous defender of freedom and a moral paradigm for others.

EXAMINING OBSERVATION, DEFINING PERCEPTION

Recently, I was engaged in conversation with a Sailor, and it became a bit lofty as we talked about the ways in which the mind works. I recalled a university lecture that I attended well over twenty-five years ago. I surmise the lecturer's statement: "The world is but the color gray. Through our eyes, what is observed is far different than what we see. Our minds process the outward stimuli and the result is our perception of it." The lecturer went on to explain this phenomenon by holding up a white sheet of paper and asking what color the sheet was. Of course, the answer was resoundingly "white!" The lecturer then asked if the class was in a blackened room, with no outward light, what the color of the same sheet of paper would be. Of course, the class said "black."

In a similar vein, those things that actually exist are regularly perceived far differently. As we are bombarded by innumerable stimuli—far more than what is natural or sufficient for us to process—we selectively allow specific provocations to influence and stimulate appropriate responses. Our biases influence us in a parochial way. We say, "We believe what we believe because of our belief in it!" And, so it is for those who are gullible: they are easily beguiled. When we fail to open our minds, we'll see what others want us to see. We love to be entertained and we at times long to escape reality, so we watch reality television and follow political theater, believing it to be authentic. Political statesmen there are few, but there are many entertainers, garnering a few laughs; however, recurrently netting our disdain, they are practiced illusionists rather than venerable political figures, living the regal life, repeatedly forgoing service to their constituencies, who are focused on image and fortune. Yet, if our vision is limited and our perception bias-based, you'll not recognize when deception presents itself and we'll be the ones deceived. The following quote by English novelist Aldous Huxley illustrates the sentiments above as "there are things known and there are things unknown, and in between are the doors of perception." Still, if you keep your eyes open and your mind sharp, you'll perceive the difference between deception and reality, realizing that to find the truth, there is only one way to do the right thing.

We look at ourselves countless times each day. We view the world as we look at it, but it is the mind that processes that which we see. As our vision is narrow-minded, we believe that what is within view is all that is to be seen. We often fail to look beyond, to broaden the aperture of the mind to include the peripheral. We loathe being wrong though we know it be; we convince ourselves still that we are right. No longer do we accept being wrong, as we frequently seek to change the narrative in order to shift the message that others perceive. And, many among us shed decorum and respect and act contrary to good order and discipline and lash out. We also are so transfixed upon ourselves that our human experience has sunk to the size of a handheld high-definition monitor. And, if information is posted on the internet, we without question believe it as fact. Why is this? Because of what we see and how it is understood, we habitually avoid rational thought and inquiry. Think about the number of individuals who believe that magic is not a trick and that illusion is real!

How many among us have fallen short of the mark, laying blame on others? Pointedly, when we fail, we fail many others than ourselves. We are quick to rebuff blame and fault others for our shortfalls. The ultimate failure is not to see the opportunities that failures yield. Individuals that obtain greatness are quick to tell of their struggles and their failures. Many entrepreneurs fail again and again—demonstrating the resourcefulness and commitment to press onward, holding true to faith, and believing in themselves— persevere, and achieve the unimaginable. We measure success in its immediacy rather than the pilgrimage. Along the way and with each step earned, with toil defined and with setback noted, we define ourselves as we become examples for others. When we are quick to see fame, we fail to appreciate the struggle. As leaders, we must consider what others see in us. It must be understood that others see much more in us than we often see in ourselves. The way in which we view the world, how others see us, and how we see ourselves defines who we are. If what defines you is an amalgam of who you really are— one's conscience, morals, values, and character—believe me, others will spend much effort examining observation, defining perception as they perceive you, positively and as a standard to emulate while upholding our core values while serving selflessly. Remember, there is no illusion when doing what is right, and your accomplishments hold no tricks. Rather, your efforts forge the way for others to follow.

NOSTALGIA IS A LONG TIME COMING

August 28, 2017

In the summer of 2017, I attended my fortieth high school reunion. Having received a notice via the mail and being quite nostalgic, I thought this would be a good time to attend a reunion for the first time and reunite with fellow classmates. Knowing how much I have changed over the years, I was eager to see those I had not seen since 1977. The evening was enjoyable, though it ended far earlier than the late-night parties that were reminisced about. A few people were immediately recognized while others evoked great surprise when we were reunited. Hugs and handshakes resulted in immediate familiarity. Recalling fond memories, we realized how swiftly life has moved on, as photographs of children and grandchildren were beheld. Reviewing the 1977 yearbook, I found the following passage: "Those who live without memories have missed life." As in life, not all recollections of high school are fond. During the evening, I recalled heartache and heartbreak, confrontation and failure, disappointment and disillusionment. Yet, as in life, we merge our personal experiences and subsume them in accordance with those that bring delight. Those we hope to forget fall behind, continuing to define us nonetheless.

Positioned at vantage points in the dining area were two video screens, one displaying photographs of past reunions and the other photographs of graduates who have passed away. I viewed the scrolling photographs of those departed numerous times throughout the evening and was saddened to learn of those familiar whose lives were so short. One graduate died shortly after graduation, others passed away in their twenties and thirties, and few passing away only recently. I looked at their young faces with their bright smiles, and I felt especially mournful. Life cut short by unknown circumstances, with a full life ahead, perhaps cheated by time as unbeknownst personal accomplishments and benefits to society were never realized. Their youthful lives all held such promise, yet with the rest of their lives ahead, abbreviated were their days. I wondered what were their dreams and aspirations; what did they believe they would accomplish in life, and what of their expectations of a long life with reward and success? Were they content with the lives they lived? Did they have any misgivings about the way they lived their lives? How did they pass? What were the circumstances? And, from their lives, what is their legacy? When we are nostalgic, we soon ponder our own mortality, and we soon realize that when considering our lives ahead, we hope our time on earth will be longer than can be imagined. Facing reality, we somberly grasp that our days are fleeting. As we contemplate our mortality, we speculate on our legacy and wonder how we will be remembered, imagining what will remain as a testament to our life's toil.

As my gaze fixated on the scrolling photographs of those departed, I wondered about their last days, their misgivings, and their realization about the end of their lives. Did they have time to put their affairs in order? Did they have time to say goodbye to their loved ones? Or did they die abruptly? Were family members at their side, or did they pass alone, being unable to bid farewell to their loved ones? Here now is the point of this memo: being nostalgic and considering mortality, the words of the American writer Bernie Siegel are fitting: "An awareness of one's mortality can lead you to wake up and live an authentic, meaningful life." After a very enjoyable evening, while traveling home, I continued to think about the photographs of the deceased. Again, I affirmed as truth that no matter the number of our days, life will in fact always be cut short!

It is imperative that we focus our attention to the inevitable outcome in life. With numbered days, the crucial task before each of us is to live a life that is right. We are seen as we live, and our actions are being recorded through the eyes of others. You will be remembered through the perceptions of those who observe your every move. What you said, what you did, and how you behaved years ago will be the topic of discussions that we'll rarely be privy to. Seldom do we realize the impact of our lives on the lives of others. Our interactions truly affect others. If we live rightly, we'll serve more than ourselves. In so doing, we'll offer ourselves to those beyond our immediate perceived sphere of influence.

Serve rightfully and with purpose, and you'll extend grace beyond yourself. When we serve others, they in turn will extend themselves in an exponential manner. If we faithfully serve, we will be defined by our devotion, and living according to the tenets of our faith, hearts will be softened and clenched fists opened to accept a helping hand. Live to serve others, and your legacy will exist far beyond your years. Ponder then the eventuality in life, as one day photographs will be viewed and remembrances exchanged in memorial to your life, a life lived purposefully and justly and lived while serving others. May it be for you that nostalgia is a long time coming!

WHY WE STAND!

Recognizing the political firestorm that is today evident, I will forgo injecting further my disdain for the behaviors of certain celebrities. I will, however, focus proudly and with adoration of the enduring symbol of freedom, democratic principles, and the greatest nation on the face of the earth. We stand for the anthem and salute the fabric of our nation. We pledge our allegiance and reaffirm our commitment to uphold and defend the Constitution while we freely offer ourselves in the service of others. We do so because it needs to be done. In times of disaster, and in times of war, we display the emblematic symbol recognized around the globe. When individuals have been disadvantaged, when all seems lost, uplifted are they when they see our flag at the horizon, for they know that what is to be offered is their salvation. Those who legally immigrate to our country stand with overwhelming pride as they become Americans. It is right that we honor the flag and our national anthem. Americans across the country fly the "Flag of Our Fathers." I for one and for all fly our flag each day.

Around the globe, there are people from all nations who dream of a place such as America where unprecedented opportunity and unparalleled freedom and liberties are constitutionally guaranteed for all. Why, then, do many of our citizens on the world stage blatantly disrespect our nation and all those who treasure our national symbols? Quick to voice the constitutional right to do so, many do so because it is vogue. Still others do so as they "know not what they do." Because you can does not mean that you should! Similarly, because I can vocalize profanity, it is wrong to do so. Yet, being fashionable, today, foul language is spoken in familial settings; and to voice dissent is to be considered prudish. The spectrum of acceptability and decency has certainly swung afar.

Consider the founding fathers, who prayerfully and with considerable forethought guaranteed liberties for the ages. Today, outward expressions of faith are forbidden, mocked, and from some spur outright contempt. When I was a child, the Pledge of Allegiance and a time for prayer began each school day. We stood tall due to instilled values of honor and respect. The respect for those in authority was undeniable. As a young man, I was raised to be thankful for the blessings bestowed upon me and revere those who served our country and who preserved those blessings. Over my lifetime, which includes being a young teenager during the Vietnam War, I witnessed much demonstration, violence, and even injustice. What makes America great is its ability to overcome past transgressions through the rule of law and on behest of all initiate change for the better.

Yes, amendment came as America redressed past grievances. In America, unparalleled opportunities exist for all, but require an individual to invest themselves for the long term through dedication, resolve, skill, faith, and trial and error, overcoming failure time and time again. We live not in a caste society, although for some self-imposed limitations, envy and anger, quick handedness, manipulation, and selfishness, although yielding quick personal gain at the expense of others in the long term, hinder the betterment of society. Over the years, rancorous debate involving civil liberties and the right to act contrary to societal norms has pitted the dissenter against the establishment. What emerged from acrimonious discord were defining wedge issues that clearly delineated the divergence among the points of view while relying upon the rule of law, constitutional safeguards, and patriotic themes, radicals criticize the very symbols that define our American exceptionalism.

We stand because we recognize our noble past and the greatness of the American democratic experiment. We stand because we salute our veterans who have given immeasurably for both Americans and those who live on foreign soil. We stand not in defiance, but rather we stand because of our respect and deference for our flag. We stand united as men and women of the military honoring our past and importantly as an example for young eyes that look to us as heroes. We stand with bowed head, not in shame but in prayer. We kneel as we pass our folded flag to a Gold Star Mother or Father, to a Gold Star family member not submissively but rather reverently as we offer sincere gratitude on behalf of a grateful nation. We stand in the wind and rain as the flag is raised and again as our flag is lowered. We stand when celebrities will not. And, most importantly, we stand in defense of those whose disdain is clearly evident. We stand firm when others may run, and we stand tall moving forward against all odds to defend those who disrespect our flag, our anthem, and our nation. It is because of our commitment to stand whether saluting or with hand over our hearts that defines us for our courage, our strength, our community, and our humanity. We rightly stand because it is the honorable thing to do.

WHY WE FACE THE FRAY

November 27, 2017

Again this year, the observance of Veterans Day is a solemn reminder to offer thanks and praise to those who have been called to a vocation of service. Called to serve at home or abroad, afield or afloat, men and women from divergent backgrounds join together to defend our cherished freedoms and to offer others the means to lift themselves from the afflictions of tyranny. This year, we remember those who have given so much though knowing the risks, pursuing the goal of enriching the lives of others, empowering the powerless, providing comfort to the weary, and enabling those whose lives have been ravaged by the maniacal despots who subjugate the helpless while plundering the underprivileged for their own rewards.

Around the globe, veterans have served during times of war and times of peace. They have willingly forfeited time with family and loved ones, going afar for months on end, uncertain of what may await. Remaining undaunted, they pressed on, meeting adversity, danger, and even death head-on. Willing to do the right thing even when facing overwhelming odds, the finest among us have committed to an ethos of service before self. When it is hard, they move forward; when it is dangerous, they disregard the peril; when others cry out, they answer the call; and when others doubt, they are certain because whatever the matter, it is done because it need be.

For those outside of the military, many wonder why young men and women would risk everything, facing such daunting odds for an uncertain return. What is it that drives military members to enter the fray, unto the breach, experiencing the taste of choking dust and the sting of acrid smoke? When others fall with deafening screams, thunderous detonations, and the whizz of bullets all around, they move ever forward into battle, why do they do this? Why cast off self-preservation and think solely of others? Far from home, risking life and limb to secure a better life for those unknown while saying what may be their final farewell to loved ones, they board planes, cross the brow of ships, and deploy—yes, momentarily saddened by leaving—but determined to fulfill their missions and return to the arms of loved ones and a grateful nation.

A few weeks ago, Army Sergeant Bowe Bergdhal's saga came to an end as he admitted and pled guilty to charges of desertion and misbehavior before the enemy while he served in Afghanistan. Some may wonder why I would write about a soldier who admitted to desertion while conveying my sentiments about veterans and their honorable and selfless service. As furious as I am about Bergdahl's desertion, this case is another example of why righteous men and women risk their lives in the search for a lesser man: because it was the right thing that needed to be done. When Bergdahl went missing, every military member in Afghanistan was aware of his disappearance, and many were specifically assigned to assist with the location of his whereabouts. Several men searching for Bergdahl were wounded, and others killed during the search. Bergdahl's location was a critical requirement that would entail military and diplomatic efforts.

Over the five years of his captivity, two distinct camps voiced support or rancor. Regardless of one's position, warriors risked their lives in order to bring an American home. What was done by those who risked themselves in the search for Bergdahl is best summed up by the words of Gen. Douglas MacArthur who stated, "Duty, Honor, Country. Those three hallowed words reverently dictate what you ought to be, what you can be, what you will be." What was done in order to find a missing man whose whereabouts were unknown, which included sacrifice, toil, and bloodshed define a military focused on doing the right thing during a time when political musings can turn opaque what must be done.

Though less than 1 percent of our total population serves in the military and far less have served in combat environments, over the past seventeen years, millions among us have deployed answering the call to arms. The reasons for serving certainly vary, yet all who serve swear to uphold and defend the Constitution from all enemies foreign and domestic. From the first time we raised our right hand and repeated the words of enlistment or commission, we stated our affirmation knowing that we've volunteered for what might come. The nation is forever indebted to veterans for their contributions ensuring the safety and security of our nation's citizenry. During times of war and times of peace, when nature delivers catastrophe, when the disadvantaged requires remedy, when all seems lost, our veterans have served honorably and with distinction, giving more of themselves knowing that compensation for their service, their aid, and their support never appears equal on a balance sheet. For those who may ask why we do what we do, a simple answer, poignant and enduring need be stated. In the words of Abraham Lincoln, "You cannot escape the responsibility of tomorrow by evading it today"; and those who have and continue to serve have been charged to secure the blessings of freedom, opportunity, safety, and security for tomorrow.

Today, there are many among us who are engaged in an epic struggle. These men and women fight for our nation's continued security, prosperity, and very way of life. We fight for those who also seek what we hold as self-evident. It is our American ethos that instills in us all that those who are not among us as Americans are with us as a collective race. For we are willing to encourage a life made better that only liberty can provide. Selflessness and sacrifice are touchstones that define who we are as Americans and from which the foundation of our grand republic is built. We volunteer; we promote liberty without prejudice, and we give more of ourselves so that liberty can endure.

So then, in order to guarantee all that we hold dear and assure our nation's prosperity, we must as those before us and as those who follow in our footsteps prevail. We do this as was done upon distant seas and on foreign shores for those who desire a free life of their own. As did former patriots endeavor, we must remain vigilant and act boldly, for in the immortal words of former president Dwight D. Eisenhower: "History does not long entrust the care of freedom to the weak or the timid." May we all reaffirm our commitment to selfless purposeful service, to the Navy, and for our nation!

IT'S UP TO YOU!

I often talk with Sailors about their journey ahead; and during these conversations, apprehension, worry, and sometimes even dread is often conveyed. These young men and women worry about the future, their experiences, the demands that will be levied against them, and meeting expectations of those appointed over them. These are challenging times, and Sailors face many uncertainties, with long periods of separations and, for some, hardship, heartache, and heart-break. They carefully consider where they will serve and the means to balance personal pursuits with professional responsibilities. What will the future hold? What of the hazards, the perils, the joys, and the rewards? We rationalize what awaits us, and we contemplate the pros and cons, within time deciding the best of choices and obligating to a new adventure. Not all locales will be to our immediate liking, and for some, acclimation may be a difficult endeavor due to divergent cultures, customs, and a way of life that is less than desirable. Much has been said as of late about countries that are of particular negative notoriety. Often, though, we fail to truly appreciate our surroundings. During my decades of military service, I've visited more than one country whose culture was at first disenchanting. Regardless of the dirt, disease, and debasement, in every location I've found remarkable opportunities to serve the people who have endured extreme hardships and unprecedented depravity that a lesser person could not endure. In these locations, some being war zones, I've found unparalleled opportunities to extend humanity. From these experiences and truly because of the remarkable people who reside there, who have overcome such hardship of which without their assistance I could not have persevered, I've offered my best to better their lives, and they in turn have made me a better man. The place and its condition are always secondary to the people whose tenacity enables them to struggle on and inspire us all.

It's up to you to realize what must be accomplished. But often we are stalled due to inhibition and uncertainty. My father would tell me, "Butch, get going to get it done!" True, there is much to be done though much more than one person can do. If, however, you focus on your contribution, effort, and active engagement, then progress will be made. Over the years, I've learned that Sailors know what must be done, and having the ability to get it done, they will often allow indecision to inhibit success. Others knowing what is right, though it may be the hard way, will ponder then waver, ultimately doing what is easier though eventually unsuitable. Believe this statement: "There is one way to do the right thing, and it is up to you to rightly do it." Life is a test of our commitment, and when life presents a path that is less than desirable, though ultimately rewarding, we must trudge on. Time and again, Sailors will look at the challenge, believe it hard, and become overwhelmed, backpedal, and distance themselves from that which perhaps is their destiny. Doubt will eventually preclude good fortune.

I will tell Sailors that life is hard, but by doing the hard thing, you will enable others to do that which is harder. We must realize that what we do enables others to surpass what we've done and be seen as enviable examples that others will rightly follow. There will be times that will challenge, and there will be events that will discourage. Yet, these are the times that will reward those who can muster the will, rely on faith, and commit to seeing it through. If one tenders the question, "What must be done?" My response will be, "Change the world through your selfless offering!" Imagine an attitude based on seven words that truly is a foundational construct that if faithfully executed can indeed make a world of difference.

Recently, I was engaged in conversation with a young person, and we talked about world travel. I was asked the location of the most enjoyable place that I have visited. I thought for a brief spell and remarked that Thailand was such a place. I also offered that I have found my time in Afghanistan to be the most memorable. My remark elicited quite a bewildered stare! I then mentioned that Afghanistan is such a place where one can truly offer humanity to generations that have suffered greatly and is a place in need of our best efforts. Befuddled by my response, I offered that recently, over 100 innocent men, women, and children were murdered by an extremist in a bombing. Undoubtedly, such a place is truly in need of an offering of humanity, and a genuine act of kindness can mend the broken and change a heart. Of course, unfamiliarity and indecision will yield nothing, as it is easy to turn away from it. Truly, there is much to do, much to address, and much to accept. What I offer to you is this: "In order to make a difference in this world, it's simply up to you!"

WHY I LOVE AMERICA

Given the troubles of the day, all too often we can become disheartened and allow malaise to overshadow the opportunities that are waiting fulfillment. True, we live in difficult times where we are under assault from the forces of greed and evil. There are those among us who commit heinous crimes, acts so despicable and reprehensible that I too am overcome at times with despair. My heart hurts for the victims, and I pray for them and their families. Yet, we must not allow ourselves to wallow in victimhood. I am also confident that justice will be served and those responsible will be reckoned with. We must not allow such evil to cast its shadow of hopelessness over our land with powers that seek to pull our society apart.

Consequently, there are individuals who conspire to bring down our pillars of culture and fundamentally change our American identity. Recently, much has been said about the greatness of America, which has resulted in an uproarious debate. Late-night media types mock America, scoff at our prominence, and disparage those who believe that our best days are before us. Many among us scoff at American exceptionalism for to do so is for some inflammatory and divisive. These agitators often rally against the Constitution when political expediency capitalizes on misfortune while citing its provisions when it suits them. True, they have the right to free speech, and we have the right not to listen. And, THAT is why I love America.

Why I love America? From main streets with maple-tree-lined roads, to the grandeur of towering man-made structures and the splendor of the open plains, rugged lofty mountains, and cascading rivers; from the great expanse to the wave from a neighbor, we being different, yet still the same, share our American experience of growing up, growing old, our families addressing struggle with success, overcoming heartache and heartbreak, hearing the laughter of newborns and the needs of the elderly, offering compassion, being empathetic while redressing apathy, while giving of ourselves to those overcome by misfortune and uniting around those less fortunate. In America, an amalgam of cultures and customs, achievement is based on hard work and the hard life, seizing opportunity while refraining from opportunism, and giving more of ourselves for the next generation. A place where we are free, and a place where boundaries are self-imposed, where we are welcome to worship as we determine, where different faiths are practiced without being shrouded in secret, where we can live and love as it pleases us, where intolerance is overcome by generosity, and where we do not have to hide who we are. America: a place of history, of struggle, and also strife; where division has been overcome by unity, and where the proper path is before us and for those who freely choose to accept that life will not be easy and that upon our way in life we will be tested. Where hardship also waits, but where toil will define our strength. Yes, there may be an easier way, but the proper path is not necessarily the easy way forward. Why I love America? Because I have been blessed with a good life, and I have also been blessed with the ability to know that if I share my good fortune, when others benefit, we all advance. A place where consequences are defined, where the rule of law is applied to the advantage of the citizenry, and where humanity is offered to all regardless of circumstance or stature; a place where the extension of goodwill is foremost before an allowance of favor, and where forgiveness is both a matter of faith and fact.

True, things have changed over time. America is definitely different then when I was a boy. Back then, write was right as I was taught cursive. I was taught to be respectful of authority. As a boy, as I inevitably did wrong, I would be punished by both parents and those who were charged to lead and teach me. I was taught to explore, and I was taught to have fun outdoors. I responded rightly to the beckoning of my parents who were both honored and treasured. I considered the embarrassment to my parents before I acted out, and when I got into trouble, I learned from my mistakes and accepted the consequences. When in school, the environment was well ordered and the only "safe place" was under my desk during Cold War-era air raid drills. I got into fistfights and with the dispute settled remained friends with my opponent. I was taught to revere the flag, respect our veterans, and that service to our nation was of a higher order. In the service of our nation, I am charged to offer the best in me to those I serve and serve with.

Why I love America? Because of our nation's prominence, we offer to the world unprecedented aid and assistance. Despite the adversary, whether at home or abroad, we offer support and extend ourselves to those who have been presented a distorted view of our benevolence. Blessedly, as an American, I can still decide to go my way, forgo an onslaught of negative influences that would take me from my quest if I was a lesser man, and remain free to define myself as I wish. Because of my upbringing and from it all, for which I am especially thankful of those who have influenced me, it is for the adoration of family and for our nation that I write "Why I Love America."

A CONVERSATION WITH MY FATHER

March 30, 2018

My father was the most influential man in my life. As a youngster, there were many male characters that I would idolize due to their onscreen antics, but the one man who was real to life and part of my every day was my father. He was as witty as he was stern. Yes, he was a disciplinarian, but as a simple man, he offered me sage advice and the truth about life. How blessed was I as he truly loved me. Though he was a man of average stature, his charisma enabled him to stand taller in my eyes. Fortunate was I, as he spent much time with me conversing about life and the proper way for me to make my own way. Over the years, I have often quoted my father within the lines of these memos; and I proudly noted his sentiments, always prefacing his words with a sentimental nickname that he called me: "Butch." In December of 2006, my father passed away. Though departed, he remains close to my heart and in my thoughts. He was a fine man, and I consider myself blessed being his son. I do, however, miss our conversations and telephone calls. Every so often, my father will visit me in my dreams; when he does, the message is one of direction, reminding me that no matter the challenge, I must see it through and get it done.

After twelve years of writing these memos and having decided that this edition would be the last, I've pulled together my father's quotes. As we all deliberate what life has in store for us, I considered hypothetically what my father would share with me if I could sit down and discuss with him my life and the best way to navigate through my elder years. So imagine my father and me sitting on the porch of our upstate New York home, the warmth of the midmorning sun filtering through a gentle breeze and the dense maples and pines. If I could, I would ask my father the following about life.

First, I would ask, "With difficult days ahead, what would be the best way to pursue the path before me?"

"Well, Butch," he would say, "get going to get it done! As a grown man, bootstraps are meant to be pulled up by the wearer. And, before you go forward, have no regrets when looking back, only great optimism when looking forward. For those things you dread in your past, may they remain behind you as you enthusiastically consider what with favor awaits."

The second question I would ask would be, "How do you approach the uncertainty that awaits us all in life?" With a wry smile, my father would offer, "Butch, take an opportunity before it's out of reach! If you focus on the horizon, you'll soon see how close it truly is. Believe me, better days will be found at your focal point!" I would reply, "But, Dad, better days may be far off, but how do I keep focus on the horizon as I wear bifocals!" He would say, "Come on now, Butch. Stop the shenanigans! If you prefer extraordinary vision, you must keep an eye on the path ahead, and watch where you're going. Remember this: if you're going to move forward, take a big step! And, don't forget to take an opportunity before it's out of reach!"

A question that I would surely ask my father, a question that all of us ponder from time to time, was, "Dad, as I contemplate the years ahead, I would ask, what's in store for me?" My father would surely offer, "Listen, Butch, you've got to make time to do what is right. Remember, you're the maker of your own making. Though the days ahead for you may be short, you've got to make the time. If you think there's not enough of it, you better make it for yourself. You must consider that one day you'll be blindsided by the unexpected, and when the unforeseen arrives, the true measure of a man is not in his size, but by the amount he has given of himself. It's not what you've done, but how you did it that makes 'cents' to a man's worth."

Finally, as I contemplate the question that all of us consider about the meaning of our lives, my father would tell me, "It's best to leave behind something in this world other than a grave marker; for all possessions are in the end trivial, yet your actions are fundamental to preserving who you were long after you are gone." As this is my last memo, I trust this theoretical conversation with my father will be contemplated long after you turn to another page. Know that it has been a tremendous privilege to share my thoughts with readers around the globe over the past twelve years. For you and to those with whom you may share these memoirs, I wish a life filled with joy, wonder, fulfillment, and of course, for you and those you hold dearly, many blessings.

RETIREMENT ADDRESS

March 22, 2019

When reflecting upon my career, I offer that I can best describe it as having been truly unimaginable. I have served with the most elite warriors, those chiefly talented, intelligent, and those who are patriots and humble servants. When I reflect upon my career and I consider the medals, the awards, and accolades bestowed upon me, I humbly submit that I have not singularly earned any such recognition as I have been a member of teams who were presented unparalleled service opportunities. Though I have been granted special acknowledgment over the years, for which I am truly grateful, I owe credit to those with whom I was privileged to serve by your side. For this again, I am so very thankful.

But yet, as I reflect upon my years of service, though unimaginably fulfilling, I am not without remorse. For I often contemplate: Could I have done more, should I have given more, and if I could do it all again, would I offer myself differently in certain situations? Though not to dwell on the past, with remorse comes recourse, and over the years, this recourse has come from my heavenly Father, whose gentle hand has been upon me, guiding me, leading me along my life's path, enabling me to see when my vision was clouded by doubt, and who while facing peril kept me from harm, and whose guidance came not from a voice the power of which can move mountains, but rather from one who was always at my side, a gentle whisper offering me always a better way. Facing trial and tribulation, it has been the necessity of service that enabled me along my chartered course, all the while in the service of others, always attentive to faith, flag, and family. And, for this, I am especially and eternally grateful to all with who served with me over the course of my Navy career.

Having offered a theme of thanksgiving, and as witnesses to the events of this day, I offer the following appeal: may God bless each and every member of our Armed Forces, your families, and those you hold dearly, and may God richly bless America, this day, and for all days hereafter.

Although having spoken from the stage at the Information Warfare Training Command over the years offering remarks for training, professional assemblies as well as many ceremonies, March 22, 2019 marked the day that I would offer remarks during a ceremony commemorating my years of service. The theme of those remarks were of thanksgiving, extending my gratitude to those whom I have served with, befriended, those here who have taught me much, and those I have been deployed with around the globe, and especially those with whom I served who enriched my life and most certainly enabled my career, enabling me to become a better man in the service of others.

Throughout my years, I've listened to my mentors who guided me, inspired me, and moved me to pace beyond my next planned footstep. Whether it was operating a beef cattle farm to returning to college as a Sunday school teacher or enlisting in the US Navy, I've sought the advice and counsel of my mentors, and with reliance on faith, with all intent to succeed, did I take a chance in order to embolden my life in the service of others. I am especially thankful to those who have motivated me to best

my last effort in order that I should serve purposefully and selflessly, confidently focused on the careers of others. In reflection, and while serving the needs of others, always mindful of the necessity to give of my best, the tenets of faith, flag, and family have especially enabled me.

Acknowledgments

I am so very grateful to my mother and father who were so instrumental in shaping the man that I became. From their service to our nation during World War II and their volunteerism toward civil defense, my affinity with community service became apparent. As a young boy, my world was at one time the family property, expanding as I grew older. New friends from the village of Saint Remy continued to shape me during my adolescent years, and today, friendships remain with those who reside in that quaint upstate New York area. I have written about the influence that the local church had upon me as I attended Sunday school and later as a Sunday school teacher. I thank the congregation for their weekly prayers for my safety and well-being. That special little church is idyllic as is the village where I was raised. I have been truly sustained by those I grew up with, grew older with and apart, and for those who have gone on ahead of me.

I would be negligent if I did not acknowledge the heartaches and heartbreaks incurred along the way, the mistakes, the misgivings, the luck, and truly providence that has shaped me. During these times of turmoil, I found relief and reprieve in the relationship with God as I have been truly blessed beyond measure and highly favored. I would be less than truthful if I did not acknowledge the failures in my life as they too have shaped me and again I believe divinely so, as these failures rightly placed me on the proper path. As I grew older and my sphere of activity broadened, so too did the number of individual relationships grow; their effect upon me refined the man that I would become. There are those who have passed away that were instrumental in my life and include my grandmother, great-aunt, of course, my mother and father, and my brother who visit me frequently in thought and shape still today my behavior as a man.

With my own family, for which I am especially thankful, I am so very beholden to my loving wife, who has maintained our family during my frequent and long periods of separation over the years of my military service. I am proud to tell others that my beloved wife was the first to review these memos prior to release, and her guidance and direction enabled me to offer my sentiments to many with confidence. I am, of course, inspired daily by my darling *Apo*, whom this book is dedicated as well as too her children's children. This now not-so-little girl has motivated me in a very big way! I truly am a better man because of my wonderful *Apo*.

This book, of course, would not have been made possible on my own volition. I have been rightly inspired by the many men and women that I have served with over the course of my career. They will remain an ever-present force within me as I begin the next phase of my life of service to our military, our nation, and the world community.

Endnotes

1   David Breashears, *High Exposure: An Enduring Passion for Everest and Unforgiving Places* (New York: Simon & Schuster, 1999).

2   Breashears, 149.

3   Breashears, 250.

4   Breashears, 167.

5   Michael M. Phillips, *The Gift of Valor: A War Story* (New York: Broadway Books, 2005), 234.

6   http://www.arlingtoncemetery.net/asrowan.htm Arlington National Cemetery Website, Andrew Summers Rowan.

7   www.frankbuckles.org.

8   www.usmemorialday.org.

About the Author

Originally from Saint Remy, New York, Robert E. Jordan graduated from the State University of New York at Albany, earning a bachelor's of science degree in political science, and was inducted into the Golden Key National Honor Society in December 1992. In February 1993, he enlisted in the US Navy. During his career of twenty-six years, he served afloat and afield: as an instructor, a Senior Enlisted Leader and Master Chief Petty Officer, and as a Chief Warrant Officer. Having served  five tours of duty in Afghanistan, he also served aboard USS *Wasp* (LHD 1), USS *Saipan* (LHA 2), and two tours aboard USS *Dwight D. Eisenhower* (CVN 69). His service included the Western Pacific region, the Mediterranean and Adriatic Seas, and the Arabian Gulf. Prior to retirement from the Navy, Chief Warrant Officer Jordan served at the Pentagon.

During his career, Chief Warrant Officer Jordan was awarded numerous personal awards, to include the VADM Rufus B. Taylor Award, the RADM Edwin T. Layton Award, and the Military Intelligence Corps Knowlton Award in recognition of his excellence in leadership, mentorship, and intelligence instruction. In addition, he and the teams that he served with were recognized by the Department of Defense for service throughout the Afghanistan Theater of Operations.

Respectfully referred to as "Father Bob," Chief Warrant Officer Jordan was a mentor to many throughout the course of his career. Once a month for twelve years, Father Bob wrote a memo focused on the topics of Faith, Flag, and Family sharing with his fellow service members the tenets of purposeful selfless service. The reach of his message came to extend far beyond his originally intended scope, as his messages were shared again and again around the globe. Today, they are gathered together in this collection as a gift of his legacy for his beautiful granddaughter, and her children's children.